T0035124

BATTLING THE BIG LIE

How Fox, Facebook, and the MAGA Media Are Destroying America

DAN PFEIFFER

TWELVE

New York   Boston

For Jack—whose joy and curiosity light up the world

Copyright © 2022 by Daniel Pfeiffer

Cover design by Jim Datz
Cover photographs: © Jon Hicks/Stone and Jon Cherry/Getty Images News,
via Getty Images
Cover copyright © 2023 by Hachette Book Group, Inc.

Hachette Book Group supports the right to free expression and the value of copyright. The purpose of copyright is to encourage writers and artists to produce the creative works that enrich our culture.

The scanning, uploading, and distribution of this book without permission is a theft of the author's intellectual property. If you would like permission to use material from the book (other than for review purposes), please contact permissions@hbgusa.com. Thank you for your support of the author's rights.

Twelve
Hachette Book Group
1290 Avenue of the Americas, New York, NY 10104
twelvebooks.com
twitter.com/twelvebooks

Originally published in hardcover and ebook by Twelve in June 2022
First trade paperback edition: June 2023

Twelve is an imprint of Grand Central Publishing. The Twelve name and logo are trademarks of Hachette Book Group, Inc.

The publisher is not responsible for websites (or their content) that are not owned by the publisher.

The Hachette Speakers Bureau provides a wide range of authors for speaking events. To find out more, go to hachettespeakersbureau.com or email HachetteSpeakers@hbgusa.com.

Twelve books may be purchased in bulk for business, educational, or promotional use. For information, please contact your local bookseller or the Hachette Book Group Special Markets Department at special.markets@hbgusa.com.

Library of Congress Control Number: 2022931656

ISBNs: 9781538707982 (trade paperback), 9781538707999 (ebook)

Printed in the United States of America

LSC-C

Printing 1, 2023

Contents

Introduction   v

I. What Happened

1. Canaries in the Information Coal Mines   3
2. From Russia with Love   18
3. How Trump Almost Stole the 2020 Election   25
4. A Short History of the Long War on Truth   48
5. Why Republicans Need to Lie to Win   61
6. The Anatomy of the MAGA Megaphone   71
7. The Best Disinformation Money Can Buy   95
8. Roger Ailes and the Evil Genius of Faux Journalism   115

II. How It Happened

9. Disinformation and the Destruction of Local News   133
10. Facebook: Too Big to Succeed   151
11. Poking Holes in Facebook's Defenses   178
12. The Media's Conservative Bias   189
13. Debunking the Dumbest Myth:
    Why MSNBC Is Not "Liberal Fox"   203

14. Message versus Megaphone:
    The Real Reason Dems Suck at Messaging   212

III. What We Do about It

15. The High Stakes of the Battle against the Big Lie   229

16. Get on a War Footing and Win Hearts and Minds   235

17. A Modern Model of Journalism   248

18. Preaching to the Progressive Choir   266

19. Starve the Trolls: How Liberals Can Stop Being
    Owned Online   290

20. Build an Army of Keyboard Warriors   301

21. Signs of Hope   310

Epilogue   315

Acknowledgments   323

Introduction

January 6, 2021, was one of the darkest days in American history. On that cold, cloudy day, more than two thousand Americans, many of them armed, stormed the US Capitol to stop the certification of the election that made Joe Biden president and Donald Trump a giant loser.

After smashing windows and breaking down doors, the mob ransacked offices, desecrated property, hunted members of Congress, and chanted "Hang Mike Pence!" A murderous rage pulsated through the crowd. Though many carried "Blue Lives Matter" flags to demonstrate their support for law enforcement, the crowd turned on anyone who stood in the way of their insurrection. Two Capitol Police officers died. Others were beaten down to the pavement with lead pipes, rocks, and ironically, even the pole from an American flag. Some rioters slinked through the halls with zip ties and Tasers, hunting for members of Congress to take hostage and potentially execute. And in case the parallels to a Jim Crow lynch mob were too subtle, a gallows was erected on Capitol grounds.

The viral photo of a man parading throughout the Capitol Building waving a Confederate flag perfectly captured the violence and sedition of that day. More than 150 years after the conclusion of the Civil War, insurrectionists had breached the Capitol and flown the flag of treason. The rioters came within minutes of entering the House Chamber while members were still on the floor. Vice President Pence was evacuated with only moments to spare. An opposing force took the US Capitol for the first time since the War of 1812. After it was all over, the fragility of the American ideal was presented in glaring relief.

The mob included avowed white supremacists, antigovernment paramilitaries, QAnon adherents, and MAGA fanatics in full regalia. There were elected officials, right-wing personalities, and a Texas socialite who had chartered a private plane to join the insurrection. The whole thing was funded in part by the heiress to a grocery store fortune. Participants came from all walks of life and every corner of the country. And despite their unique experiences, they had one thing in common: They had all fallen for the Big Lie; they all believed, without a single doubt, that the election had been stolen from Donald Trump.

There were various iterations of this lie. Some believed Democratic officials in big cities had stuffed ballot boxes; others believed thousands of dead people had voted with help from family members. Conspiracy theories abounded: Trump votes were purged. Voting machines flipped thousands of ballots to Biden. Some swore that China, Venezuela, and a global cabal of Communists and celebrities had played a role in stealing the election from Trump. Each theory was more absurd than the last.[1]

The stolen election argument was debunked over and over. There was zero evidence to support the allegations. Every court rejected the claims—including the courts of judges appointed by President Trump himself. Republican election officials dismissed the claims and testified to the integrity of the election.

None of it mattered. Nothing could shake Trump supporters' faith in these unfounded claims. The militant agitators at the Capitol were

---

1 Speaking of absurd: When I was writing my first book, I used footnotes to entertain myself with the jokes and asides I thought the publisher would never let me use. I forgot to delete them before submitting the first draft, and they all ended up in the final bound book. Readers seemed not to hate them, so here we go again.

immune to the truth, facts, opposing viewpoints, or evidence. They were willing to break the law, destroy property, and commit murder for a lie—and one so easily disproven.

After the rioters left and the property damage was repaired, the people who promoted the Big Lie denounced the violence without reflecting on the role they had played in fomenting it. These same people began recommending a peaceful transfer of power. They finally started referring to Joe Biden as "President-elect." Most Republicans attended Biden's inauguration. Even Sen. Ted Cruz, a leader of the insurrection, showed up to rinse the blood off his hands.

In the immediate aftermath of the insurrection, Republicans bemoaned the violence and denounced the perpetrators. Some even had the temerity to mention Trump's name.

But this period of awareness was fleeting.[2]

Before long, history was rewritten. Republicans, on Capitol Hill and out in the country, convinced themselves that the whole thing was not a violent extremist attack on democracy, and the question of who was at fault became a subject for debate. Some in the press, with their own deranged balance, covered this lack of accountability as if the Capitol riot were a he-said-she-said argument instead of a clear and indisputable event born out of the words and tweets of a president who spread lies, incited rioters, and then refused to send help as his own vice president feared for his life from a mob of his voters.

Few Republican elected officials were willing to take on the lies or the biggest liars. When Trump was impeached for his role in inciting the violence, only 10 House Republicans voted to hold him accountable. Less than 10 percent of the Republicans in Congress were willing to publicly sanction President Trump for dispatching his supporters to murder them.

Within months, the majority of people who had voted for Trump

---

2 Like "don't blink" levels of fleeting.

believed the election was stolen. Seventy percent of Republicans told pollsters that Biden was an illegitimate president. The Big Lie had become the uniting principle of the GOP, a litmus test, the price of admission to the Republican Party.

Everyone was shocked by what happened at the Capitol and by how quickly and easily it was swept away in a cloud of lies and disinformation. But they should have expected this.

I have spent twenty years in politics, working on campaigns, on Capitol Hill, and in the White House. Throughout that time, I have had a front-row seat to Republicans' efforts to bend the truth to their will. I've watched good people smeared, good policy stymied, and urgent problems go unaddressed. I've seen America elect its worst president and then almost reelect that person despite a mountain of evidence as to why that would be an epic disaster.

In my various positions, my central task has been to get the message out to the public, to present arguments in the most compelling fashion. That task is now impossible. Politics is no longer a debate about solutions to mutual problems. History, science, and math are no longer seen as immutable truths. They are subject to debate, with no right or wrong answer—like whether LeBron James is better than Michael Jordan.[3] People like to say that Democrats and Republicans now live in two separate realities, but that is incorrect. Democrats live in the real world, and Republicans live in a deeply delusional alternative ecosystem.

The insurrection and the subsequent rewriting of history are proof that the Republicans have mastered a form of politics that depends on disinformation and propaganda. They have built a megaphone that drowns out the truth and any and all dissenting views.

After all these years in politics, the Republican Party's ability to bend

---

3 There is only one answer to this question, and it's not LeBron.

reality is not just *a* problem. It is *the* problem. The insurrection at the Capitol, the inability to control COVID-19, and the rapidly accelerating threat of climate change are all products of the GOP's disinformation machine.

The lesson from the 2020 election is that the long-running Republican war on the truth is over and the Republicans have won. Most Americans didn't even know such a war was happening. Many still don't know it took place. Over a period of decades, the Republican Party built up a massive propaganda and disinformation apparatus that allows them to dominate politics despite representing a shrinking share of the electorate. This "MAGA megaphone" is embodied by Fox News and powered by Facebook and gives the GOP the power to bend reality.

The vast majority of the Democratic Party's leadership, many of whom were born before the advent of television, have their heads buried in the proverbial sand. They run the same old plays from the same outdated playbook with the same poor results. Too many are comforted by Joe Biden's victory in 2020, and too few are asking how it is possible that Trump, despite massively mishandling a pandemic that killed hundreds of thousands of Americans by Election Day, narrowly lost that race. A shift of 40,000 votes over four states, and Donald Trump would have been reelected.

Let me be even clearer: The Democratic Party isn't just losing. We are getting our asses kicked.

The 2016 election should have been the moment of reckoning for the Democratic Party, the media, and anyone who cares about democracy. Setting aside the fact that America elected a corrupt, racist reality TV star, other cracks in the U.S. system were appearing by then. The polls were wrong. Political observers[4] made incorrect assumptions about the durability of the coalition that had elected Barack Obama only four years before. And yes, there were some black swan

---

4 Me, me, me.

events, like Russia's hacking and Jim Comey's fuckery, that may have tipped the election, but something much bigger happened, and nearly everyone missed it. A universe of alternative information had come to reside on Facebook, on Fox, and in the digital lives of millions of Americans. In that universe, Hillary Clinton was a criminal, Donald Trump was a hero, all immigrants were terrorists, and everyone was coming for the rights and privileges of white Americans. This universe was not accounted for in political strategy or communications planning. In the "real world" of facts communicated to the public by "objective" journalists, the case against Donald Trump was open and shut. He was corrupt, dishonest, and dumb. Perhaps most important, he was obviously and completely full of shit. He said he was anti-immigration, but he hired undocumented people to work at his hotels and vineyard. He called himself a populist, but he promoted tax cuts for the wealthy and owned a plane with a gold toilet. He said he was above reproach because he was self-funding his campaign, but he was depending on the largesse of billionaires and selling merch to millions of his credulous supporters. It was one of the least clever cons in American history.

When Trump won, the reaction from Democrats and the media missed the point. Many Democrats bemoaned the naïveté of Trump's base, calling them cult members or arrogantly dismissing them as gullible rubes. The political press went on countless "safaris" in MAGA country, spending time in the usual hangouts, like diners and small-town bars. The goal was to understand how so many people could look at the same information about Trump's physical and intellectual capabilities and come to a different conclusion about the man. Those who didn't support Trump questioned whether he could tie his own shoelaces,[5] let alone be responsible for the world's largest nuclear arsenal.

---

5 I'm pretty sure that was Corey Lewandowski's job during the campaign. Ted Cruz now does it and is grateful for the opportunity.

Large portions of the country never heard any negative information about Trump. And if some of that information slipped through, Americans already surrounded by Trump-supporting peers were conditioned to dismiss it out of hand. They were living in a hermetically sealed information bubble. The problems of right wing propaganda and disinformation have only gotten worse—much worse.

America stands on a precipice. We are nearing the point of no return. If Democrats and the press do not fight back against the right-wing media machine bent on division and destruction, democracy has no chance of surviving.

This is the tipping point.

The problem of disinformation and conspiracy theories is long-standing and incredibly complex. Much of it predates the internet and has nothing to do with partisanship. Prior to COVID-19, antivaccine conspiracy theories were often the province of rich liberals.

I don't pretend to have all the answers or the capacity to tell the full story of how America diverged from reality. My focus is narrower and, I believe, more necessary.

This book is about how disinformation and propaganda became the dominant Republican political strategy, how it works, what it means, and how Democrats can fight back. I wrote *Battling the Big Lie* as a wake-up call and a call to arms for Democrats sick of losing the message wars. It's impossible to understand American politics without knowledge of the history and inner workings of the MAGA megaphone.

If Democrats, and the country, can't find a way to narrow the right wing's media advantage, nothing else we do will matter. We can raise more money, have better candidates, run better ads, have the best message in the world—and still lose. Over the next couple of elections, democracy and the planet will be on the line.

We cannot afford to lose.

I. WHAT HAPPENED

———

I

Canaries in the Information
Coal Mines

My entire career in politics has been on the front lines of this battle. Unfortunately, it has taken me years[1] to fully comprehend what we are up against.

When I started more than twenty years ago, there was order to the communications chaos. The internet was new. Mark Zuckerberg had yet to unleash his relentless greed and invasive algorithms on the world. Most people got their news from the same newsstands and the same coffee spots. On my first major campaign, the 2000 presidential election between Al Gore and George W. Bush, the staff gathered at the end of every day to watch the evening news together. What aired on NBC, ABC, and CBS was our most reliable barometer of how the public was viewing the campaign. If the coverage was good for us, it meant we were winning. If the coverage was bad, we were losing. The Republican campaign engaged in the same exercise at the same time with the same calculus. Voters—Republicans, Democrats, and independents—passed judgment on the candidates based on the same information delivered from the same sources. While America was—as it has always been—quite divided, that division existed as a

---

1 Way too many years.

disagreement over a shared set of facts and a mutual understanding of the challenges.

Fox News was around back then. Internet news sites existed, but they were an ancillary part of politics. When I traveled to staff an event or attend a debate, I neglected my emails for up to a week.[2] If someone needed me, they would page me, and I would call them back on a pay phone or a landline—the campaign did not issue cell phones to all staff. Our rapid-response operation involved a "tracker," who would follow Bush around the country to videotape his remarks in the hope of catching the candidate in a gaffe we could exploit in campaign ads. This is still a central part of campaigns, but *rapid* is a relative term. After capturing Bush on tape, the tracker would have to drive to a FedEx office and overnight the tape back to headquarters, where our research staff would watch it in its entirety—on a VCR! The researchers would then send notes to the communications staff. Our response would come twenty-four to forty-eight hours later.

By 2004, things had changed dramatically. That year, I worked in South Dakota. The goal was to reelect Tom Daschle, the Democratic Senate majority leader and top Republican target. Before the GOP demagogued Nancy Pelosi, Alexandria Ocasio-Cortez, and Ilhan Omar, Tom Daschle was Republicans' enemy number one. Daschle was the face of the Democratic Party and was running for reelection in a red state. South Dakota was rapidly getting redder. A brutal race ensued, with millions of dollars' worth of negative ads running for well over a year. Republicans saw an opportunity to take out one of their leading antagonists. No Senate leader had lost reelection in a half century. The stakes were high, and the rhetoric was heated. At one point, the campaign manager for John Thune, Daschle's opponent, got in my face so aggressively that the assembled press thought we

_____

2 It would be nice to still have this excuse.

were about to come to blows.[3] That campaign also marks the first time I encountered disinformation as a political strategy.

Two years before, Tim Johnson, the state's other Democratic senator, defeated Thune by a margin of 524 votes. Thune had been recruited to run by Karl Rove and George W. Bush. He was a self-proclaimed high school basketball legend[4] and a rising political star. Republicans could not fathom how their golden boy lost to Johnson, a senator with a relatively low profile, Republicans were unwilling to accept the legitimacy of the election. They blamed two things: voter fraud on the state's Native American reservations and media bias. During his presidency, Trump ran this 2004 playbook, but he didn't write it.

South Dakota is a sparsely populated state with a minuscule media footprint.[5] There are only two media markets and, during that campaign, fewer than a dozen daily newspapers.[6] The most influential of these outlets was the Sioux Falls *Argus Leader*. The *Argus Leader* was the largest newspaper in the state and the only one with the resources to cover politics locally and in Washington. As far back as Tom Daschle's 1978 election to Congress, South Dakota Republicans were convinced that the *Argus Leader* was pro-Democrat and pro-Daschle.

With Thune running against Daschle, Republicans planned to neutralize the perceived Democratic advantage in the media. Early in the campaign, a series of blogs covering the race popped up under generic names like *South Dakota Politics* and *Daschle v. Thune*. Most of the blogs' contributors remained anonymous, and their content was

3 His name was Dick Wadhams, which explains in part why he went through life with such a bad attitude. If he had gone by "Richard," he might have had a sunnier disposition.
4 An *actual* legend would have played his college ball somewhere other than the Bible Institute of Los Angeles (not exactly a powerhouse).
5 It is also so goddamn cold there in winter that its residents need special heaters to keep their car engines from freezing.
6 Far fewer now.

a steady stream of anti-Daschle propaganda and accusations of bias against the *Argus Leader*, its editor, and David Kranz, the state's leading political columnist. As the campaign went on, these blogs became a larger part of the political conversation. Unprompted, reporters brought them up with me, asking for a response to this accusation or that allegation. It didn't matter that the blogs were nothing more than the rantings of online activists. Many in South Dakota treated them as part of the legitimate media. The *Argus Leader* was shaken. Its credibility and integrity were at risk. Its editors had let the conservative blogs bully them into assigning a reporter with near-zero political experience to cover a high-profile campaign. This decision had dramatic implications. Throughout the campaign, the paper responded to the criticism by overcompensating with negative stories about Daschle.

The bloggers, whose identities as GOP activists and Thune supporters eventually emerged, gathered at a conference in Sioux Falls to pass a resolution regarding the *Argus Leader*. They wrote: "WHEREAS, the Sioux Falls Argus Leader has become a powerful print media monopoly in Southeastern South Dakota; WHEREAS, a pattern of chronic political bias has been uncovered at the Argus Leader; WHEREAS, many stories reported nationally which are critical of US senator Tom Daschle are not reported by the Argus Leader." The bloggers even developed a partnership with Jeff Gannon, a reporter from an unknown website called Talon News, to publish a series of investigative pieces that came directly from the Thune campaign's opposition research. It emerged later that Talon News was a conservative front organization and that Gannon was operating under a pseudonym to obscure his past as a paid escort.[7]

---

7 Gannon's past was irrelevant, but his use of a pseudonym was notable because it implied that he obtained his White House press credentials under false pretenses.

This all seemed like small-time mischief. I was annoyed by the secrecy and weaseling of these conservative players, but dismissive of the broader political impact. I believed this was a rare, one-off incident.

I was dead wrong.

One of the blogs "broke" a blockbuster story reminiscent of the sort of absurd, but lethally effective disinformation present in the Trump era. The blog *Daschle v. Thune* claimed that Daschle had promised to support the return of the Black Hills of South Dakota to the Sioux Nation in exchange for the voter turnout necessary to win the election.

Now, South Dakota has a sordid history of discrimination and demagoguery toward its Native American population. Traditionally, upward of 9 in 10 votes from the Native American reservations located in the state went to Democrats. Painting Democrats as too friendly to the community was a tried-and-true GOP tactic, but there was no evidence to support the outrageous charge.[8] Though based on specious hearsay and anonymous sources, the charge rocketed through the political community and was picked up by the national conservative press. Future Trump flunkies, like radio host Hugh Hewitt, amplified the boom of disinformation.

My approach to this conspiracy theory came out of the crisis communications playbook of the day: Ignore it lest you give it more oxygen. I did not want to feed the fire. I could not have known that the embers were already hot and primed to burn.

While political junkies and media types checked these blogs several times a day, the public barely knew they existed, and few cared about what they reported. This notion comforted me until I sat down in a dingy conference room in a run-down hotel in Rapid City to watch

---

8 To be clear, that land was stolen from the Sioux, and they deserve compensation.

a focus group of undecided South Dakota voters. I love focus groups. They are far from a perfect tool, but if you watch enough of them, you can get a real feel for how your voters are thinking. These groups usually make you feel a little better about politics. Most voters, you'll find, live in blissful ignorance of the dumb shit that drives cable TV and gossipy websites like Politico.[9] I was a bit cocky, and confident that this focus group would validate my belief that these blogs that sucked up so much of my time, that lied and pandered, were inconsequential.

Most of the focus group participants had previously voted for Daschle but were now undecided. When the moderator asked them why they were questioning their previous support for Daschle, one older woman with a classic South Dakota accent and slightly blue hair said, "Well, I love Tom, but I don't know why he wants to give away the Black Hills."

Holy shit, I thought. *What are the odds that we've ended up with one of the tiny handful of blog readers in our focus group?*

But then the man sitting next to her chimed in: "I was wondering that, too. Tom has been to my farm, and the Tom I knew would never do that. Washington has changed him."

Fuck. It was then that I realized Daschle might lose. Something bigger was going on, and I had completely missed it. The old rules didn't apply anymore.

When Thune narrowly won, the conservative bloggers did a victory lap, patting themselves on the back. They believed they were grassroots journalists taking on the powerful Democratic elite. But that Black Hills story was bullshit. This wasn't journalism, and it wasn't grassroots. After the election, it was revealed that two of the

---

9 Not to mention what trends on Twitter, the lowest form of information on the planet (other than what trends on Facebook).

bloggers, Jason Van Beek and Jon Lauck, were paid by the Thune campaign for their work taking down Daschle and bludgeoning the local media. This was a campaign stoked by an alternative media eco-system. It was the first of its kind, but it would not be the last.

I can't blame this initiative completely for Daschle's loss. This was a tough year for the Democrats, and South Dakota is a tough state, but I am sure this disinformation played a role. After the election was over, I swore I would never get caught off guard again.

Flash-forward to 2007. I am living in Chicago and working for Barack Obama's presidential campaign. Obama represented a unique threat to the political order. He challenged Hillary Clinton and Joe Biden, among others, for the Democratic nomination. Only a few years removed from the Illinois state senate, Obama rose to the top of the presidential field in an entirely new fashion. With few connections to the party establishment and a sparse Rolodex of the big-money donors, he had not climbed the traditional ladder. Obama's speech to the 2004 Democratic National Convention turned him into a political rock star overnight. This level of instant celebrity—especially for a politician—was impossible before the age of the internet. Most people missed Obama's speech, but they were able to watch it later on You-Tube and news websites. Links to the video were forwarded via email and embedded in blogs.

The Republican Party, with its sordid history of weaponizing racial grievance, saw both an existential threat and a unique oppor-tunity in Obama's candidacy. Before Obama formally announced his campaign, Fox News launched the first attack. The network's morn-ing show, *Fox and Friends*, has all the accoutrements of a typical news program while being a right-wing clown show. Steve Doocy, one of the hosts, regurgitated an allegation that Obama had been educated in a madrassa when he lived in Indonesia as a child. No evidence was presented to back up the statement. At this point, Brian Kilmeade, one of the cohosts, offered this line: "Maybe he doesn't consider terrorists the enemy. Well, we'll see about that."[10]

Unlike in the Daschle campaign, we did not let this charge lie. We weren't afraid of giving oxygen to the fire. The segment was barely over before the Obama campaign was on the phone raising all sorts of hell with the higher-ups at Fox. We contacted progressive bloggers and others in the media to generate a backlash against *Fox and Friends*. If anyone on the campaign knew someone at Fox, they were instructed to call them up and yell at them. *Fox and Friends* eventually gave a lackluster nonapology and retracted the statements.

Later, ABC News sent a reporter to Indonesia to investigate Obama's school. As it turned out, Fox was wrong. Obama did not attend a terrorist training academy. It was a normal school. Shocking! The ABC report was fine journalism and politically beneficial in putting that particular rumor to bed. However, I was kept awake at night, disturbed that a random conspiracy theory mentioned by a Fox doofus with zero credibility could get a major network to fly across the globe to confirm that conspiracy theory. I had the nagging sense that ABC was disappointed by what they found in Indonesia.

The rest of the 2008 Obama campaign was an ongoing battle against right-wing disinformation and conspiracy theories. Early in the campaign, Paul Tewes, who led our efforts in the critical state of Iowa, called with an alarming report. His field staff were receiving a deluge of calls asking two questions about Obama: Was he Muslim, and was it true that he was born in Kenya? The callers had heard these conspiracy theories from three sources: friends and family who

---

10 Amazingly, these two yahoos are still hosting *Fox and Friends* despite being quite dumb and very punchable.

listened to talk radio, friends and family who read conservative news on the internet, and forwarded emails.

The first question is inherently offensive. Whether Obama was Christian, Jewish, or Muslim should have been of no consequence. But for many Democrats, the question was as much about electability in the post-9/11 era as it was about religious bigotry. The second question was an existential threat to the candidacy. If Obama had been born in Kenya, he would have been constitutionally ineligible for the US presidency. This may come as a surprise, but political parties do not want to nominate presidential candidates who cannot serve as president.[11] If Iowa Democrats who loved Obama were hearing and consuming these rumors, imagine the impact they were having with independent voters and more conservative Democrats in places like Ohio and Florida. Once again, we leapt into action, creating a website eventually called Fight the Smears. (While launching a website sounds like an outdated response now, at the time, it was seen as innovative.) On it, we posted a copy of Obama's birth certificate—indisputable evidence that he was born in Hawaii and therefore eligible for the presidency. We wanted to give our supporters the tools to push back on the disinformation. If someone forwarded you an email chain saying Obama wasn't born in the United States, all you had to do was hit Reply All and attach the birth certificate downloaded from our site. This was rudimentary, but it was the first attempt to fight viral disinformation with viral facts. Among Democrats, at least, we were able quell the furor and win the Iowa caucus.

Later in the campaign, the Republicans tried to "swift boat" Obama. *Swift boating* refers to the strategy George W. Bush's campaign used in 2004 to turn John Kerry's heroic service in Vietnam against him. During that election, a book was released (by a conservative publishing

---

11 The GOP, however, had a real habit of nominating people who should *not* serve.

house) titled *Unfit for Command: Swift Boat Veterans Speak Out against John Kerry*. The book featured fellow Vietnam veterans who criticized Kerry for his time as an outspoken critic of the war and falsely and maliciously accused him of lying to win his commendations. The Kerry campaign, following the same outdated playbook I had used in 2004, simply ignored the lies. Lacking a vigorous response, the charges stuck. Throughout the campaign, Kerry used his military service as proof that he could protect a country still living in fear of another 9/11. Within weeks, that central pillar of Kerry's campaign quickly crumbled.

The right wing tried to run an updated, and racist, version of that play against Obama. Jerome Corsi,[12] one of the authors of Kerry's demise, wrote a book titled *The Obama Nation: Leftist Politics and the Cult of Personality*. The book was filled with racist false allegations and painted Obama as an anti-American, Black militant Manchurian candidate. Corsi is a well-known nutcase and a shitty writer, but when your campaign is trying to elect a Black man with the middle name "Hussein," no threat can be ignored.

But we were not going to be swift boated. The Obama campaign acquired a galley copy of Corsi's book through a publishing industry insider, and our research staff went to work with a line-by-line rebuttal. We packaged the final product as a digital book with the clever[13] title *Unfit for Publication*, distributed it to the press, and posted it on the Fight the Smears site. Despite a vigorous book tour that, fittingly, included stops on a white-supremacist radio show and an interview with the final boss of conspiracy theorists, Alex Jones, and with conservative political operatives furiously fanning the flames, *Obama Nation* was a political dud.

---

12 Corsi would reemerge years later as part of the coterie of creeps involved in the Trump campaign's efforts to work with Russia to defeat Hillary Clinton.
13 Cleverness is in the eye of the beholder.

After Obama's landslide victory, our internet-based communications and rapid-response strategies were hailed as innovations. Democrats had stood on the losing end of the message wars for most of the
last thirty years. Now it felt like we had finally cracked the code and
could fight back against an emerging strain of GOP disinformation.

We were wrong. We had won the battle but lost the war.

The Big Lie of Birtherism

Less than three years after Obama's taking office, I stood at the lectern
in the White House Briefing Room flanked by White House counsel
Bob Bauer, admitting defeat in the most public and humiliating way
possible. The purpose of our appearance was to succumb to growing pressure from conspiracy theorists and release Obama's birth
certificate.

Wait, didn't we do that during the campaign? Wasn't that one of
those innovative rapid-response strategies over which we had almost
broken our arms patting ourselves on the back?

Yep.

Publicly releasing the president's birth certificate had done nothing
to solve the problem. The conspiracy theory and the disinformation
peddlers changed the terms without blinking an eye. "Sure, Obama
released his birth certificate. But why won't he release the *long-form*
version of the birth certificate? What is he hiding?"[14] This was a truly
absurd claim, a distinction without a difference. But Corsi and other
trolls, who resided primarily in the dark recesses of the internet, had
kept the "birther movement" alive.

It was Donald Trump—at the time a reality television star, faux
businessman, and loudmouthed son of Queens who was famous for

---

14 Everything is so damn stupid.

being famous[15]—who brought the conspiracy to the forefront. Trump made his rounds promoting the upcoming season of *Celebrity Apprentice*, a show in which a B-list celebrity hosts a competition among a group of C- and D-list celebrities for a fake job and real money. During these media appearances, Trump pushed the notion, contrary to all available evidence, that Obama was born in Kenya. A compliant press, addicted to celebrity gossip and conflict, lapped it up and amplified Trump's false claims with only a modicum of scrutiny. The whole spectacle was great for ratings and clicks, and more media outlets covered it.

This should have been the moment when we realized Trump was a serious presidential competitor. Reporters asked White House spokespeople about it. They shouted ridiculous questions at Obama. There is no dumber, more intellectually lazy question than "Mr. President, what is your response to Donald Trump's claim that you were born in Kenya?" Alas, many media outlets didn't send their best or brightest to cover the White House. The whole affair quickly became an annoying distraction. At Obama's behest, we worked with the state of Hawaii to acquire a copy of the long-form version of the birth certificate released during the campaign. We then scheduled a surprise press conference at which Bauer and I released the birth certificate, explained how we had obtained it, and why Obama had decided to release it. Later that day, Obama went to the Briefing Room to chide the press for covering "carnival barkers."[16]

The press turned on Trump. He became a laughingstock, he was no longer booked for interviews (with the exception of Fox News), and his nascent run for president was abandoned. It wasn't pretty, but once again, we had struck a blow against a malicious disinformation

---

15 Paris Hilton, but less savvy with schlockier eponymous hotels.
16 "Carnival barker" is the most apt description of Trump to date (other than "asshole").

campaign. The release of the birth certificate dominated the news and put the issue to bed.

Or did it?

An NBC/Survey Monkey poll released in October 2016 found that 72 percent of Republicans doubted whether Obama was born in America. It's easy to dismiss this finding as another piece of evidence of Republicans losing their collective minds. I get that. But the situation was more nuanced.

I remember seeing that poll make its rounds on Twitter. My first reaction was "This explains why Trump so easily won the nomination." But as I thought about the implications of the poll, I took a brief[17] respite from my overwhelming confidence in Hillary Clinton's inevitable victory. Nearly three quarters of Republicans was a much, much larger group than the lunatic fringe of Fox addicts and Breitbart readers. And if this many people could believe something so dumb, what other conspiracy theories could be taking hold?

There is no doubt: our pushback on the birther conspiracy and the traditional media's aggressive fact-checking required a more forceful approach and better timing. There would always be people who believed the BS, just as there would always be people who believed the moon landing was faked or that Tupac and Biggie were alive and living in the Caribbean. Conspiracy theories are as much a part of the American tradition as baseball, apple pie, and ill-conceived foreign invasions. Obama's birthplace was not an open question worthy of debate. His birth certificate existed for everyone to see. It had been validated by every available authority. The press spent the Obama years fact-checking every statement to the contrary and informing the public that Obama was born in the United States. It should be impossible to believe otherwise, yet three quarters of one of America's two political

---

17 All too brief.

parties were unwilling to accept reality. They were living, and consuming information, in an entirely different dimension. There were two reasons for this: either a large chunk of the American population was not seeing accurate information, or they were so distrustful of the information they were seeing that they dismissed it out of hand.

In those final weeks of ignorant bliss before Trump won, I comforted myself knowing the Obama-era Republican Party was in its death throes. A third consecutive ass-kicking would knock some sense into the party and move it away from delusion and disinformation. Right-wing Republicans convinced themselves that John McCain lost to Obama because he was too moderate. Romney lost because he had the political skills of a duck-billed platypus. Trump was running on the agenda of Fox News. (Sean Hannity even appeared with Trump at a rally, and Fox News honcho Roger Ailes prepped him for debates.[18]) In my mind, Trump's obviously inevitable defeat would empower the Republicans calling for more moderation and less racism.[19]

Instead, Trump's victory over Hillary Clinton, the GOP's most despised foil, became proof that propaganda and disinformation were viable options for winning. Moreover, they were the *only* way to win.

Politics would never be the same again.

Five years, two impeachments, one insurrection, and a closer-than-expected 2020 election later, Democrats, the press, and the public still haven't fully reckoned with the Republicans' plague on the public consciousness. The problems have only worsened.

I have become more and more convinced that if we continue to lose the information wars, Democrats and democracy will be doomed. There will be more Big Lies, more violence, and little progress on climate change or any other progressive priorities.

---

18 After getting fired from Fox News for sexual misconduct and myriad misdeeds. I think I know what Ailes and Trump bonded over.
19 Those folks are now mostly retired or working for MSNBC.

Since the 2016 elections, Democrats have asked many rhetorical questions about the state of our politics: How does Trump get away with everything? How did he win? Why did he almost win again in 2020, despite four years of corruption and incompetence? Why do Republicans think Biden cheated? Why won't some people get vaccinated or wear a mask? Why does nothing seem to matter?

I could go on and on, but while these questions feel unanswerable, they aren't. The answer to all of them is the same: the right-wing disinformation machine. This "MAGA megaphone" is the most powerful force in politics. Up until the moment Democrats have an answer to Fox, Facebook, and the MAGA media, we will always be on the losing side.

Our answers to these questions begin with an understanding of what we are up against.

2

From Russia with Love

In its purest form, politics is supposed to be an argument—two sides using facts and anecdotes to make a case to the public about the best solution to a policy problem. The side that makes the best argument wins. It's that simple.

With the possible exception of the Lincoln–Douglas debates, *The West Wing*, and some stuff that probably happened in Ancient Greece, I'm not sure politics has ever lived up to this idealized vision. There have always been media manipulators, bad actors, and new technologies to complicate the simple. But for the vast majority of my two decades in this rotten business, political persuasion was possible. You couldn't win over everyone, but with a well-conceived argument backed by data and delivered by a compelling messenger, you could win over enough of them. Partisan media existed—it always has, always will—but Republicans and Democrats fought over the same media terrain. We fought over which campaign would lead the evening news. We both courted local newspaper columnists and competed for coverage on local news. Both sides cared about who scored the cover of *Time* and *Newsweek*.[1] By the time I left the White House in 2015, the ground had fundamentally shifted in ways that seemed equal parts disorienting and dangerous.

---

1 Imagine that?

Change shouldn't be a surprise or be inherently feared. The decade I worked with President Obama coincided with the greatest innovation in media since the invention of the printing press. When I joined the Obama campaign in early 2007, I was issued a BlackBerry; the iPhone had not yet been invented.

John McCain, Obama's opponent in that election, was a relic of the old media era.[2] He loved long, rambling chats with reporters aboard his campaign bus and once jokingly described the establishment media as his "base." The fact that McCain's "Straight Talk Express" campaign was only two presidential campaigns removed from Donald Trump's "the press is the enemy of the people" rhetoric speaks to how quickly things changed.

Technological innovation upending the media landscape is nothing new. Over the course of a century, we moved from print to radio to TV to digital. These shifts were big and came with pluses and minuses for the communicators and the consumers, but the fundamental rules stayed the same. Republican and Democratic voters mostly turned to the same sources for information. Republican and Democratic politicians used the same media to speak to the public. Everyone existed in the same information ecosystem.

I can see how this trip down memory lane can seem like both a paean to the old, outdated media and a "Get off my lawn" moment for an aging political flack. But beyond my personal nostalgia, the most recent shifts are different from anything that has come before. Things in media and politics have fundamentally changed, and those changes threaten democracy and the planet. Almost nothing I learned when I first started in politics is operative today. Political communication has transitioned from public relations to information warfare. Republicans and Democrats no longer consume the same media. We no longer

---

2 He didn't use the internet.

agree on a set of objective facts. The very idea of a "fact" is now questioned. For many Republicans, math and science are to be questioned and, ultimately, dismissed if they run counter to partisan ideology. Truth is in the eye of the beholder. Information bubbles exist. Radicalization happens online. People start watching a few videos about a topic of interest, and a few months later, they storm the US Capitol or try to convince family and friends to avoid submitting to one of Bill Gates's mind-control experiments via the COVID-19 vaccine.[3]

The fact that our media environment is a dystopian hellscape comes as a surprise to no one. Whether you are a junkie or a political noncombatant; whether you read every story and never miss a Sunday show or you don't pay attention to the news, you know that things are a mess. You simply can't avoid it. Every family gathering involves an awkward encounter with a relative whose brain has been pickled by Fox News or YouTube. We've all logged on to Facebook to discover that a high school classmate, an ex, or our dentist has been up at all hours of the night posting conspiracy memes. And who can forget the early days of the COVID-19 pandemic, when it was impossible to find consistent information or clear guidance on how to keep ourselves and our families safe? When the public needed information the most, the press and social media were awash in misinformation, conspiracy theories, half-truths, and panic porn.

In other words, the American information ecosystem is fundamentally broken. It is a legitimate crisis that threatens anything and everything.

While it's impossible to miss the existence of our broken information ecosystem, the conversation about it is detached from the reality and the origins of the crisis. Like a tractor beam, the political media

---

3 Obviously, Gates isn't using the vaccine for his mind-control experiments. He is using 5G. (I'm kidding, I think.)

pulls every conversation toward the dumbest-possible version of what needs to be discussed. To be fair, the ways in which changes in technology and politics have broken the collective American brain are complex and multilayered. Much of the Republican complicity in this situation is obscured by rhetorical smoke screens and secret funding streams.

This is a tricky topic for a lot of Democrats to tackle, because it forces us to question some of our basic principles about how politics should work. To reckon with the new reality will require tearing down many of the political institutions and structures on which we have come to rely. We will also need to adopt some of the methods and strategies we spent the Trump years decrying.[4]

The traditional media, which are charged with telling the story, are culturally and psychologically unable to do so. No media outlet wants to write a real-time account of its own creeping irrelevance and potential demise. Asking the *New York Times* or the *Washington Post* to write a full account of the Republican war on truth would be the equivalent of asking someone to write their own obituary with a focus on all the life decisions they made that contributed to their impending death.

The whole conversation becomes circular, with a bunch of self-serving tropes that miss the bigger picture. You can't solve a problem you don't understand. And I don't think there is problem in American life that requires a more urgent solution. The Republican war on truth is an existential threat to everything.

And despite all that has happened, most people still don't even use the right terms to describe what's happening. That's a problem.

---

4 No, not more tweeting from the toilet.

Russia 2016 to Trump 2020

The terms *disinformation* and *misinformation* are often used inter-changeably and incorrectly. But you don't need to be a lexicographer[5] to know that both words mean "incorrect information." Disinformation and misinformation are abundant in our media ecosystem and on social media. They are both giant problems that make it nearly impossible for anyone but the most media literate to receive consistently accurate information on topics of interest.

The difference lies in much more than one letter.

Misinformation refers to incorrect information that is inadvertently spread; *disinformation*, to information intended to deceive. The growing prevalence of misinformation is the product of a bunch of societal, cultural, technological, and economic trends. With the advent of social media, the hollowing out of traditional media, and a broad-based erosion in trust in institutions, more people are viewing content and then passing it along to even more people with a single click. The old days, when most information came from a small menu of trusted sources (the local newspaper; the three broadcast networks with their famous, reputable anchors; and authorities in the community), are over. These days, it's nearly impossible to know whom or what to trust, so consumers of information are constantly spreading incorrect info to the people in their lives via Facebook, text, or at the dinner table. People have been getting things wrong since the beginning of time. What's changed is the speed at which that (mis)information spreads.

When I was a kid, someone whom I won't name (Hi, Dad!) told me that it could be too cold to snow. Like any gullible youth, I believed this "fact." For years, when the weather came up in conversation, I would

---

5 Or a master at the *New York Times* Spelling Bee or Wordle (an addiction I picked up during the pandemic).

periodically pass this information on. I can't imagine it happened that often; maybe I told this to a dozen people over a decade or so. If any one of those people believed me, they might have told a few people themselves. This was misinformation. I wasn't trying to deceive anyone. I truly believed what I was saying;[6] I was just wrong. However, if a similar thing happened today, I could misinform a much larger group, much faster, by tweeting that it can be too cold to snow. How many of us have hit the Share or RT button too quickly and passed along something that was wholly incorrect or missing so much content that it was deceptive?

Disinformation is something very different. It is a specific and deliberate strategy to pull the wool over people's eyes by knowingly putting out incorrect information. Many readers probably first heard the term *disinformation* in relation to Russian interference in the 2016 election. The Internet Research Agency (IRA), a Russian government–backed troll farm[7]—that's a real thing—used the avarice and obstinance of social media platforms to wage an intense disinformation campaign to help Donald Trump win the 2016 election. While Special Counsel Robert Mueller failed to find enough evidence to indict Donald Trump, Mueller did indict the IRA for election interference. There is no question that Russia actively interfered to help Trump. Admitting this obvious and provable fact might get you excommunicated from the Republican Party, but that doesn't mean it isn't true.

The Russian strategy was a classic example of how to use disinformation to achieve a desired political outcome. As the election approached, Donald Trump's best hope was diminished turnout for Hillary Clinton, particularly among Black voters. But in recent years, approximately 9 in 10 Black voters had supported the Democratic nominee. With a slight drop in turnout potentially being the difference in the election,

---

6 I'm still so convinced this might be true that I googled it at least a dozen different times in the writing and editing of this book. And yes, it's still not true.
7 Some would call Fox News a "Murdoch-backed troll farm."

the Russians went to work. They created fake Twitter and Facebook accounts impersonating Black Americans. Accounts like "Blacktivist" and "BlackMattersUS" criticized Clinton from the left and portrayed her as insufficiently supportive of civil rights. Other posts told Black voters not to vote at all. According to a report from the Senate Intelligence Committee, Russian operatives ran a (nearly illegible) Facebook ad that read, "Not one represents Black People. Don't go to vote. Only this way we can change the way of things." The ad was targeted at Facebook users who had expressed an interest in Martin Luther King Jr., Malcolm X, and civil rights.

The Russian strategy of using disinformation to dissuade worked. According to the Pew Research Center's analysis of the 2016 election, "The Black voter turnout rate declined for the first time in twenty years in a presidential election, falling to 59.6% in 2016 after reaching a record-high 66.6% in 2012. The 7-percentage-point decline from the previous presidential election is the largest on record for Blacks."

The Russians were likely pushing on an open door. Some decline in Black voter turnout after two elections with the first Black president at the top of the ticket was close to inevitable. Elections are too complex to attribute to a single factor. However, in an election decided by fewer than 80,000 votes spread across three states, it would be naïve to dismiss the impact of such a strategic and well-coordinated effort.

This is not an idle trip down memory lane to revisit the most painful election in history.[8] Disinformation is not a just a Russian strategy. It has been a central part of the Republican playbook for a long time. In fact, Trump, the Republicans, and the MAGA media picked up right where the Russians left off. In 2020, the external threat from the Russian government became an internal threat from the Republican Party.

And it almost worked.

---

8 No one needs that.

3

How Trump Almost Stole the 2020 Election

On Election Eve 2020, I participated in a Zoom call with the staff of Crooked Media. Many staff on the call had been working for nearly four years for this night. They had joined the progressive media company after the shock of Trump's victory, looking for a way to make a difference. I loved seeing Crooked fight back against the right-wing media forces that enabled Trump's rise. This election was going to be the culmination of a lot of blood, sweat, and tears. It was a moment of anticipation and anxiety—and because of the pandemic, we were all experiencing it apart. People were Zooming in from home. Some of the staff had decamped from California, where the company was located, and were working from the perhaps more spacious (and affordable) homes of family and friends. This Zoom call was as close as we were going to come to the communal experience that makes the exhausting work of political campaigns feel worth it.

Tanya Somanader, Crooked Media's chief content officer and political strategist, asked me to offer her staffers my Election Eve analysis. I was looking forward to the opportunity to address the amazing young people who had worked so hard over the years. The success of Crooked Media as a political force was due to their hard work; they had changed the game. But the invitation put me in a tough position. My natural demeanor is negative. I would rather expect the worst and hope for the best. In addition to being incredibly superstitious,[1] I had been scarred by my overly optimistic and wholly incorrect assessments of the 2016 election. Still, all the fundamentals of electoral analysis suggested a sizable Biden victory. I didn't want to get hopes up or rain on anyone's parade. Who needs some grumpy old guy making you more nervous on the most nerve-wracking day of your career?

After thinking about this dilemma for way too long, I decided to play it straight:[2]

...as we sit here tonight, Joe Biden is better positioned to win than any candidate since Bill Clinton in 1996.[3] His lead in the polling average nationally and in the battleground states is historically larger. Biden has multiple paths to the requisite 270 votes, and Trump has one. And he is losing by more than five points in the states he needs to win.

And if you don't believe the public polls, look at the campaigns. Biden was campaigning in Iowa and Ohio on the last day.

Last but not least, we are in the middle of a pandemic that has killed more than 100,000 Americans. Trump failed to prepare for it, and his response has been to dismiss it, tell people to drink bleach, and generally act like a clown. Every time he opens his mouth or tweets, he makes an in-kind contribution to the Biden campaign. But—and this is the ultimate but—there has never been, and hopefully will never be, another election like this. The pandemic's impact on campaigning, voting, and turnout are the ultimate X factor.

---

1 I have calluses on my knuckles from knocking on wood.
2 A decision I very much regretted at about midnight Pacific Standard Time.
3 A reference that meant almost nothing to staff born after an election that happened while I was still in college. Ouch!

Everything I said was pretty much correct. Despite the apparent optimism over the outcome, mine was nothing more than a cold-blooded analysis of the data. It says a lot about how much the data favored Biden that I felt compelled to be so positive. Now, of course, I was technically right but spiritually wrong. Biden won, but it was much, much closer than I imagined or the fundamentals suggested.

In the weeks after the election, I wrestled with what I, and everyone else, had missed. Sure, the polls were very wrong, but we all knew to be skeptical of polls after 2016. The real issue was that Trump had increased his turnout despite doing almost every single thing wrong by the traditional rules of politics. He was unpopular, untrustworthy, and seen as thoroughly incompetent on the single-biggest issue in the race. Yet, a shift of fewer than 44,000 votes in four states, and Trump would have been reelected.[4]

What I missed in my analysis was that while I lived in one version of reality, where Trump was an incompetent fool sticking his thumb in the eye of the electorate, a huge segment of the electorate lived in an alternative version of reality, one where up was down and black was white. While I had spent much of my career in politics raising the alarm about the power of Fox News and other right-wing media, I truly underestimated how powerful the disinformation machine had become. Trump, with the help of his friends at Fox and Facebook, made people forget, or at least misunderstand, that it was the pandemic costing them their jobs, livelihoods, and the lives of their friends and family.

The postelection analyses of the closer-than-expected race focused on the political potency of GOP attacks about defunding the police, the impact of late-breaking news about Hunter Biden, and Trump's appeal to working-class voters, including the Black and

---

4 And I would be writing this book on pieces of toilet paper in my cell at Gitmo.

Latino voters who had long been a part of the Democratic coalition. But there was too little discussion of why these things mattered.

While everyone was focused on stopping the Russian interference that played a role in 2016, Trump and the Republicans had taken the Russian playbook, updated it, and run an even more powerful disinformation campaign than Putin ever did. Republicans used disinformation to nearly steal an election they should have lost handily—and there was little discussion of how Democrats almost let it happen.

There were three parts to Trump's 2020 disinformation strategy:

1. Make the pandemic disappear;
2. Set the stage for the Big Lie; and
3. Depress turnout among Black and Latino voters.

This Is Not the Pandemic You Are Looking For

In February 2020, Donald Trump looked like a slight favorite for reelection. Democrats were engaged in a divisive primary that threatened to go on for months. Trump was an incumbent president with a strong economy and a massive campaign war chest. And incumbent presidents running on strong economies with massive war chests almost never lose.

Then COVID-19 hit. America was unprepared and slow to respond. The pandemic preparedness handbook that President Obama's staff had left for Trump was gathering dust on a shelf. The pandemic unit Obama had built within the National Security Council was unceremoniously disbanded by Trump years earlier. Trump himself ignored warnings from the intelligence community and health experts. Until that point, he had been pretty lucky. The majority of the crises he confronted had been political and self-created.[5] His first three-plus years

---

5 And created mostly via tweet.

were a nearly unprecedented run of peace and prosperity. The onset of the pandemic was a deadly piece of prima facie evidence of the dangers of having a reality TV star as president.

The pandemic also eviscerated Trump's best (or only) argument for reelection: the strong economy. Polls showed that bipartisan majorities approved of Trump's handling of the economy and preferred him on economic issues over Democrats, including Joe Biden. The truth is that all Trump had done was not screw up the Obama economy, and in fact, job creation had slowed since the end of the Obama administration.[6] But within weeks of the emergence of COVID-19, the economy was devastated. America was in a historic recession with whole sectors of the economy shut down due to the pandemic.

The pandemic was an existential threat to Trump's prospects for reelection. The president had two options: either roll up his sleeves and do the hard work of addressing the novel coronavirus, saving lives, and fixing the economy; or try to convince just enough voters that the pandemic wasn't his fault and wasn't that big a deal.

Given the choice between hard work and lying, which do you think Donald J. Trump chose?

On its face, convincing people, even hard-core MAGA supporters, to ignore a pandemic killing thousands of Americans every day was absurd and impossible. But Trump almost pulled it off. There was a period early in the pandemic when Trump was appointment viewing. The White House Coronavirus Task Force was doing daily press briefings. Other than Mike Pence, the political version of the human appendix, these briefings were quite informative. There were updates on case rates, the latest findings on how the virus spread, and information on the availability of tests and personal protective equipment.

---

6 I am professionally obligated to point this out. Preserving and burnishing the Obama legacy will be my task for the balance of my years on this planet.

It was reassuring to know that there were competent, nonpartisan experts like Anthony Fauci working in a government populated with rejects from the Fox News expanded universe.

With an anxious public locked in their homes and craving information about the virus, the cable networks carried these briefings live. Even in the middle of a raging pandemic, Donald Trump's primary presidential activity was watching cable news.

Yet, once Trump saw all the cameras glued to Vice President Mike Pence, Fauci, and others, he invited himself to attend. It was classic Trump—his insatiable need for media attention getting in the way of his strategic objective, which in this case was blaming Pence for anything that went wrong during the pandemic.[7] Once Trump started showing up, the pandemic press briefing went from an occasion for hope and information to one of despair and disinformation. But as the ratings indicate, most people still couldn't avert their eyes. The press briefings became like a regularly scheduled rubbernecking at a car crash carried out live on cable TV. Of Trump's many gaffes, misstatements, and temper tantrums, none stood out more than the Great Bleach Incident of 2020.

During this now-notorious press briefing, Bill Bryan, a Department of Homeland Security official, was explaining to the press the impact of sunlight and disinfectant on coronavirus found on surfaces. Trump, standing off to the side, was waiting for his turn at the lectern. He had designated himself emcee for these briefings, which made sense—he had little else to offer. In fact, Trump had reportedly stopped attending the regular task force meetings and was now getting (at best) a CliffsNotes version of them delivered by political staffers.[8]

---

7 A precursor to Trump's revving up his mob of supporters to murder Mike Pence on January 6.
8 Trump found the experts tedious, presumably because of all their polysyllabic words.

As Bryan finished his presentation, Trump strode to the lectern. His task was either to hand off to the next speaker or open the room up for questions from the assembled members of the media. The look on Trump's face as he prepared to speak was priceless. He looked so proud of himself, as if he personally had discovered cold fusion.[9] But then he opened his mouth and disaster ensued: "A question that probably some of you are thinking of if you're totally into that world," Trump began, clearly thinking of the question himself:

So, supposing we hit the body with a tremendous—whether it's ultraviolet or just very powerful light—and I think you said that that hasn't been checked, but you're going to test it. And then I said, supposing you brought the light inside the body, which you can do either through the skin or in some other way, and I think you said you're going to test that, too. Sounds interesting, right? And then I see the disinfectant, where it knocks it out in a minute. One minute. And is there a way we can do something like that, by injection inside or almost a cleaning. Because you see it gets in the lungs, and it does a tremendous number on the lungs. So it would be interesting to check that.

If you put aside the fact that this dimwit had the ability then to blow up a country with nuclear weapons, his statements during this briefing are truly funny. In that moment, we were allowed to watch President Homer Simpson's pea brain at work in real time. If bleach kills COVID-19 outside the body, why not put bleach *inside* the body? Boom! Problem solved.

(While most of the attention and ridicule was focused on the bleach

---

9 Or his father finally said, "I love you." Is that too mean? Do I care? Can you be too mean to Trump?

part of Trump's inquiry, I would have loved some follow-up questions about how exactly he planned to get sunlight inside the body.[10])

The reaction to the "bleach moment" was typical of Trump's messaging: while liberals laughed, Trump supporters listened, and numerous reports of Trump supporters getting sick from ingesting bleach or other disinfectants followed. Liberals viewed this incident as evidence of the gullibility of Trump supporters as opposed to the power of the messaging and the messenger.

Trump's suggesting that anyone inject bleach in the human body was a dumb statement from a dumb person, but it is an alarmingly amusing anecdote that speaks to how he used disinformation to blunt the damage from the pandemic. I don't want to be one of those pundits who reverse-engineer strategic significance from Trump's verbal and digital diarrhea. It's clear from the video that Trump's "inject bleach" moment was not part of some master plan. It was merely spur-of-the-moment idiocy. Still, the instinct to endorse bleach injection as a cure for COVID-19 fit a pattern. From its onset, Trump had tried to minimize the dangers of the pandemic for one simple reason: the safer people felt, the sooner they would start venturing out and spending money, and the sooner the economy would bounce back.

A less clumsy version of this strategy was when Trump and his allies in the MAGA media began relentlessly hocking hydroxychloroquine as a treatment for COVID-19 disease, even though its safety was repeatedly questioned by Trump's own Food and Drug Administration. Trump supporters (including Trump-supporting doctors) rushed out to buy as much hydroxychloroquine as they could find, creating a run on a drug that wasn't even fully approved to treat COVID-19. The presence of a possible cure was supposed to encourage people to take more risks, spend more money, and get America back to normal faster.

---

10 Okay, maybe I don't really want to know the answer to that question.

Now, it probably goes without saying that this strategy had some downsides. Encouraging people to return to normalcy before there were vaccines and before the infection rates had gone down only prolonged the pandemic and delayed the return to normalcy. But no one had ever accused Donald Trump of being a strategic genius. Trump cared only about the election; the loss of American life was inconsequential. He would gladly have taken a higher death count if it meant a lower unemployment rate.[11]

For similar reasons, Trump and right-wing media personalities continued dismissing the efficacy and acceptability of masks. The image of people wearing masks became, for Trump, the physical manifestation of his failure to prepare for and respond to the pandemic. Seeing people wearing masks felt, to Trump at least, like seeing them running around wearing T-shirts reading, "Trump Failed."[12]

When Joe Biden was photographed wearing a mask for the first time, Brit Hume, a once-respected[13] Fox News analyst, tweeted the photo with the caption "This might help explain why Trump doesn't like to wear a mask in public." Hume's tweet immediately went viral, getting lift from high-profile Trump supporters (and from angry liberals inadvertently spreading it via hate engagement). In the view of Fox News, mask wearing was beta behavior, a sign of weakness. Trump's minions did everything they could to discourage people from wearing masks. Despite the fact that mask-wearing was the recommended guidance from his own government, Trump refused to wear one in public for months—even when infected with COVID-19.

In theory, an escalating death toll is an impossible political problem for an incumbent president. But the right-wing media helped solve

---

11 Much as GOP-supporting corporations would gladly have taken a higher death count if it meant a lower tax rate.

12 A missed merch opportunity for Crooked Media.

13 "Once," as in at one moment before now but after the beginning of time.

this problem for Trump. As the death toll started to rise well above the overly rosy predictions of the Trump administration, conspiracy theories about the accuracy of the count started spreading on the internet and in the right-wing media. Right-wing outlets latched on to an esoteric technicality of how New York and other states counted COVID-19 deaths. While the conspiracy theories started in the dark corners of the internet, they quickly traveled to Fox News. Brit Hume and Tucker Carlson argued that the death tolls were inflated by blue-state bureaucrats looking to hurt Trump. The claim was that just because someone had died *with* COVID-19, it didn't mean they had died *of* COVID-19. This was, of course, a bad-faith argument from people who certainly knew better, but gaslighting the pandemic was a political priority for right-wing media, which had gotten very rich in the Trump era. These claims were amplified on social media by high-profile Trumpists.

Because of a shortage of tests and an unusually high number of deaths from "pneumonia" before medical professionals knew to test for the novel coronavirus, every health expert believed that the official death toll actually *underestimated* the number of people who had died from COVID-19. But, once again, the right-wing media was successfully making people disbelieve what they were seeing. An Axios/Ipsos poll from July 2020 found that one third of Americans believed the death count was inflated. This included 61 percent of people who watched Fox. Only 7 percent of people who watched CNN thought the count inflated.

In addition to an unmasked populace and an escalating death toll, Trump's efforts to minimize the pandemic faced one diminutive but garrulous obstacle: Dr. Anthony Fauci. The longtime director of the National Institute of Allergy and Infectious Diseases became a bona fide celebrity in the early days of the pandemic and was omnipresent in the media. For the majority of Americans who didn't trust their president, Fauci, with his comforting demeanor and actionable advice, became a beacon of hope in a dark time. Polls showed that Fauci was the most trusted person in America. Fauci worship became a thing. You could buy votive candles bearing saintly images of the doctor, and his visage was printed on T-shirts and found in online avatars. While respect for Fauci's brilliance and long career was more than warranted, the deification was bizarre.[14]

Trump is naturally envious of anyone who gets better press coverage or generates more enthusiasm[15] than he does, but Fauci presented a political problem for Trump as well. While Trump was minimizing the dangers of the pandemic and peddling false hope, Fauci was repeatedly using his very large platform to warn people about the seriousness of the virus and the need to adhere to social distancing and masking guidelines. His every utterance was a rebuke of the president's dominant message. Fauci was so respected that even Trump knew he was essentially untouchable. Firing Fauci would have prompted a bipartisan uproar on the Hill, led to the resignation of a number of members of the White House Coronavirus Task Force, and caused a media firestorm.[16]

At first, Trump tried to silence Fauci. The Vice President's Office, which was responsible for signing off on Fauci's media interviews, stopped greenlighting those opportunities.[17] Then Fauci stopped coming to the daily task force press briefings. The result was Trump

---

14 There's probably a lot of overlap between the people who bought Fauci candles and those with prints of RBG greeting John McCain in heaven hanging in their homes.

15 This is certainly why he chose Mike Pence, a man that makes plain yogurt seem exciting, as his VP.

16 Fauci was *great* for ratings and clicks. Note: this is not the only reason he was a returning guest on *Pod Save America*. It's not *not* the reason, either.

17 Pence's office wouldn't return calls from the *Pod Save America* producer, which may be related to the fact that I have repeatedly referred to Pence as a "homophobic tub of paste" in multiple forums.

and his aides getting asked nonstop questions about Fauci's where-abouts, his standing, and if and when he was getting fired. Even in absentia, Fauci was distracting from Trump's message.

Trump was in a political vise—so, his MAGA media minions went to work discrediting Fauci. The hashtag FireFauci started trending online. Fox News and right-wing media personalities started highlighting mistakes Fauci may have made at the outset of the pandemic. They called him a member of the "deep state" trying to undermine Trump from the inside. There were conspiracies circulating about Fauci's role in funding a lab in the Wuhan province of China that may have been the original source for the virus. Laura Ingraham, and others argued that Fauci's calls for social distancing measures, which slowed economic growth, were born of his secret support for Joe Biden. Trusting Fauci—which most of the country did—became a sign of disloyalty to Donald Trump. Fauci's approval rating took a huge hit with Republicans, who now believed that he was an enemy of Trump and Trumpism. As a result, Trump—the man who had recommended injecting bleach—became the most trusted voice for news on the pandemic for Republicans.[18]

The evil beauty of the right-wing media bubble is that it is hermetically sealed. Republicans can deliver one message to the base via Fox and Facebook and offer a different message to the masses. Because he had no filter or impulse control, Trump rarely took advantage of this opportunity. At the very same time that Trump's allies were trashing Fauci to the Republican base, Trump's campaign started airing a television ad with a clip of Fauci saying about Trump's pandemic response, "I can't imagine that anybody could be doing more."

Then Trump himself contracted COVID-19—perhaps the most

---

18 By early 2022, less than half of Americans trusted Fauci, which speaks to the power of the MAGA megaphone.

predictable thing ever to happen—and (allegedly) knowingly exposed a large group of people, including his staff, the Secret Service, Gold Star families, and Joe Biden. Former New Jersey governor Chris Christie got COVID-19 and almost died from it. When he was in the hospital with the virus, Trump called him. Did the president inquire about his health? Offer help of any kind? Nope. Trump only wanted to make sure Christie wasn't going to tell people he had caught the virus from him.

The fact that Trump got COVID-19 and lived to tell about it became part of the disinformation strategy. *See? It's not so bad! He got it and returned to the campaign trail before too long.* What Trump and his media allies failed to mention was that the president had access to some of the best doctors in the world, while convalescing at one of the best hospitals in the world, and he was treated with a very expensive experimental drug unavailable to all but the most powerful.

It speaks to the power of the disinformation apparatus that Trump was able to turn his catching COVID-19 because he was too stubborn and stupid to follow his own government's guidelines into an argument for his reelection.

Disinformation to Break Up the Democratic Coalition

With all due respect to Pitbull, Gloria Estefan, Miami Sound Machine, Rick Ross, and Walt Disney, Florida is the absolute worst. As Democrats across the country settled into their couches to watch what the polls (incorrectly) told us[19] would be the ass-kicking Donald Trump deserved, the first sign that something might be amiss came from Florida. The polling in the run-up to the election was pretty consistent; Biden had a small but steady lead in the Sunshine State. The last *New York Times*/Siena College poll of Florida, the theoretical gold standard

---

19 LOL.

in media polling,[20] had Biden winning the state by 3 points. Joe Biden didn't need to win Florida,[21] but it would have been sweet. Florida counts quickly and reports early. If Biden were victorious there, Democrats could get the champagne out of the freezer. Trump had basically no path to 270 electoral votes without Florida. There was also an emotional significance. In 2016, it was the early results from Florida that shook our mistaken confidence in Hillary Clinton's inevitable victory. Every Democrat can remember that moment on Election Night 2016, when the world started to fall apart. There is nothing I wanted more than to not have that feeling again. Florida was the test, and once again, Florida failed us.

The state is always close. Everyone knows what happened to Al Gore in Florida in 2000. And the state wasn't called for Obama until days after the election in 2012. A big chunk of Democratic votes is in Miami-Dade County.[22] The rhythm of Florida Election Nights is mind-numbingly familiar: Dems jump out to an early lead, Republicans quickly gain the advantage as the red rural counties report their votes, and then we wait for Miami-Dade to come in.

The 2020 election, however, was different. When the Miami-Dade votes started coming in, something looked very different. Trump was winning a shocking number of votes. Even more surprisingly, the more Hispanic the precinct, the better Trump performed.

Florida, with its large Cuban American population, is unique. But the Rio Grande Valley of Texas, with its overwhelming Hispanic population, also moved in Trump's direction. He even improved on his numbers in rural counties with large Black populations. In major urban areas like Philadelphia, Detroit, and Milwaukee, Trump did

---

20 Also LOL.

21 You know this because he didn't win Florida. And now he gets from A to B via Air Force One instead of United Airlines.

22 I will let you guess which major city is in Miami-Dade County. (Hint: It's not Dade.) My self-hate grows with each passing dad joke.

marginally better than in 2016. The racist in chief who spent four years demagoguing immigrants, called African nations "shithole" countries, and referred to the people peacefully protesting structural racism and police brutality as "thugs" did better with Black, Latino, and Asian voters.

What the F was going on? Did nothing make sense?

Biden won anyway—but barely. On Twitter, in the media, and in text chains and Zoom calls hosted by Democratic Party operatives,[23] a vigorous debate broke out over how Trump had done the impossible. Was it Trump's economic message? Had Biden and the Democrats missed pandemic fatigue among working-class voters? Were the Dems too woke? Not woke enough? There is some truth to all these. These communities are not monolithic. Trying to find a singular reason that a Cuban American in Miami, a Mexican American in Texas, an older Black man in rural North Carolina, or a young Black woman in Philly didn't vote for Joe Biden is a fool's errand. But there is one thing these communities have in common: they were all the targets of a well-funded, strategic, under-the-radar disinformation campaign.

I am not arguing that disinformation is the only reason, or even the main reason, Democrats lost ground with the voters who made up the backbone of our coalition for decades. There is no question that our strategy was flawed, our outreach was lacking, and our message was at times condescending. But disinformation played an important role, too, and if the party doesn't understand what Republicans did and how they did it, we will continue to lose ground we can't afford to lose.

Postelection, a number of academic efforts were made to document how disinformation targeted communities of color. Black and Latino political strategists urged the mostly white political pundits dominating cable and Twitter to acknowledge that there was more at

---

23 Also podcasts. How could I forget podcasts?

play than voters being wooed by Donald Trump's charms or turned off by Biden's decades-old record on crime.

The use of disinformation to target communities of color was much more widespread and strategic than many people realize. The scope of the effort is stunning and happened largely below the radar and with limited attention from the bulk of the media and the Democratic Party.

Voter Depression

There is nothing new about Republican forces trying to stop people from voting. Voter suppression has been a core part of GOP strategy since about five minutes after President Lyndon Johnson signed the Voting Rights Act. Poll taxes, voter ID laws, threats of violence, and a scarcity of polling places and voting machines are all part of the playbook.

Disinformation is also part of the voter suppression strategy. Shadowy groups send out mailers and robocalls with intentionally incorrect information about where, when, and how to vote. These communications misstate voter registration deadlines, the date of elections, and the addresses of polling places. In 2020, a group called Project 1599[24] sent robocalls targeted at Black voters in Michigan, Pennsylvania, and elsewhere that falsely claimed that voters who cast their ballots by mail would have their information shared with law enforcement and collection agencies seeking warrants and unpaid debts.

These offline efforts have a long history. They are definitely illegal, even in a world where the Supreme Court has turned the Voting Rights Act into an ineffective and unenforceable husk. Luckily, in 2021 the yahoos behind the Project 1599 calls were charged with a crime.

---

24 Project 1599 was founded by Jacob Wohl, a Trump-supporting dirty trickster. Wohl's bungling criminality makes the people who post videos of themselves committing crimes look like El Chapo.

For the Republican operatives who want to stop people from voting and not get charged with a crime, there is another strategy, one that exists in a legal gray area. If voter suppression means stopping people who want to vote from casting their ballot, voter depression means using disinformation to convince people not to vote at all. The Russians used this tactic to great effect in 2016, with efforts targeted at Black voters, young voters, and supporters of Bernie Sanders disenchanted with Hillary Clinton. The social media platforms that were played for fools by Putin in 2016 invested time and energy in stopping future foreign interference. But, being the fools they are, they were played once again in 2020. This time, though, the interference was coming from inside the house! Some of it was implicit; some was explicit; some was from mysterious sources; some was from right-wing media figures looking for attention as much as political advantage—but all of it was part of an effort to convince primarily Black voters to stay home.

In 2016, Trump's victory was so narrow that the margin could be attributed to almost anything. But if there was one thing the Trump campaign feared more than anything else, it was an increase in turnout among Black voters. Even a slight increase in Black turnout over 2016 spelled doom for Trump.

Reducing Black turnout or keeping it at 2016 levels seemed possible. Right-wing media influencers and Trump surrogates went to work. The goal was to sow division and disinterest between Black voters and the Democratic Party, a page ripped right out of the Russian playbook from 2016. As the Senate Intelligence Committee wrote in its bipartisan[25] report on Russian interference, "No single group of Americans was targeted by IRA [the Kremlin-backed Internet Research Agency] information operatives more than African Americans. By far,

---

25 Imagine that!

race and related issues were the preferred target of the information warfare campaign designed to divide the country in 2016."

In 2020, right-wing digital operatives picked up where the Russians left off. Trump-supporting Black social media influencers targeted their audiences with arguments about why the Democrats had not and would not deliver for the Black community. Very few bothered to make the positive case for Trump. Facebook groups for Black Americans were flooded with arguments designed to encourage voters to stay home. Any complaints or criticisms about Biden, his record, or his agenda from Black people, whether genuine or performative cynicism, were amplified by the right-wing media and MAGA influencers with large followings, like the Trump children and media provocateur Dan Bongino.

Joe Biden's decision to pick Kamala Harris, the first Black woman to serve on a major-party ticket, increased the peril for Team Trump. In a form of political and digital jujitsu, the Trump campaign and its allies tried to weaponize Harris's record as San Francisco district attorney and California attorney general. Leveraging a heated debate from the Democratic primary, memes and hashtags referred to Harris as "Kamala the Cop" or "Copala Harris." Criticisms of her record were hyperbolized and spread on Black Twitter and in other online communities without context or rebuttal. In the run-up to the election, a photo mosaic of Harris's face, purportedly made up of photos of "All the Black Men She Locked Up and Kept in Prison Past Their Release Date for Jail Labor," went viral. The image was a fraud. Upon closer examination, the meme appeared to have used the same few images over and over.

Similarly, the Republican campaign to sow doubts over the integrity of mail-in ballots was largely targeted at Black voters, who have a well-earned historic distrust of the process. Dissuading people from the safer, more secure vote-by-mail options put in place due to the pandemic could lead to a lower turnout. Fears of COVID-19, fewer polling places, and longer lines in precincts with disproportionately large Black populations meant that someone who didn't avail themselves of the vote-by-mail or early-voting option could end up being turned away or leaving because of insanely long lines.

While the overwhelming focus was on dissuading people from voting, Trump supporters also used disinformation to create a false impression of Black support for Trump. In the weeks before the election, Twitter suspended a network of fake accounts pretending to be Black Trump supporters. These accounts, which used stolen and stock photos, posted positive content about Trump and were shared by Trump allies. The genesis of this network is unknown, but it is yet another example of pro-Trump disinformation targeted at Black voters. Another image that went viral late in the campaign was a photo of rappers 50 Cent and Ice Cube wearing "Make America Great Again" swag. The photo was widely shared on social media, including by Donald Trump's son Eric. There was only one problem: it had been doctored. While Ice Cube had made some vaguely positive statements about his conversations with Trump, and while 50 Cent had endorsed Trump (based on a gigantic misunderstanding of Biden's tax plan) before disavowing him, neither rapper formally endorsed President Trump; nor had they worn the hats shown in the photo.

Like the decision to have Tim Scott, the only Black Republican in the Senate, deliver the keynote speech at the Republican National Convention, the goal of these efforts was to create a false impression of Black support for Trump and Black disdain for Biden and Harris. It's hard to know what role these efforts played, but Biden received the same level of support from Black voters that Clinton received in 2016—but down from Obama in 2008 and 2012. This was enough to make the race a coin flip that, fortunately, Biden won. Biden's victory makes it easy to say these efforts failed, but consider this: the efforts from pro-Trump forces targeting Black voters were just as successful as the Russian interference campaign in 2016.

Disinformación

In 2018, I was unusually optimistic about Florida. Democrats had a legitimate chance to win the governorship for the first time this century[26] with an exciting progressive candidate in Andrew Gillum. Sen. Bill Nelson, the least exciting astronaut in American history, had a good chance at reelection because he was facing the outgoing Republican governor in what promised to be a bad year for sitting Republican politicians.

A few weeks before the election, I was talking to someone involved in Florida politics. This operative did not share my optimism or agree with the larger political universe that was bullish on Gillum and Nelson. When I asked why, they responded with one word: *socialism.*

I was immediately and foolishly dismissive. As a natural pessimist, I thought I could spot someone looking for a reason to worry. Republicans have been playing the socialist card for years. They used it to attack Obama repeatedly—though our polling was very clear that voters did not buy it—and Trump called Democrats socialists, a message Fox readily amplified. Still, few people outside the Republican base believed it. With the emergence of Bernie Sanders, a self-described Democratic Socialist, as a Democratic Party leader, the salience of the issue was raised. But the idea that one could persuade actual swing voters that Democratic candidates were socialist seemed far-fetched. In my experience, the much more impactful (and accurate) criticism of the party was that we were too close to powerful capitalist powers like Wall Street, the pharmaceutical industry, and Big Tech.

---

26 Yes, you read that correctly.

"But Florida is different. Trust me," the Florida operative insisted. I should have trusted him. The results in Florida in 2018—the only battleground state where Democrats fared poorly—are proof. Unbeknownst to me and a lot of other Democrats, the Trump campaign and other Republican groups were running a consistent campaign branding the Democrats as socialists. What made these efforts different, and more effective, was that they were mostly in Spanish and targeted at Florida voters with roots in Cuba and Venezuela, voters who had lived under the yoke of socialism or who had family still in those countries. To these voters, socialism was not a dumb right-wing talking point. It was a part of their lives. Even if the Republicans were unable to convince voters that Democrats were actual socialists in the Karl Marx, nationalizing-industries sense of the term, they could convince voters that Democrats were soft on socialists at home and abroad. I mean, heck, they had socialists in their own party.

In 2018, Gillum and Nelson lost very close elections with all the political wind at their back because nearly 5 in 10 Florida Hispanics joined with a majority of white voters to vote Republican. There was a marked increase in Republican Hispanic support from previous elections.

In 2020, the Trump campaign and its allies doubled and tripled down on the socialism disinformation strategy. How candidates deal with socialist regimes like Venezuela's is a legitimate campaign issue. The nature of their economic programs is a subject worthy of debate, but that is not what happened in Florida. The right-wing efforts were designed to confuse and mislead. They did not exist in the gray areas of truth, where campaign messaging sometimes wanders. They were disinformation, pure and simple. Here are some of the examples:

- A group called Cubanos por Donald Trump shared a photo of Biden kneeling while surrounded by people in native

Haitian attire. The caption read, "Who wants a commander in chief that kneels before foreign leaders?" Except, Biden wasn't in Haiti. He was in Miami, at the Haitian Cultural Center, and he was kneeling to pay tribute to George Floyd and the fight against structural racism.

■   The Trump campaign ran an ad in the Miami media market that juxtaposed quotes from Biden with those from socialist leaders like Hugo Chávez and Nicolás Maduro of Venezuela that ended with the very subtle tagline "Biden = Socialism."

■   A false Spanish-language ad from the Trump campaign, targeted at Florida's Venezuelan American population, claimed that Venezuela's socialist rulers were backing Biden's election. According to ProPublica, the ad was watched more than one hundred thousand times on YouTube in the eight days before the election. These views of this faux-explosive revelation only increased with the organic sharing that occurred on Facebook, WhatsApp, and in family group chats.

■   Carinés Moncada, a host on a popular Spanish-language Florida radio station, asserted that one of the cofounders of Black Lives Matter practiced 'Brujería' or witchcraft and that "whoever votes for Biden, unfortunately, is supporting that." This absurd but powerful claim was taken directly from Punch, a right-wing news website known for pushing conspiracy theories.

A lot of the disinformation revolved around Biden's support for socialism, his mental acuity, and misinformation about COVID-19. This disinfo was pushed by what the *New York Times* described as a "crop of right-wing Spanish-language websites that are designed to look like nonpartisan news outlets." Other reports found wild conspiracy theories going viral on WhatsApp groups, including one about Biden being unable to serve as president due to his Catholic faith.

This disinformation campaign is not the only reason Biden lost Florida by a larger than expected margin, but it *is* a reason. And Democrats ignore it at our peril. In the years since, there has been very little Democratic Party–wide response to what happened, no concerted effort to build better defenses or go on the offensive. Just as we did after 2016, we are sticking our heads back in the sand without doing anything and hoping for a better outcome. Democrats tend to see stopping the spread of disinformation in English, Spanish, or any other language as the job of the mainstream media. We see the effectiveness of this tactic as evidence of the voters' stupidity, rather than as a failure of our strategy.

And what are the Republicans doing?

In early 2021, One America News, the billionaire-funded right-wing cable network that markets itself as the place for people who think Fox News isn't pro-Trump enough, announced plans to launch a Spanish-language network that should be up and running well before the 2024 election is under way.

4

A Short History of the Long War on Truth

During his first formal press conference since his inauguration, Donald Trump strode to the lectern in the East Room looking almost like a president. For anyone who pays attention to politics, the image of an American leader walking up to that big wooden lectern with the Presidential Seal (known as the "Blue Goose") is a familiar one. We have seen many presidents make that walk to sign historic legislation, address national crises, and announce future[1] Supreme Court justices.

The purpose of Trump's press conference that day—other than to remind everyone that his 2016 election victory wasn't a fever dream—was to announce a totally fake, immediately ignored, and never-again-discussed plan to address the conflict of interest in a sitting US president with ongoing business interests.

Before too long, the press conference devolved into a shouting match between Trump and CNN correspondent Jim Acosta.[2] As the questioning grew more heated, Trump transformed from a newly elected president into an angry school bus driver who had been on the

---

1 Before you tweet at me, the nomination of Merrick Garland was announced in the Rose Garden. His fate, however, was determined by Mitch McConnell's constitutional arson more than the location of the ceremony (I think/hope).

2 Acosta had chosen himself as chief combatant in Trump's war against the media, a sign that the war was over before it truly began.

job a few years too long.[3] "Fake news," he shouted over and over, as if it were his safe word.

He would go on in that press conference to spout lie after lie, and in the weeks that followed spread conspiracy theories about the election, falsely claiming that:

- Hillary Clinton had not won the popular vote due to millions of votes from undocumented immigrants;
- Barack Obama had *wiretapped* his phone; and
- His pitifully small inauguration crowd was the largest in history.[4]

As often as these statements were fact-checked and debunked, a significant portion of the Republican base believes them to this day.

During the campaign, Trump ran successfully against the press. He turned their disdain for him into a political asset, evidence that he really was an outsider trying to upend the political system. While candidates, and particularly Republican candidates, had critiqued media outlets in the past,[5] Trump brought a new and dangerous vitriol to the sport. He banned certain media outlets from his events. He attacked reporters by name on Twitter and in front of rally crowds. And he targeted women and reporters of color with particularly nasty vigor. At one point, he directed his supporters to harm the reporters in attendance at one of his rallies. Indeed, Trump rallygoers often chanted "CNN sucks!"[6]

Trump's campaign tactics were gross and, more important,

---

3 Think the Chris Farley character in *Billy Madison*.

4 Remember Sean Spicer? That's okay. No one else does, either.

5 Vice President Dick Cheney, a major league asshole, was once caught on a hot mic calling a *New York Times* reporter a "major league asshole."

6 An open question is whether this was partisan vitriol or just the natural reaction of people who had seen former CNN anchor Chris Cuomo both ask and answer the questions in his interviews—an impressive parlor trick, but absolutely miserable TV.

dangerous. To see a man with the power to declare wars use the White House to bully and attack the media was deeply troubling. When foreign leaders rant about the dangers of a free press, they are added to a list at the State Department. Now we had come to expect the same behavior from the president of the United States. It was shocking to see a president act with such cruelty and arrogance.

An American president waging war on the media felt like something entirely new. But this wasn't the beginning. It was a natural endgame in a decades-long conservative war against the very idea of objective truth.

Why the GOP Wages War on Truth

For better or worse,[7] the fourth estate is the self-appointed guardian of truth. It is supposed to separate fact from fiction and hold the powerful accountable. This is the romanticized *All the President's Men/Spotlight* version of the press's role in American life. Reality is more complicated than a Hollywood movie plot, but that doesn't make it fundamentally wrong. A vibrant free press is a necessary ingredient for a well-functioning democracy.

A lot of this book is about the media's failures,[8] but that shouldn't distract from their very real accomplishments. It was the media that exposed the Watergate scandal and later took down Nixon. It was the media that uncovered the lies being told about the Vietnam War. It was they who released the Pentagon Papers, at great legal risk. And the media uncovered the excesses of the post-9/11 security state.

The press is not perfect now, nor has it ever been. In the past, it was

---

7 It's definitely not for the better.
8 Don't worry, media. There will be a lot on the failures of the Democratic Party, too (one of your favorite subjects).

often too cozy with the powerful and told stories almost exclusively from the perspective of white men. From the very beginning, journalism was often used to further the motives of the rich and improve the bottom line of major corporations. NBC is owned by a cable company; ABC is part of the Disney empire. The *Washington Post* is a hobby of sorts for one of the richest men in the world. None of this is new; the term *media baron* exists for a reason.

American history is littered with overly saccharine quotes about the role of the press, but this quote from Franklin Delano Roosevelt is worth repeating, because it explains why the Republicans spend so much time waging war against the press: "Freedom of conscience, of education, of speech, of assembly are among the very fundamentals of democracy and all of them would be nullified should freedom of the press ever be successfully challenged."

There is a sense among a lot of political observers that the Republican attacks on the media are just performance art, a cheap way to fire up the base that is done with a wink and a nod. *Sure, they love to beat us up, but they don't really mean it, right?*

This is why, particularly before Trump, so many in the media took these attacks so lightly. But this response misses the much more dangerous reality. Eroding trust in the media is a necessary precondition for Republican political success for two reasons.

First, the GOP has a truth problem. A factual presentation of the positions of both parties is very bad for Republicans. While there are issues worthy of debate, where people of good faith on both sides can disagree, on some core issues, Republicans are just objectively wrong. They push an agenda of tax cuts for the rich even though the three times that approach has been tried in modern history have been abject failures with anemic growth and explosive deficits. They have been running just as strong on national security, even though 9/11 and the

Iraq War happened on their watch.[9] The Republican energy plan, which is a sop to the oil and gas companies that fund their campaigns, is destroying the planet. In addition to being wrong on the facts, the GOP is on the wrong side of public opinion on nearly every issue of consequence. Therefore, Republicans need to ensure that the public never hears what they are actually for. When the message is bad, shoot the messenger.[10]

The second problem for the Republicans is one of math. They are a minority party in a theoretically majoritarian system. If people are allowed to vote freely, and if all those votes are counted, the Republicans have very little chance to hold on to power. They can either change their positions to be more appealing, or they can try to subvert democracy. Time and again, the Republicans have chosen the latter. As the overwhelmingly white GOP stares down a near future where white people are no longer the majority, the Republicans have become brazenly authoritarian.

It all boils down to a simple political syllogism: Democracy is bad for Republicans. The press is good for democracy. Therefore, the press is bad for Republicans.

Republican political success depends on eroding the credibility and reach of a free and independent press. Information control is the first move of any tinpot authoritarian hoping to mold the minds of a populace. Take control of the newspaper, the printing presses, the radio, and the TV stations.

Hungary, a country that slid into authoritarianism, has disturbing parallels to the United States under Trump. Viktor Orbán has taken nearly complete control of the media. The public broadcasters are now pro-Orbán propagandists. Nearly five hundred of the country's media

---

9 Always remember the horror of President George W. Bush—whose reputation and historical standing has unfortunately improved in recent years.
10 This was a figurative approach until Trump made it dangerously literal.

outlets have been consolidated under the roof of one pro-Orbán foundation. Reporters Without Borders made Orbán the first European Union member on its Enemies of Press Freedom list—joining leaders like Syria's Bashar al Assad, Russia's Vladimir Putin, and North Korea's Kim Jong-un.

Similarly aggressive measures are consistent with Donald Trump's behavior (or that of the next Trump-like figure to demagogue their way into the Oval Office). Trump has always had dictator[11] envy. He salivated at the idea of sending CNN's Jim Acosta to Gitmo, and the rabid supporters at his rallies, who chant "CNN sucks" and "Fake news" at the press pen, rejoice at the idea of a Trump hostile takeover. But so far, that's a pipe dream. As for many countries, freedom of the press is written into our Constitution. *Unlike* with those countries, our Constitution is difficult to change. So, because Republicans cannot take over the press with force, they've chosen a different path.

They can destroy its credibility, nullify its influence, reduce its drive to protect democracy. They can force the press to look the other way.

The Big Lies that dominate American politics are the results of a two-part long-term plan to win political power, eroding the very concept of objective truth by destroying the truth-tellers.

Part One: Sow Distrust

Republicans spent decades accusing the media of liberal bias to justify the failure of their political efforts and the unpopularity of their agenda. These complaints were made in bad faith and were disconnected from reality.

---

11 I am going to assume you see what I did there, but as Jon Lovett (an actual funny person) has told me (a non-funny person) on multiple ocassions before, if you have to point out the joke, it's probably not a good one.

Every politician complains about their press coverage, but during Barry Goldwater's 1964 campaign for president, attacking the press became both a political strategy and a convenient explanation. For decades, restive conservatives had been champing at the bit for one of their own to run. After two terms of the moderate and somewhat apolitical Dwight Eisenhower and Richard Nixon's loss in 1960, the right wing found its champion in Goldwater, a senator from Arizona. By 1964, Republicans had lost five of the previous seven presidential elections, and those on the Right barely counted the two Eisenhower wins because Ike failed many of the base's litmus tests. It was an article of faith within the Republican grassroots that the country was waiting for a rock-ribbed, red-blooded conservative. Goldwater was all that and more. He ran on a platform of repealing popular New Deal programs, undermining Social Security, opposing the Civil Rights Act, and engaging in aggressive confrontation with the Soviet Union. Politically, he was the forerunner to Donald Trump. As Trump endeared himself to the GOP base via Fox News, Facebook, and Twitter, Goldwater became the darling of the Far Right by making frequent appearances on the radio program of a conservative host named Clarence Manion. (In the Trump analogy, Manion was Goldwater's Steve Bannon.) In addition to his influential radio program, Manion shepherded Goldwater's 1960 book, *The Conscience of a Conservative*, through the publishing process, including handpicking its ghostwriter.[12] The book was popular with Republican readers and vaulted Goldwater to the 1964 nomination despite strong opposition from the party establishment.

This probably won't come as a surprise, but conservative activists were dead wrong about what the country was looking for in a

---

12 The need for a ghostwriter is also a parallel with Trump, who can barely read, let alone write a book.

president. Goldwater lost to President Lyndon Johnson in one of biggest landslides in history, winning only six states and losing the popular vote by 23 points. The Right needed something or someone to blame, because the alternative was to face reality: the American public was not buying what they were selling. The media was the easy and obvious target. Goldwater spent much of the campaign attacking the media. They were part of the "establishment" he was trying (and failing) to use as a foil. His campaign press secretary even handed out pins to the reporters covering his campaign that read, "Eastern Liberal Press."[13] The argument during and after the campaign was that Goldwater couldn't receive a fair hearing because of endemic liberal bias. The idea that the media was powerful enough to dictate a 486–52 Electoral College victory is patently absurd, but projection is easier than self-reflection.

The Republican war against the media reached a new level when Richard Nixon, a paranoid crook, ascended to the Oval Office. Like Goldwater, Nixon treated the media as his enemy. Every problem could be explained by biased reporters. Spiro Agnew, Nixon's vice president, was the hatchet man, frequently dispatched to attack the media. He famously called them "nattering nabobs of negativism."[14] The press's behavior makes it hard to disagree. Now, Nixon's main complaint concerned well-sourced revelations about a massive criminal conspiracy to abuse power and obstruct justice.

The White House tapes released during the Watergate investigation contain hours of Nixon ranting about the press and fantasizing about ways to eliminate their freedoms and scrutiny. This sounds eerily similar to Donald Trump's Twitter feed (RIP). Nixon's idle threats to jail and punish reporters are as well known as his Enemies

---

13 I imagine the Trump-era versions of this pins would have said "Enemy of the People."
14 Agnew was a crook and a generally terrible vice president, but "nattering nabobs of negativism" is a pitch-perfect description.

List (which also included reporters), but the Nixon initiative that most successfully undermined the media is less well remembered.

In 1971, *The News Twisters*, a book by *TV Guide* writer Edith Efron, was released. Efron is reported to have analyzed one hundred thousand words of broadcast television coverage of the 1968 campaign between Nixon and then-Vice President Hubert Humphrey. According to Efron's specious methods, while only 8.7 percent of the words about Nixon were deemed positive by Efron, more than 50 percent of the words about Humphrey were. Notably, her research was funded in part by a conservative foundation.

In addition to stroking his ego about his poor press coverage and speaking to his deep-seated insecurities, *The News Twisters* presented Nixon with a massive political opportunity. Here was "scientific" proof of the media's bias against Republicans. He ordered his aides to make sure the book ended up on the *New York Times* Best Seller list.[15] Using campaign funds, they bought every copy they could find. Once Efron's book was deemed a best seller, it garnered more attention— and better placement in every bookstore in America.[16]

The News Twisters became a foundational text for the right-wing war on the media. By the time Bob Woodward, Carl Bernstein, and Katherine Graham took down Nixon, the Republican idea that the media was irreparably biased against them had become a core belief. This anger against the media was fomented by Republican politicians and conservative activists trying to fire up their base and explain away failures to achieve their goals. Nixon's resignation? The media's fault.

---

15 Funnily enough, the Republican National Committee did the exact same thing with Donald Trump Jr.'s absurd book.
16 While this is not how I would like to make it onto the *New York Times* Best Seller list, I would have no objection if President Biden took a similar interest.

Gerald Ford's loss? Liberal news bias. Support for liberal programs like Medicare and Social Security? Coastal media elites.

Convincing their base that their failure was the media's fault created an environment where conservative politicians could do no wrong.

Part Two: Building the Bubble[17]

Once you have sown distrust in the traditional media, you need to create a place for people to go get "information." Enter Ronald Reagan, the president whose sterling reputation is most at odds with his abysmal performance.

The former B-movie actor and California governor was a master media manipulator who used the ascendant conservative media ecosystem to maintain his relevance despite losing the 1976 Republican primary. Reagan's rise within the Republican Party was a direct result of a televised speech he gave in support of Barry Goldwater in 1964. The speech, "A Time for Choosing," became legendary among Republicans and rocketed to conservative icon status an actor best known for costarring in a film with a chimpanzee.[18]

The newly elected Reagan attempted to strike a lethal blow in the war Goldwater had helped start. The Republican war on the media held a core concern: objective reporting of facts hurt Republicans. The Fairness Doctrine, a rule implemented by the Federal Communications Commission (FCC), was the mechanism that enforced objectivity on the airwaves

---

17 Do you *build* a bubble? Should it be *blow* a bubble? There are very real limits to some of these metaphors.

18 There are more parallels between Trump and Reagan than a lot of Never Trump Republicans would like to admit. Starring beside an ape is not less embarrassing than hosting a game show to determine whether Gilbert Gottfried, Lil Jon, or Dennis Rodman has the best business chops. (When you read that sentence, you have to wonder how America survived 2017–2021. Well, we almost didn't.)

and therefore quickly became the object of Republican ire. Under the doctrine, in exchange for using the public airwaves, broadcasters were required to do two things: dedicate some airtime to controversial issues deemed to be in the public interest *and* show contrasting viewpoints on those issues. The Fairness Doctrine was vague and sporadically enforced, but it was a bulwark against the rise of inherently ideological media. Despite the success of Manion and others, the Fairness Doctrine limited the size and scope of the alternative media ecosystem that conservatives were so desperate to build. When conservative radio hosts ignored the doctrine, their stations were forced into offering equal time to opposing views.

Reagan solved this problem. In 1987, under the leadership of the conservative activists appointed by Reagan, the FCC abolished the Fairness Doctrine. The vote was 4–0. Three of the commissioners were appointed by Reagan; the fourth was a Nixon appointee.

The end of the Fairness Doctrine had a massive, immediate impact on the media environment. Right-wing radio flourished, becoming a dominant and disturbingly influential forum. As historians Julian Zelizer and Kevin Kruse have pointed out in the *Washington Post*, "there were only a couple of all-talk radio stations in America in 1960; by 1995, there were 1,130."

While cable television was not technically covered by the Fairness Doctrine, it's unlikely that Fox News would exist if Reagan's FCC hadn't ended the doctrine. Fox changed the game, supercharging the worst elements of conservative media. It wasn't trying to advocate for a point of view. It was a political weapon in the hands of the Republican Party's most ruthless strategist. That weapon was deployed against Democrats and the media in equal measure.[19] The mere existence of

---

19 The number of DC political reporters who defend Fox News "reporters," despite the fact that no one has done more damage to their credibility than Fox, is truly stunning.

Fox News was (in the mind of its viewers) prima facie evidence that the rest of the media was biased and incapable of fairness and balance.

When a Republican was in the White House, whether Bush or Trump, Fox blamed any negative press coverage of that president on liberal bias. If the media dared criticize the conduct of the wars in Afghanistan or Iraq, Fox personalities (news and opinion) suggested it was part of a reflexive anti-American bias. When a Democrat was in the White House, Fox shamed the rest of the media for not covering the picayune "scandals" and outlandish conspiracy theories that dominated its own airwaves.

For more than twenty years, Fox held the largest audience of a cable news network by a country mile. It weaponized its platform with ruthless effectiveness and cemented its status by convincing its loyal viewers that getting information anywhere else was tantamount to apostasy.

Without right-wing media, there is no President Donald Trump. He tested his talking points and built his brand with regular interviews on *Fox and Friends* and *The Rush Limbaugh Show*. His nativist, anti-immigration agenda won him the nomination and presidency in 2016. These ideas were not created in a think tank. This agenda was the result of the right-wing media's feedback loop.

A reality-based media losing this war seems inevitable now. Yet Trump's constant and aggressive attacks on the media only finished a job started decades ago. Previous Republican politicians spoke with more nuance and subtlety than Trump, despite sharing his goals. This was by necessity. As much as GOP politicians hated it, they needed the traditional media in order to reach people. They depended on their local media to get elected and on the Sunday shows and CNN to maintain national relevance.

Then Trump taught them that the internet had supercharged the right-wing echo chamber. Republicans no longer needed the "fake news" media. In fact, it was in their interest to be more aggressive in destroying it. No more subtlety. No more paeans to the media at fancy black-tie press dinners. It was kill or be killed.

This was devastatingly effective. According to the Pew Research Center, the number of media-trusting Republicans was cut in half from 2016 to 2021. Put another way, fewer than four in ten Republicans still trust the national media. This shocking number holds huge implications for democracy.

Several generations of Republicans helped create this environment, and they could not have succeeded without a series of miscalculations born of naïveté and cowardice from the media itself. It wasn't a war the traditional media powers were destined to lose, but it was one they seemed incapable of winning.

5

Why Republicans Need to Lie to Win

Donald Trump is a liar. He's the biggest liar in the history of politics. He makes Richard Nixon look like George Washington. Despite the reluctance of the folks who run the *New York Times* to use the L-word, there is no disputing that Trump is a liar. The *Washington Post* Fact Checker recorded more than 30,000 Trump lies during his four years as president. That's an average of 21 lies per day. On the day before the 2020 election, the *Post* found, Trump made 503 false or misleading statements—a lie for every three minutes of the day if he never slept.

Democrats obsessed over Trump's constant lies and lamented his avoidance of any repercussions. For progressives, the idea that lying works as a political strategy is deeply depressing. We so desperately want to believe in the existence of rules and in the power of referees to dole out consequences for misdeeds. In arguments with our Trump-loving uncles and neighbors, we are always pointing to Trump's obvious and provable lies and then raging in disbelief when his supporters are unmoved.

We need leaders who speak the truth and can be trusted, particularly in a time of crisis. The consequences of Trump's lies were deadly during the COVID-19 pandemic. People didn't wear masks or socially distance because the president had said the deadly virus wasn't that deadly. This will be tough to explain to subsequent generations, but some of Trump's supporters even started ingesting horse deworming pills as a possible cure for COVID-19.[1]

The same dynamic played out in equally dangerous ways during the violent assault on the Capitol. Trump lied, and people died.

But the obsession over Trump's lies misses the bigger point. Trump is a terribly shitty liar. COVID-19 truthers and Capitol rioters aside, almost everyone knew Trump was lying, his supporters included. He couldn't keep his lies or his face straight. It was political performance art. In the end, Trump's lies were a distraction. Pushing back against them was like treating the symptom but ignoring the disease.

These presidential prevarications are just a small part of the broader conservative disinformation strategy that pre- and postdates Donald Trump. Historically, "Big Lie" originally referred to the Nazi propaganda about Jews that led to the Holocaust, but it has come to refer specifically to the conspiracy theories about the 2020 presidential election.

Modern Republicanism is based on the embrace of one Big Lie after another: climate change isn't real, supply-side economics works, immigrants are dangerous, Barack Obama wasn't born in the United States—the list goes on and on, and it is easy to recite because these lies were pounded into the American consciousness for decades. Large portions of the populace and the majority of Republicans still believe them.

The conservative movement invested billions in building up a vast and varied disinformation apparatus—buying up television networks, investing in websites, promoting YouTubers, and so on. And they all push out these Big Lies.

The existence of their media empire is no secret. Everyone knows

---

1 I never know whether we are living in a Coen brothers movie or on the set of *Arrested Development* (and yes, I know I'm dating myself with these references).

Fox is evil,[2] that Ben Shapiro is a troll, that YouTube and Facebook are hellscapes of disinformation and racist right-wing clickbait. And we know conservatives lie. They also spend a lot of time and money ensuring that people don't hear the truth—but why? Why go to such lengths to pull the wool over people's eyes?

The answer to that question is simple.

The Republicans have no choice. They recently controlled the House, Senate, White House, and most statehouses, but Republicanism suffers from a terminal diagnosis. The GOP represents a rapidly shrinking minority of Americans.

Republican political figures, both current and former, are less popular to the American public than their Democratic counterparts. Donald Trump is the only president in the history of the Gallup poll never to achieve a 50 percent approval. Republican Senate leader Mitch McConnell is broadly despised. The hatred of McConnell, the legislative Grim Reaper, is one the few things that unites Democrats and Republicans.[3]

Additionally, the Republican position on taxes, immigration, climate change, the minimum wage, guns, and health care has gotten steadily less popular. To put a finer point on it, the Republican base is shrinking, and most people hate their politicians and their party. There is no way for Republicans to win national elections without bastardizing the US democratic system. Therefore, they need to rely on two specific and extraordinary measures to hang on to power.

The first measure consists of voter suppression, gerrymandering,

---

2 It feels harsh to call someone evil, but I don't know of a more appropriate term to describe a network that sows distrust in lifesaving vaccines that their own executives, hosts, and staff have all received.

3 That a majority of Trump voters despises McConnell is one of the few things that give me hope about bridging the partisan divide in this country.

and the geographic advantages of the Electoral College and the Senate. Disinformation is the second.

If there is a fair hearing on the issues, Republicans will lose. They must defame Democrats, hide their own positions, and keep their shrinking white base fired up with a steady dose of racist agitprop.

One of the primary purposes of this disinformation strategy is to paper over a potentially fatal contradiction. The Republicans depend on a populist working-class base, but their policy agenda asks those very same working-class voters to pay for tax cuts for corporations and the wealthy. This tension is simply irreconcilable. If elections were centered on the contrasting economic positions of the party, the Republicans would get clobbered. So, they obfuscate and distract. They move the conversation to the cultural issues that unite their base and divide ours.

Republicans learned this lesson the hard way in 2012. Heading into that election, they were confident they could make Barack Obama a one-term wonder. The economy improved under Obama, but not as quickly as the public hoped. When Obama's reelection campaign got underway, unemployment was over 8 percent and the country was still in shock from the 2008 financial crisis. Mitt Romney, the Republican nominee, wanted to make the election a referendum on Obama's economic performance. We welcomed the challenge.

Well, *welcome* might be a strong word. Romney was, on paper, a formidable opponent,[4] a halfhearted moderate with a successful business record and a famous name. The economy was Obama's greatest weakness, but it was also Romney's. The former private equity executive made millions buying companies and selling off the parts, often leaving the workers to fend for themselves. He had a penchant for saying things that reinforced his status as an out-of-touch rich guy who

---

4 I said "on paper."

didn't know or care about the hoi polloi.[5] During the campaign, Romney said or did everything on this list:

- Stated he liked "being able to fire people."
- Got into a heated argument with a fairgoer about whether corporations were people.
- Rolled out a tax policy that gave multimillionaires like him a huge tax cut while raising taxes on the middle class.
- Argued that Obama should have let the US auto industry go bankrupt, which would have cost tens of thousands of jobs in the industrial Midwest.
- Chose as his vice president Paul Ryan, a man so committed to privatizing Medicare that he named a Medicare privatization plan after himself.

Instead of the referendum Romney and the Republicans yearned for, the election became a choice between two competing economic theories. Romney's trickle-down economics on steroids versus Obama's focus on the middle class. We in the Obama campaign nicknamed the debate "top down v. middle out."[6]

In the end, the problem wasn't that Romney was a shitty candidate (he was) who ran a shitty campaign (he did).[7] The problem for the Republicans was that the campaign focused entirely on the economy, the issue that exposes the contradiction between GOP policies and political imperatives.

---

5 Although I can't prove it, Romney probably uses the term *hoi polloi* without irony. In fact, he strikes me as someone incapable of understanding irony.

6 In hindsight, this is some overly focused grouped messaging mush. But Obama won so who am I to question it?

7 I know Romney has been a very rare voice of courage in recent years, but he has a long way to go to expiate his sins, including his courtship of Donald Trump and the birtherism that helped put Trump on the path to the presidency.

By (accurately) painting Romney as a plutocrat fighting for his fellow plutocrats, Obama claimed the populist mantle and easily won reelection, winning even Pennsylvania, Ohio, Iowa, Michigan, and Wisconsin with relative ease.[8]

Though the Republicans had significantly more money to spend,[9] Obama and the Democrats dictated the terms of the debate. Obama turned out an emerging electorate of diverse young voters and won in rural, very white midwestern areas on the strength of his economic message. And Republicans paid the price. They lost the election they believed they should have won.

Afterward, Republicans dissected Romney's political carcass to determine cause of death. The Republican National Committee released a report that called for the party to be less racist (LOL). Others tried to figure out why the app the Romney campaign had built to facilitate Election Day turnout, crashed. There were analyses of data, technology, and campaign spending. Republicans were simply out-messaged in quality and quantity. Romney spent the campaign responding to Obama. Part of this was a problem of his own making. The Republican nominee struggled to keep his Gucci loafer[10] from being lodged in his own mouth. Unfortunately for his campaign, the Democrats understood how to communicate in the internet age. Republican operatives and the right-wing billionaires paying them concluded that if they were ever going to win another election, they would need to increase their media firepower. They could never again allow the Democrats to control the narrative. The Republicans needed the ability to change the subject to the issues that animated their base.

---

8 The fact that Barack Hussein Obama won Iowa and Ohio twice is very hard to explain to people only ten years later.

9 Karl Rove famously flushed several hundred million dollars down the toilet.

10 The fact-checkers could find no evidence that Romney wore loafers, let alone Gucci loafers, but I am taking some artistic license to paint a picture. I know you get it, even if they don't.

Too many voters had stayed home in 2012 because they believed Romney was more likely to fire them than fight for them.[11]

What came next were more media outlets, better data, more digital ads, and a souped-up messaging operation. Democrats were foolishly dismissive of these efforts. There was no way the GOP could catch up in just four years.

Oops.

Four years later, the economy was barely an afterthought in the presidential campaign. Donald Trump's platform did not focus on retaining the strength of Obama's economy or building on the progress of the outgoing president. Instead, Trump and Hillary Clinton waged a battle over immigration, Muslim bans, and email servers. Trump painted an apocalyptic image of "American carnage," a country under assault from immigrants, terrorists, and inner-city criminals that bore no resemblance to reality. It was false and very racist.[12] It drove clicks, shares, and cable ratings. Hillary Clinton was the subject of countless conspiracy theories. Republicans pushed false stories: Clinton had been endorsed by ISIS; she was the mastermind of a global sex-trafficking ring run out of a pizza parlor; she was guilty of murder;[13] she drank children's blood.

Fox News personalities claimed that Clinton had suffered a traumatic brain injury four years prior and was being propped up on the campaign trail by Huma Abedin, her top aide, a Muslim. Abedin herself was the subject of virulently racist attacks from the Right. These contradicting messages simultaneously painted Clinton as a criminal

---

11 A version of this message, which I've just made up, could have been a good 2016 anti-Trump message.

12 A feature, not a bug, as the tech bros say.

13 #Clintonbodycount, a frequent trending topic on Twitter, should have been a warning sign about the election (and Twitter).

mastermind and too enfeebled to campaign. This hardly mattered to the recipients of this propaganda.

Under constant assault from Trump and a newly empowered Facebook-friendly right-wing media, the Clinton campaign never got out of a defensive crouch. They spent all their time parrying the attacks, and Trump won an election he had no business winning. The Facebook targeting strategy worked. By controlling the narrative and centering the campaign on racially divisive cultural issues, Trump turned out Republican voters, won over a shocking number of people who had voted for Obama in 2012, and helped convince more than 4 million 2012 Obama voters to stay home.

The 2016 election proved that disinformation-based politics was a necessary ingredient of Republican success. The lesson was learned. The disinformation efforts got bolder in 2020, and the Right has tripled down since Trump's narrower-than-expected loss.

President Joe Biden, a moderate older white man, was an elusive target for a Republican Party that used race to attack Obama and gender to attack Clinton. Early in the Biden presidency, the Right struggled to get their folks amped up about the new president. But there was simply nothing scary about "Uncle Joe" from Scranton. The Republican message had long been that America was changing and that change was bad for white Americans.[14] But for a lot of voters, Joe Biden was more of a throwback than a leap forward. So, the Republicans had to go out and invent something to scare their voters. Enter critical race theory (CRT), an esoteric legal theory that is part of law school curricula. Like most dumb racist controversies, this one started on Fox News.

After the protests over structural racism and the murders of George Floyd, Breonna Taylor, and others by police officers in 2020, a

---

14 The people whom the Republicans call "real Americans."

national conversation broke out about how racism should be taught in schools. Seemingly out of the blue, the Trump administration issued a presidential memorandum[15] warning federal government agencies against the use of CRT. This memo received a lot of coverage in the right-wing press. So, in Pavlovian fashion, Trump followed it up with an executive order banning any training materials that asserted that the United States was fundamentally racist. He waded so aggressively into this heretofore unknown topic because of an interview he'd seen on Fox News.[16] In it, Tucker Carlson spoke with Christopher Rufo, a conservative activist, who predicted, without evidence, that liberals would soon be indoctrinating students in critical race theory.

After Trump's loss, the right-wing disinformation machine went into overdrive. Even though critical race theory was not being taught in a single public school in America, Fox and Republican politicians went about creating moral panic. Local politicians passed laws banning the teaching of something that wasn't being taught. Parents stormed local school board meetings. Critical race theory became a central part of the 2021 Virginia governor's race. Republican Glenn Youngkin ran ads about it and mentioned it in nearly every speech. Media Matters estimates that Fox News ran nearly one hundred segments on CRT in Virginia that spring, even though it wasn't being taught in Virginia schools. Many Democrats were dismissive of the issue—because, once again, it was completely made-up Fox News BS. But it stuck.

In the run-up to the election, Crooked Media conducted a poll with Change Research, a Democratic polling firm, that showed just how deeply this fake issue had penetrated. Nine in 10 Youngkin supporters believed that critical race theory was a significant threat. Additionally, more than half of undecided voters and a third of Biden voters

---

15 Something that has all the legal force of a well-crafted tweet.
16 Of course.

who were not planning to support the Democratic nominee said it was at least a medium-size threat. Weaponizing critical race theory helped Youngkin win a state that Biden had won by 10 points in 2020, a stunning victory that spoke to the power of disinformation as a political strategy.

To recap: in a little over a year, Trump and the MAGA media took an entirely made-up issue from a random Fox interview and turned it into a national crusade that changed laws in more than a dozen states and helped flip the governorship in a state Republicans had won only once this century.

That's the "why." There is no other option. True, conservatives *could* abandon their unpopular corporatist policies and racist rhetoric,[17] but that would anger their donors and their base. Unfortunately, this also requires a modicum of courage and introspection. So, rampant disinformation and propaganda it is!

---

17 I *could* call this the "Billionaires and Bigots" strategy. Perhaps I should...

6

The Anatomy of the MAGA Megaphone

Turn on Fox News on any given night and you'll find a series of buffoons interviewing other buffoons about the same thing over and over again. The conversation is dumb, the jokes are unfunny, and the production value has a real *Wayne's World* vibe. The whole thing is the opposite of *America's Got Talent*.

A visit to the right-wing corners of Facebook makes the schlock on Fox look like high art. The MAGA media personalities are a rogue's gallery of misfits. Dan Bongino looks like the guy who scared you straight from steroid use in high school, Ben Shapiro makes Ted Cruz seem charismatic, and Steve Bannon seems to have stopped bathing during the Trump presidency. It's hard to square this cacophonous collection of dunderheads with the tremendous success of right-wing disinformation as a political strategy. Did these clowns stumble ass-backward into stealing elections?

On the surface, MAGA media appears to be a loosely connected, incoherent mishmash of militants, grifters, and attention merchants. The only consistencies appear to be racist agitprop and a sense that Democrats are colluding with an array of nonwhite actors to bring about the fall of (white) civilization.

But behind the noise, there's strategic logic and ruthless efficiency to the disinformation machine. The Big Liars pushing the Big Lies have four very specific political goals, and they have great success advancing them. This is why Trump won in 2016, survived multiple impeachments, and remains a politically relevant figure despite losing reelection and spearheading a deadly, albeit failed, insurrection. On a dime, the Right switched from promoting President Trump to hobbling President Biden.

Goal One: Reject the Evidence

In the summer of 2018, Donald Trump was enmeshed in an array of self-generated controversies. For the most part, the Trump presidency was one long, bad news cycle. The irony was lost on the reporters who frequently referred to Trump as a "master media manipulator." This was a particularly tough period. Trump's EPA administrator resigned in scandal; Special Counsel Robert Mueller indicted thirteen Russians for interfering in the 2016 election, undermining Trump's claim that no such interference had occurred; and the president caused a massive firestorm by siding with Vladimir Putin over his own intelligence agencies during a summit in Helsinki, Finland.[1] It was against this backdrop that Trump strode to the lectern at the Veterans of Foreign Wars convention in Kansas City, Missouri, to present before a theoretically friendly audience in a very Republican state. In 2016, Trump won veteran households by 26 points, and he won Missouri by double digits. Traditionally, presidents attending the VFW convention deliver addresses on foreign policy. These addresses are normally filled with paeans to veterans and recitations of the benefits delivered to them— an opportunity to right a lilting ship.

Of course, Trump barely touched on these issues. He gave a

---

1 I know these things happened. I even remember tweeting about them (kill me), but it's still really hard to believe they all happened to one shitty president.

rambling, incoherent, campaign-style speech that almost certainly violated campaign finance law. Like all Trump speeches, this one was filled with lies, exaggerations, and misstatements—with one very notable exception. In an offhand, unprepared aside that certainly wasn't on the teleprompter before him, he uttered perhaps the most honest statement of his presidency: "Don't believe the crap you see from these people, the fake news. . . . Just remember, what you are seeing and what you are reading is not happening."

This quote is the Rosetta Stone of Republican political strategy. Trump, who has always struggled to distinguish between inside and outside thoughts, admitted out loud what Roger Ailes and his ilk had spent decades trying to achieve under the cover of "fair and balanced" journalism: *Don't trust anyone else. Don't believe your eyes or your ears. Believe only what we tell you.* Indeed, Trump's statement was a less eloquent version of the famous quote from George Orwell's *1984*: "The party told you to reject the evidence of your eyes and ears. It was their final, most essential command."

In other words, the Right wants to create a disinformation bubble in which they control what info reaches their voters. In the fictional state depicted by Orwell, it's possible simply to shut down all sources of information that contradict the view of the state. America is still a democracy,[2] and Republicans may not be able to shut down the media outlets and other information sources that contradict the party line,[3] but they can convince the public to shut them out.

To restrict information in this way requires sowing distrust in every institution other than right-wing media outlets and Republican politicians. Winning the war on truth depends on defeating the truth-tellers.

---

2 For now.
3 Not yet.

Therefore, Republicans continually attack the media that reports facts about them. This effort has been so successful that, for most Republicans, a story's appearance on CNN or in the *New York Times* is proof that it is false. It doesn't matter how obviously or provably true said information may be. Anything the "fake news" reports is, by definition, false. Prior to Trump, Republicans tried to make this case with more subtlety. They screamed about "liberal bias" and turned every minor journalistic mistake into an example of said bias. For Fox News to be believed, they needed CNN to be *dis*believed. Trump, as the least subtle human on the planet, just said the quiet part out loud... all the time. Every bad story was a whole-cloth creation by the biased news media. Anonymous sources didn't exist. Every poll that had Trump losing was fake.[4]

Planting distrust in institutions is why the Republicans often employ antigovernment rhetoric. Many people think that the last century or so of American politics has been a battle over the size of government. Democrats want an expanded social safety net and more government intervention, while Republicans want to shrink government to enable the free market. This is the central narrative for most political reporting. It is also dangerously wrong.

The battle over government is not about the size of government, but the *role* of government. Republicans want the government to serve as a bulwark against the growing political and economic power of a diversifying America they view as an existential threat to their primarily white, Christian base. The Republican narrative depends on reinforcing lies and fear of the government.

The Republican Party disregards science for similar reasons. Addressing the existential threat of climate change poses a similarly existential threat to the fossil fuel interests that bankroll the

---

4 Okay, this one was closer to correct than most of us would like to admit.

Republican Party. There is no solution for climate change that doesn't require oil barons to make less money. Therefore, the Republicans adopted a two-step plan. First, deny, deny, and deny the existence of climate change. No need to solve a problem that doesn't exist. But because the existence of climate change is the overwhelming consensus among scientists, the only option is to wage a war on science, too. Don't believe the scientists or the increasing frequency of forest fires, hurricanes, and unprecedented weather events. But the Republican war on science is not just a rhetorical one. To buttress the wholly incorrect idea that climate change is not a threat, fossil fuel companies have funded "scientific" front groups to put out questionable information. Republican administrations have suppressed scientific research and silenced scientists who contradicted Republican policy aims. Putting aside the potential planetary apocalypse, the distrust of scientists is directly related to the millions of Americans who have refused to get the lifesaving COVID-19 vaccine or adhere to masking and social distancing guidelines put forward by the scientists.

So, you can't trust the media, scientists, or the government. Before too long, there will be a war on math to justify some Republican tax cut. Or a Fox segment like "Is Gravity a Liberal Conspiracy?"[5] The Republican embrace of antivaccine conspiracy theories is a great example of how this dynamic works.

When Obama was running for reelection, he used to say privately to his aides that one of his great fears with regard to losing the race was that he would have done all the work to save the economy, and Mitt Romney would get to reap all the benefits. Trump had a similar dilemma and feared he would not get credit for the single element of pandemic management he didn't royally screw up.

---

5 This will end with Fox host Jesse Watters jumping out of a second-story window to prove the point.

To say Trump cannot boast a lot of presidential accomplishments is the understatement of the century, but he (or at least some people who work for him) deserve some credit for the rapid development of the COVID-19 vaccine under Project Warp Speed.[6]

If Trump had been reelected,[7] the Republican Party and Fox News would have been huge boosters of the vaccine program. Carlson would have gotten his shots live on air. Ron Johnson and Rand Paul would have been running vaccine clinics out of their offices. The D-list MAGA celebrities would have been doing PSAs on OAN and Newsmax.

But Trump lost reelection before the vaccines were in full circulation. Yes, the vaccines were made on Trump's watch, but people would benefit from them under Biden. Republicans therefore had a political imperative to undermine the vaccines and prolong the pandemic in order to increase their chances of regaining Congress and the White House.

Without blinking an eye, the Right went from patting Trump on the back for creating the vaccines to trying to convince people that the vaccines were potentially dangerous. Republican elected officials proudly refused to get vaccinated. MAGA media personalities spread disinformation about the efficacy of the vaccines and their side effects. When someone who happened to be vaccinated died, the Right immediately and incorrectly claimed causation and spread the story online. In the parlance of Steve Bannon, they flooded the zone with shit.

No one has done more to discredit the vaccines than Tucker Carlson,[8] who regularly invites on his show discredited conspiracy theorists like Alex Berenson. Berenson, whom *The Atlantic* dubbed "the

6 I am going to take a wild guess that Trump was not deeply involved in the process, did not read the research, and didn't attend the meetings at which the decisions were made.
7 Or had been successful in his attempts to steal the election.
8 Podcaster Joe Rogan is a very close second.

Pandemic's Wrongest Man," is a former *New York Times* reporter who has desperately sought relevance by becoming a champion of the antivaccine movement. Other Fox hosts are less explicit but nearly as dangerous. The network hosts, even on the faux-news side, are constantly interviewing vaccine-skeptical "experts," asking them "questions" about the imaginary dangers, instead of the real impact, of the COVID-19 vaccines.

While there is no doubt some of these Republicans come by their lunacy naturally, most of them are lying. We know this because, while Trump was in office, Republicans and their media allies praised the vaccines. The *Washington Post* compiled an incredible list of soon-to-be vaccine skeptics praising the vaccine under Trump:

- In December, Sen. Ron Johnson (R-Wis.) praised the Trump administration's "brilliant" Operation Warp Speed for helping expedite the development of coronavirus vaccines. Since then, Johnson has inflated the number of adverse reactions and deaths linked to the vaccines.

- Rep. Ronny Jackson (R-Tex.), a former White House physician, told Fox News in November that he would get vaccinated to contribute to herd immunity. By July, Jackson was warning Fox viewers that "this is still an experimental vaccine being used under an emergency use authorization."

- In March, Rep. Marjorie Taylor Greene (R-Ga.) praised former president Donald Trump for saving lives with the coronavirus vaccines. By July, Greene was telling Americans not to get vaccinated.

To put a finer point on the hypocrisy, Rupert Murdoch was one of the first people on earth to receive a vaccine against COVID-19. The fact that Murdoch can profit off the death of his viewers yet be secure in his own immunity is more evidence that he is one of history's great villains. His network has also railed against the idea of vaccine mandates or passports. Yet Fox has a vaccine mandate for its own employees.

The efforts to sow distrust in the vaccines have been devastatingly effective. Polls show that Republicans are significantly less likely to get vaccinated and that Republicans who consume right-wing media are even less likely. Republicans make up the vast majority of the unvaccinated in the United States and have, therefore, borne the brunt of the pandemic.

A National Public Radio analysis found that people who lived in counties where Trump won at least 60 percent of the vote in 2020 died from COVID-19 disease at a rate more than two and a half times greater than those in counties who voted for Joe Biden. The more pro-Trump the county, the higher the death rate.

Putting aside the historic evil of killing people for political gain,[9] the fact that the Republicans were able convince Trump supporters not to get a vaccine developed on Trump's watch that Trump himself received shows just how effective they can be at sowing distrust in the institutions that threaten them.

A side note: Sometimes the monster comes for Dr. Frankenstein. During a late-August 2021 rally, Trump did something that bordered on responsible and encouraged attendees to get vaccinated, telling the crowd, "I recommend taking the vaccines. I did it. It's good. Take the vaccines." The attendees—many wearing "Make America Great Again" hats and other Trump swag—did something unprecedented for a Trump rally: they booed their Dear Leader.[10]

---

9 I know it's quite hard to put that aside.

10 I am not proud of this, but watching Trump's tiny, hardened heart break in real time is quite enjoyable.

Goal Two: Flood the Zone with Shit

The second element of the GOP disinformation strategy was crassly, but correctly, described by Trump adviser Steve Bannon in 2018 as "flood the zone with shit." Bannon's comment was a preview of the Republican response to Donald Trump's first impeachment. The former president was caught strong-arming the Ukrainian president to dig up dirt on Joe Biden in exchange for the release of promised aid. This is a textbook example of a presidential high crime worthy of impeachment and removal. Even for Trump, the brazen nature of the crime was something to behold. No code words were used. There was no subtlety. No plausible deniability. It was pure extortion, a (very) poorly written scene from a wannabe Scorsese. Trump was offering the Ukrainian president a very clear quid pro quo. The Ukrainians could either open a farcical investigation into Joe Biden's son Hunter or risk losing the military assistance necessary to ward off a Russian invasion.

The transcript of the call caused a political firestorm unlike anything else to that point in Trump's presidency. After more than two years of resisting the grassroots pressure to impeach him, Speaker of the House Nancy Pelosi quickly moved to open impeachment proceedings.

After dodging even a modicum of accountability for attempted collusion with the Russians, praising Nazis, steering taxpayer dollars to his hotels, and being accused of multiple credible allegations of sexual assault—and after a half dozen or so of his aides ended up in prison or resigned in scandal—it seemed like his time was up. Trump would finally pay the political piper.

Less than a year after a midterm in which Trump was an anvil around his party's neck, and with the 2020 elections looming, how could Republicans defend conduct that would have made Richard Nixon blush?

The Republicans were not cowering. They were cocky. The Republican leaders in the House and Senate announced that they would not remove the president no matter what the inquiry found.[11]

Trump and the Republicans knew that truth and rock-solid evidence were no match for their modern media strategy. Steve Bannon, the architect of Trump's 2016 victory, described this strategy to journalist Michael Lewis as follows: "The Democrats don't matter. The real opposition is the media. And the way to deal with them is to flood the zone with shit."

Bannon's quote perfectly describes how Republicans hacked the traditional media and hijacked social media. Voters are inundated with a constant stream of conflicting information. They are groomed to have an inherent distrust of politicians and the media. It's disorienting and disconcerting. This strategy involves the use in some quarters of "alternative facts," a term coined by Trump Senior Adviser Kellyanne Conway[12] on Trump's first weekend in the White House to justify White House press secretary Sean Spicer's career-dooming lie that Trump had drawn the largest inauguration crowd in history. Conway called this an "alternative fact." The willingness of Republicans to describe something easily proven false by photo evidence as a "fact" speaks to the confidence they have in their ability to wash away the truth with a flood of shit.[13]

The Republicans adopted the "flood the zone with shit" strategy because they understand three core truths about politics in the age of the internet:

---

11 If the president's being caught on tape committing the crime were not enough, what else could the inquiry possibly have found? A note in crayon?

12 Senior Adviser was my old title in the Obama White House. I like to believe that is the only thing Conway and I have in common.

13 "Shit" is an overly generous descriptor.

First, even the most sophisticated news consumers struggle to differentiate news from opinion to determine which sources are credible and which aren't. Discerning truth from lies and information from disinformation is daunting. When you combine this confusion with the cynicism that comes from years of being told not to trust the media or politicians, many give up and tune out.

Second, partisan affiliation is the dominant identity for most people. In other words, being a Republican or Democrat (or pro-Trump or anti-Trump) is more important than the policy positions undergirding the parties. (When Trump became the party's standard-bearer, Republicans went from being overwhelmingly pro-trade to anti-trade.) Therefore, the voters most likely to turn out are looking for permission to stick with their partisan team. There is no need for a coherent narrative. Even the thinnest, least believable reed will do.

Third, and finally, the Right understands that information warfare in the age of Facebook is a game of quantity over quality. So many right-wing digital media outlets have sprung up in recent years. Breitbart (which was where Bannon cut his fangs), the Daily Caller, the *Federalist*, Gateway Pundit, and dozens of others flood the zone at a furious pace.

Each of these three political truths is more outrageous than the last. Facts aren't checked. Misspellings aren't corrected. There is a barrage of bullshit to confuse and confound. But it's not just hackish conspiracy theory sites desperately seeking a Trump retweet. There is also a parade of books from Republican commentators, Fox News personalities, and politicians creating an alternative reality filled with conspiracy theories and fan fiction where Trump is a conquering hero against a cabal of liberal elite socialists and deep-state operatives. Once putatively respected columnists, the *Wall Street Journal*'s Kimberley Strassel, the *Washington Examiner*'s Byron York, and *National*

Review's Rich Lowry[14] have all morphed into MAGA fabulists spreading disinformation from their august media perches with unearned legitimacy.

During the first impeachment hearing, Republicans took an open-and-shut case based on a transcribed phone call voluntarily released and turned it into a fog of fake news and alternative realities. There were attacks on Hunter Biden, an attempt to turn Joe Biden's record of fighting corruption in Ukraine on its head, and a smear campaign against the whistleblower who revealed the scandal for having a meeting with a Democratic congressman. In a truly stunning example of the power of disinformation, the Republicans convinced large swaths of the country (and virtually every Republican in Congress) that Trump's phone call to the president of Ukraine was appropriate because, they asserted, it was Ukraine, not Russia, that had interfered in the 2016 election.

Think about that for a second.

Despite Trump's protestations to the contrary, it is an established fact that the Russians interfered in the 2016 election. But with the help of Rudy Giuliani and a coterie of conspiracy theorists, Trump spun a complex, patently absurd tale and claimed it was the Ukrainians. This fabrication involved claims of Ukrainian cooperation in the arrest of Trump's convicted criminal of a campaign manager Paul Manafort, alleged hacking by a Ukrainian company, and a missing DNC server being absconded to Kiev.

None of it makes any logical (Manafort was already being investigated), technological (ever hear of the cloud?), or geographic (the supposedly Ukrainian company is based in California, with no ties to Ukraine) sense. But confusion was the objective. These conspiracies

---

14 "Putatively" is doing a lot of work in this sentence. People who paid close attention and didn't attend a lot of DC cocktail parties held this group in low esteem for a very long time.

were fantastical enough to flood the zone with just enough shit to allow Republicans to acquit Trump of an obvious crime. While Democrats fumed, MAGA Republicans cheered, and the rest of the country just threw up their hands in confused exhaustion.

The Republicans applied this same strategy during the 2020 election and Trump's second impeachment. And the flood tide of shit continues to swell...

Goal Three: The Bigot Spigot

The third main goal of the GOP disinformation strategy is as gross and bigoted as it is obvious to anyone who watches Fox News or logs onto Facebook: keep white Americans scared shitless of nonwhite people.

View these sources on any given day, and you enter an alternative reality where Latino immigrants, Muslim terrorists, and Black criminals are terrorizing white people in their homes while overly "woke" Hollywood liberals go about erasing American history and calling white kids racist.

The election of the nation's first Black president led to a wave of white anxiety over the security of their position as the preeminent political power in the country. Fox News quickly discovered that it could monetize and weaponize this racial anxiety. On the HBO show *Succession*, which is based loosely on the Murdoch family, the racist programming on the fictional version of Fox News is called "the Bigot Spigot."

These are just a few examples of what happened when Fox News turned on the Bigot Spigot in the Obama years:

■ Something called the New Black Panthers scandal emerged. The short version of this absurdity is that on Election Day 2008, two members of a fringe organization known as the New Black

Panther Party stood outside one polling place in Philadelphia. These two people, one of them carrying a billy club, allegedly shouted racial epithets. Reports of this incident dominated right-wing radio, the Drudge Report, and Fox News. The very conservative Bush administration Department of Justice responded to this furor by opening an inquiry during its last weeks in office and then promptly tossed the hot potato into Obama's lap. The Right went out of its way to make this singular incident part of a larger conspiracy and tie Barack Obama and Eric Holder, the first Black attorney general in the history of the country, to these individuals. There were congressional inquiries. A former Bush administration lawyer wrote a book about the whole case, and Andrew Breitbart, the conservative provocateur who founded the eponymous website, relentlessly promoted photographs that showed Obama at an event with one of the two New Black Panthers. What event was it? A small meeting? A dinner party? A pickup basketball game? Nope. A 2007 civil rights march in Selma, Alabama, that featured tens of thousands of people. And because what's old is new, the Republicans played the New Black Panthers card again in 2018. With Stacy Abrams heading toward becoming the first Black woman governor in history, the Republicans began circulating pictures and videos of members of the New Black Panther Party campaigning for Abrams while carrying guns. Abrams lost by fewer than 60,000 votes.

▪ For a long time, Megyn Kelly was the star of the "news" division at Fox News. With a high-profile time slot and a reputation[15] for asking tough questions of both sides, Kelly was the face of Fox.[16] In

---

15 A not particularly well-earned reputation, in my humble opinion.
16 This is similar to being the most successful football team in the New York metropolitan area.

2013, she led her show by taking on the single biggest issue of the time: "In Slate, they have a piece on dot-com,[17] 'Santa Claus should not be a white man anymore.' And when I saw this headline I kind of laughed and I said 'this is so ridiculous. Yet another person claiming it's racist to have a white Santa,' you know. And by the way, for all you kids watching at home, Santa just is white. But this person is arguing that maybe we should also have a black Santa. But Santa is what he is, and just so you know, we're just debating this because someone wrote about it, kids." Yep, that's why she was debating it. Not because she was looking for a reason, any reason, to make white people think their way of life was under attack. (I am going out on a limb to guess that Kelly wasn't a big fan of Lin Manuel Miranda's take on Alexander Hamilton's life story.) In case you're wondering if Kelly's crusade on behalf of a white Santa was an anomaly, you need not wonder any longer. Her brief stint in mainstream journalism came to an end when, in her new role as host of a low-rated NBC News show, she defended blackface Halloween costumes.[18]

■ Numerous studies have shown that undocumented immigrants commit crimes at lower rates than American citizens. This fact is a theoretically mortal blow to the Republican anti-immigration narrative. How can you get people worked up into a lather about immigrants if those immigrants are less dangerous than the Joneses living next door? Fox News and their ilk on the right spend much time highlighting crimes involving the undocumented without ever putting the relative infrequency of such crimes into context. The tragic victims of these crimes are regular guests

---

17 The use of the term *dot-com* is almost as damning as defending the Aryan roots of Santa Claus.
18 The fact that NBC gave Kelly a Brink's truck worth of money to leave Fox is more evidence that the media is not liberal, but it may be dumb.

on Fox programming. When Donald Trump called Mexican immigrants rapists in a speech announcing his candidacy, he was simply repeating information learned from watching hours and hours of Fox News. Trump's infamous comment said more about the lingua franca of the right-wing media ecosystem than about his strategy.

Right-wing media devoted untold amounts of coverage to the death of Kate Steinle, a woman shot in broad daylight in San Francisco. Every shooting in America is one too many, and Steinle's death was certainly tragic. However, gun violence is not unusual in America. It is so commonplace in fact that most of the more than eight thousand people killed by guns in the first five months of 2021 didn't merit a mention on the national news. The Steinle case became a cause célèbre in the right-wing media for one reason and one reason only: José García Zárate, the man accused of firing the weapon that killed Steinle, was an undocumented immigrant who had been deported five times previously. García Zárate became the face of a broken immigration system and an avatar for the dangers of immigration writ large. Sen. Ted Cruz sponsored legislation called Kate's Law, and Donald Trump featured it in a horrendously racist (and completely on-brand) political ad. Ultimately, García Zárate was acquitted of the charges, and his conviction for possession of a firearm was overturned on appeal. Unfortunately, law-abiding Mexican immigrants were not so lucky to escape the consequences of the racial profiling encouraged by the right-wing media as a result of this case.

■ A study by Media Matters, which assiduously documents how Fox News covers immigration, showed that of the 1,366 total immigration segments on Fox over a twelve-week period in 2021:

◻ 605 emphasized danger, framing migrants as a threat to Americans;

☐   149 suggested migrants were an economic drain on Americans; and

☐   35 peddled racist conspiracy theories about migrant culture as a threat to American culture, including pushing the white-nationalist "great replacement" theory.

Fox is so committed to covering "illegal immigration," in fact, that it petitioned the Federal Aviation Administration to fly a drone over the border in the hope of getting grainy footage of border crossers.

■   The sweet spot of right-wing racist fearmongering is the combination of anti-immigrant sentiments with post 9/11 Islamophobia. The Right-Wing ecosystem repeatedly and breathlessly reports on alleged Muslim prayer rugs being found near the border, disregarding that there is nothing inherently wrong or dangerous about a prayer rug nor is there evidence that the purported owners of these alleged rugs are terrorists. These stories are relentlessly hyped to scare people into believing Al Qaeda and ISIS are sneaking across the border to murder unsuspecting white people. Breitbart infamously published a photo of a "Muslim prayer rug" found near the border in Arizona. The alt-right rag received the photo from a militia supporter who enjoyed patrolling the border and hunting undocumented immigrants for sport. This photo went viral on the internet and was the subject of Right-Wing media coverage.

However, it was revealed days later that the photo was not of a Muslim prayer rug, but instead an Adidas soccer jersey.[19] In a moment that confirms the existence of karma, Fox News ended

---

19 Who among us hasn't confused a prayer rug with a soccer jersey? A totally normal mistake made in good faith.

up reaping what they sowed from broadcasting these absurd Muslim prayer rug conspiracy theories. Breitbart eventually turned on Fox News and attacked them as being insufficiently racist based on a report that the cable network had installed a meditation room with prayer rugs. These were actual prayer rugs not soccer jerseys.

The need to understand Fox's imperative to scare the living daylights out of white people starts to make a hell of a lot more sense when one considers that the consequences of this racist fearmongering go far beyond politics. According to the FBI, in 2020, hate crimes reached their highest levels since 2008.

Goal Four: Weaponization of Information

The best way to think about right-wing media is not as propaganda or even disinformation, but as campaign opposition research without the middleman.

Here's a little insight into how a political campaign works: Every campaign has an opposition research department. There are two stereotypes of campaign operatives who work in opposition research. The first is of a shadowy private investigator who digs through dumpsters and peers into windows. The second is of a basement-dwelling, Mountain Dew–swilling nerd with the demeanor and fashion sense of the Comic Book Guy from *The Simpsons* or various cast members from the film *Clerks*.[20]

Neither of these caricatures is accurate.[21] Opposition researchers (or "oppo folks") are detail-oriented workaholics who pore over the records, statements, and finances of their candidate's opponent looking

---

20 I might as well tattoo "Late-stage Gen X" on my forehead.
21 Something that a researcher would love to point out.

for the silver bullet to win the campaign. To be fair, any opposition researcher will tell you that a silver bullet does not exist.[22] There is no single piece of information buried somewhere that will bring down a candidate. Donald Trump's being caught on tape bragging about sexual assault mere weeks before winning the election is evidence of this.

What these researchers do all day, every day, is find information from the past or present to buttress the campaign's chosen narrative about the opponent. For example, in 2012, Obama's campaign wanted to (accurately) paint Mitt Romney as an out-of-touch rich guy who was running for president only to help other out-of-touch rich guys get richer. Therefore, when the campaign researchers discovered that Romney planned to build an elevator in his beach house, they hid that information away like nerdy squirrels storing nuts for the winter. Why is this noteworthy? The elevator was for Romney's many, many cars. Similarly, the 2008 presidential campaign of John Edwards, the wealthy trial lawyer turned farcical advocate for the poor, took a huge hit when it was revealed that he spent four hundred dollars in campaign money on a haircut. This little nugget of information was uncovered by a researcher digging through the Edwards campaign's finance report. And Obama's presidential ambitions were almost derailed when a political rival found videos of offensive remarks made by the candidate's pastor, who had served as a mentor to the future president.

Usually, oppo research is less glamorous. The info unearthed ranges from statements uttered on the Senate floor decades ago to quotes from a local news interview. Oppo researchers had a field day

---

22 I have to say this because the very excellent researchers who worked on this book with me are former campaign oppo folks, and they wouldn't let me publish without mentioning the "no silver bullet" rule.

when Bernie Sanders's campaign found a speech Joe Biden had delivered in the 1990s suggesting a freeze on Social Security.[23]

Making these oppo hits count is a two-step process. Step one: find the devastating info. Step two: ensure voters know about the devastating info. The second step is where things usually come off the rails. The campaign press team goes looking for reporters to publish the information. Usually, the campaign doesn't want its fingerprints anywhere near the info, for fear of being branded as engaging in dirty politics.

The necessary ingredients for a successful oppo hit are: information that is newsworthy; a reporter who thinks the information is newsworthy *and* who is willing to accept the information anonymously; and most important, a reporter trustworthy enough to keep the origin secret. Even if all these are in place, the story must land on a day when the public is paying attention and there isn't too much else going on. Many times during the Obama campaign, we labored for weeks on a story we thought would damage our candidate's opponent and knock them off message for days or even weeks, only to have the story land on deaf ears.

The process of using the media to take down your political opponents is remarkably inefficient. Like many outdated communications strategies, it depends on the goodwill of media members who (correctly) do not share the interests of the campaign. As campaign staff, our interest is in communicating information we think voters need to hear about the dangerous folly of electing the other side. The media, for its part, wants to communicate something that meets their vague, amorphous standard of "newsworthiness" and that (more cynically)

---

23 A position Biden had long disavowed. Sanders himself called his campaign's attack out of bounds.

will get eyeballs and clicks. Journalism is still a business, and the bottom line still matters—maybe now more than ever.

Ultimately, this inefficiency is what led Roger Ailes to start Fox News. Before he was a despicable sexual miscreant and merchant of misinformation, Ailes was a legendary political consultant, one who (appropriately) cut his teeth working for Richard Nixon. One of Ailes's great frustrations was the inability to get the media to cover what he wanted them to cover. Why spend all day pitching media outlets when you can start your own?

Daily, the right-wing media goes looking for any piece of information, no matter how obscure or factually incorrect, that will push negative narratives about their political opponents—Democratic presidents, liberal bogeymen and, more often, bogeywomen. They love nothing more than a story that sows racial division between white people and everyone else. These right-wing oppo nuggets are like campaign ads, except instead of costing money, they make money[24]—a very sweet (and cynical) deal.

The sorts of opposition research nuggets that normally never see the light of day on traditional media become stories that drive conservative media for hours, days, and sometimes weeks at a time. These right-wing outrages du jour are usually too stupid or specious to merit coverage from the more traditional media outlets, but for the right-wing media ecosystem, this is a feature, not a bug. A media brouhaha over a ban on burgers is a good example of how this works.

In the summer of 2021, Republicans and their fossil fuel financiers had two problems: policies to address climate change were quite popular, and President Joe Biden and the Democrats were heading toward

---

24 We have truth-in-advertising laws, but no truth-in-news laws, which seems like a pretty major fucking oversight.

passing the most aggressive climate change legislation in history. Therefore, Republicans needed to make Biden's climate change plans seem extreme and dangerous—or, at least more dangerous than the planet melting beneath our feet. An opportunity presented itself when the *Daily Mail*, a garbage British tabloid that makes the *New York Post* look like *The New Yorker*, wrote an incorrect and irresponsible story about Joe Biden's plan to cut carbon emissions in half by 2030 with the following passage: "How Biden's climate plan could limit you to eat just one burger a MONTH, cost $3.5K a year per person in taxes, force you to spend $55K on an electric car and 'crush' American jobs." The *Daily Mail* article was based on a University of Michigan study about how certain changes in behavior could impact climate change, including a reduction in beef consumption. The information arsonists at the *Mail* took this study, which had no connection to Biden's plan, and asserted that to meet Biden's emissions goal, Americans could be limited to one burger a month.

The "Biden burger ban" became the dominant story on Fox News and Facebook. Republican members of Congress went to the floor of the House to promise to fight for the rights of hamburger consumers. Every MAGA media personality on YouTube and Twitter echoed this message. Millions of voters were exposed to the Big Burger Lie. It didn't matter that it was complete and total bullshit.

Now, I doubt even the most ignorant voter believed that middle-class Joe from Scranton, Pennsylvania, was going to enact a burger-a-month limit, but stories like these have an impact. They suck up oxygen that could be used to make the case for bold climate action. Instead of explaining the moral urgency or economic opportunity in transitioning to a green economy, we spend time fighting against specious BS. These stories also snag Democrats in the briar patch of Republican turf, forcing them to fight their way out. Once again, Democratic messages, policies, and politicians are more popular than

Republican ones, so when we are playing defense instead of offense, that's a win for the Republicans.

Another example of this phenomenon happened after the tragic attack on U.S. troops during the 2021 withdrawal from Afghanistan. President Biden was attending a memorial service for the thirteen Americans killed in an ISIS bombing when, for a moment during the service, he appeared to glance at his watch. The right-wing media smelled blood. As someone who has experienced unspeakable personal tragedy, Biden's empathy is legendary, and one of his greatest political assets. The misinformation merchants saw an opportunity to undermine that strength. The watch-checking image would have currency because it was a throwback to a famous moment in a 1992 presidential debate when George H. W. Bush glanced at his watch. Biden's brief glance gave people the impression that he would rather be anywhere else.

What this out-of-context image did not capture was the fact that before and after that moment, Biden was shedding tears for the lives lost. Still, the photo was posted to the internet, Facebook accounts shared the image and transformed it into a meme, the *Daily Mail* wrote an article on it, Rupert Murdoch's *New York Post* headlined a story "Biden Ripped for Apparently Glancing at Watch During Ceremony for Fallen Troops," and former Fox News personality and staunch Trump defender Lou Dobbs passed it along to his two million Twitter followers.

Without this massive, well-funded media machine, it would be nearly impossible to showcase these misleading stories to voters.

A Method to This Madness

It is essential that we understand the method embedded in the racist right-wing media madness. Its proponents are not just grifters, fame seekers, or angry people with limited impulse control. Even when the individual participants are painfully stupid (Jesse Watters), the overall hive mind operates with brilliance and a dedicated purpose that is alarmingly impressive.

This very specific, wildly successful political strategy has given Republicans the upper hand at a time when their party should be losing ground. It's how Trump got elected, and it may get him elected again. The Republican disinformation apparatus is one of the most powerful weapons in the history of politics. And too many Democrats, media members, and other stakeholders are blithely unaware of what they are up against. But the stakes are too high for us to keep turning a blind eye.

In addition to understanding why Republicans depend on disinformation and how they use it, we need to understand who is paying for it and what they are getting for their money.

7

The Best Disinformation
Money Can Buy

Few statements have been ridiculed more than Hillary Clinton's late-1990s comment about a "vast right-wing conspiracy." Clinton was being interviewed by Matt Lauer on *Today* against the backdrop of the rapidly metastasizing investigation into allegations of sexual misconduct, perjury, and obstruction of justice by her husband. In the interview, Hillary seemed to be blaming her husband's problems on a shadowy cabal of conservatives. At the time, it sounded somewhere between a wee bit paranoid and fucking bananas.

The Republicans, late-night comedians, and most of the public pounced on her. What the hell was she talking about?

President Clinton was guilty of core elements of the accusations being made against him. He *did* have an affair with a subordinate. He *did* lie under oath. And he *did* work very hard to keep the truth of this from coming to light. For that he was impeached, lost his law license, and suffered the indignity of having personal and intimate details of his life entered into the *Congressional Record*.

Her husband's guilt obscured the fact that Hillary Clinton was 100 percent correct about the existence of a "vast right-wing conspiracy." This wasn't an idle comment or an off-the-cuff dodge against a hostile and misogynistic interviewer. It was a reference to a secret

332-page memo[1] written several years earlier by a White House lawyer named Chris Lehane.[2] This memo chronicled an emerging internet-based right-wing media ecosystem. The memo laid out in tremendous detail how a network of conservative billionaires, political operatives, and lawyers worked together to turn internet-based anti-Clinton conspiracy theories into mainstream news coverage and, eventually, congressional investigations. In other words, exactly what happened to Bill Clinton.

I was working for Lehane during the White House internship[3] that started my career in politics when Clinton did the *Today Show* interview.[4] If he knew the connection between Clinton's famous comment and his earlier memo, he did not share it with his coworkers at the time.

Reading Lehane's memo all these years later is equal parts amusing and alarming. Even though the statements are less than thirty years old, they feel so outdated. One half-expects the memo to be written in Aramaic and etched on a stone tablet. I can only imagine Lehane, a fast-talking, whip-smart New Englander, trying to explain the internet to a bunch of older White House staff who were flummoxed by their own pagers and confused by the central premise of the film *You've Got Mail.*

Alarmingly, this memo perfectly summarizes the origins and structure of the modern Republican disinformation operation.

Here's essentially what Lehane wrote back then: "First, well-funded right-wing think tanks and individuals underwrite conserva-

---

1 Not sure what they did in the Clinton White House, but in the Obama White House, we tried to make our memos shorter than a Harry Potter book.

2 Lehane was my first boss in politics and is therefore to blame for all my failures.

3 Even less glamorous than it sounds.

4 Chris gets some of the credit and none of the blame for my career. I wouldn't have pursued a career in politics, let alone political communications, had it not been for his mentorship.

tive newsletters and newspapers...Next, the stories are reprinted on the internet, where they are bounced all over the world. From there, the stories are bounced into the mainstream media."

A few key revelations in this twentieth-century memo help explain what we are confronting in the twenty-first century. Of course, a lot has changed, but rich conservatives using the internet and the media as political weapons is exactly what is happening right now.

The single most important thing to understand about the right-wing media is that it is bought and paid for by wealthy interests. Then, as now, wealthy conservatives propped up a right-wing media ecosystem in order to shape the political discourse, damage Democrats, and elect politicians who would keep their tax rates low and allow their corporations to pollute the air and water.

Losing Money to Make Money

In general, the last ten years or so have been a really shitty time to get into the media business: Newspaper consumption is down. Television ratings are down. More and more people are cutting the cord with cable, denying needed revenue to its news channels. And Facebook and Google have cannibalized the advertising market that used to fund journalism.

Every month brings news of more layoffs in the world of journalism. Digital outlets that were once highly touted, like BuzzFeed, are struggling. Others are shutting down. Local newspapers are being bought up by rapacious hedge funds and harvested for parts.[5]

The economic landscape is littered with the carcasses of failed digital media companies, but new conservative media outlets seem to

---

5 I call this Romney-nomics because I still hold a grudge about 2012.

spring up daily. Despite no obvious revenue stream, many of these outlets continue to exist and, in some cases, expand.

Have conservatives figured out something about the media business that has eluded everyone else?

Nope.

Most of these right-wing media outlets are huge money losers. Nearly every single one exists primarily on the sucre of right-wing billionaires.

A second question is why would these people—people smart enough to make enough money to become billionaires in the first place, or at least not dumb enough to lose the money they inherited—keep throwing money into losing ventures? The secret to understanding the mystery is to stop thinking about these media operations as business investments. They aren't. These are not media barons in the traditional sense—that is, rich people dabbling in journalism to scratch an itch of relevance, like William Randolph Hearst or even Jeff Bezos. No, the billionaires behind these efforts are more akin to Russian oligarchs buying and selling politicians and political disinformation in new and devious ways.

The decision to pour millions into Breitbart, the Daily Caller, Newsmax, and other right-wing sites is an investment in a political outcome. It should be viewed no differently than a contribution to a super PAC or to the Republican Party. It is a very specific way of pushing conservative policies and electing conservative politicians. It isn't about an ideological preference; it is about a bottom line. These billionaires stand to make millions, if not billions, from Republican policies.

There is no chance Donald Trump gets elected without the existence of this thriving Republican media ecosystem. It's hard to overstate how profitable the reign of the racist reality TV star was for this collection of conservative oligarchs. According to an investigation by the Center for Media and Democracy, organizations associated with the wealthy Koch brothers donated at least $8 million to media outlets from 2015 to 2018. Now, $8 million is a lot of money, but it is couch cushion change to these billionaires. This relatively meager investment helped ensure that Donald Trump was elected, it helped Trump survive crisis after crisis and crime after crime, and it paid off more than a thousandfold when the Kochs reaped an estimated $1.4 billion tax break from the law Trump passed in 2018.[6] In short, it was among the most successful investments in political history.

Billionaire (Proud) Boys Club

Lehane's memo focused on Richard Mellon Scaife, the billionaire heir to the Mellon fortune, who owned and funded a passel of conservative media outlets and political efforts. In many ways, Scaife was the godfather of the anti-Clinton efforts. He funded the private investigators who dug up dirt on the Clintons, the media outlets that published the spurious results of those "investigations," and the members of Congress who launched the hearings that legitimized and publicized those "investigations." More specifically, Scaife donated more than two million dollars to the conservative magazine *The American Spectator*. That money funded something called the Arkansas Project, a yearslong investigation into the Clintons, their business dealings, and their personal lives.

The Arkansas Project led to the independent counsel investigation that eventually brought about Bill Clinton's impeachment and paved the way for George W. Bush to win the 2000 election (and really fucked up the twenty-first century). One could also argue that without

---

6 Campaign finance rules in America are merely legalized bribery and money laundering. Thanks, John Roberts!

Scaife-funded endeavors, Trump would never have been elected president. The caricature of Hillary Clinton as "Crooked Hillary," as Trump liked to call her, existed in part because of efforts Scaife had funded in the 1990s. Last but not least, Scaife even subsidized the pseudo film project that sparked the *Citizens United* Supreme Court decision that gave the wealthy and corporations the ability to purchase elections.

Scaife has long since passed, but his legacy lives on.[7] The vast right-wing conspiracy is alive and well because a bunch of very rich Republicans decided to make their impact on American politics by funding right-wing media outlets.

David and Charles Koch, the Wichita-based pseudo-libertarian fossil fuel billionaires, are the most infamous heirs to the Scaife legacy. The hundreds of millions of dollars they have spent moving the Republican Party to the right are well known. If we are unable to address climate change and, thus, the eradication of all human life, the Koch brothers, along with Rupert Murdoch, will have been among the people most responsible. I know that sounds a wee bit extreme, but I am not kidding. Most of their money is siphoned into super PACs, nonprofits, and think tanks, but they have also spread their libertarian largesse toward media entities and nonprofits that seek to influence media coverage. They have been the leaders and major funders of two right-wing donor collectives. The brothers reportedly have given more than one hundred million dollars to conservative media outlets. But Charles Koch—David passed away in 2019—spends most of their money on more traditional political endeavors.

Rupert Murdoch, owner of Fox News, the *Wall Street Journal*, and the *New York Post*, is the quintessential disinformation-funding

---

7 Bizarrely enough, he and Bill Clinton developed a late-in-life friendship and Clinton spoke at his memorial service.

billionaire. By proving that there were few public consequences to profiting off racism and planetary destruction, he paved the way for the next generation. *See, you can be the head of one the evilest*[8] *endeavors in recent history and still get invited to parties in Sun Valley and the Hamptons!* In fact, doing so will actually give you greater access to the power players in government whose decisions directly affect your bottom line. In terms of a business investment, disinformation is all upside and little downside—that is, if you don't plan to live long enough to deal with the melting planet. But over the long, sordid history of Fox, Murdoch has mostly written and cashed checks. It was Roger Ailes who was the driving force behind the network, pushing it into dangerous territory. Murdoch is a rock-ribbed conservative, but he even deigned to support a handful of Democrats when they shared his financial interests.

The true heir to the legacy of Scaife, though, is Robert Mercer, the reclusive white supremacist and hedge fund billionaire. To say Mercer is a mysterious figure in Republican politics would be an understatement. Despite his being one of the most successful hedge fund executives on Wall Street and one of the biggest funders of right-wing causes, few people know his name. Mercer is famously media shy, and according to the *Wall Street Journal*, he once told a coworker that he preferred cats to humans.[9] If Scaife was newspapers and Murdoch was television, then Mercer was the one who took right-wing disinformation into the digital age.

Mercer and his daughter Rebekah were at the center of Trump's rise. For years, they were Steve Bannon's chief patrons. According to some reports, the Mercers helped connect Bannon and Trump. They gave boatloads of money to Trump's campaigns and to outside groups

---

8 Yes, evil.
9 My friend (and probably yours) Alyssa Mastromonaco, of Obama and Crooked Media fame, thinks this is a good thing, and she has never been wrong before.

supporting him. The Mercers were also major investors in Cambridge Analytica, the controversial Trump campaign data firm that stole data from tens of millions of Facebook users. But beyond all the fundraising and connections, the Mercers' biggest contribution to Trump's victory had little to do with Trump. In 2011, after a meeting with Bannon and Andrew Breitbart, the Mercers agreed to invest ten million dollars in Breitbart, the alt-right news outlet. The Mercers' check came with one contingency: Bannon must join the board of the publication. Within a year, Andrew Breitbart had passed away, and Bannon was running the show. Under Bannon's leadership, Breitbart paved the way for Trump's nomination and eventual election.

Before 2016, the website had acted as a cudgel against any Republican who dared deviate from the rabid nativism and anti-immigrant sentiment taking over the party's base. In 2013, the Republicans were ready to pass a comprehensive immigration bill, a bill that forever altered the direction of the party. It seems hard to imagine now, but in the moment, there was real impetus for immigration reform. An autopsy of the 2012 election identified Romney's extreme immigration stances as a major contributing factor to his loss. Even Rupert Murdoch was on board with immigration reform and had his biggest blowhards, like Sean Hannity, bloviating in favor of a path to citizenship.[10] Bannon/Breitbart pushed hard in the opposite direction. Most of their ire was focused on Marco Rubio, the Florida senator and presidential aspirant whom *Time* dubbed the "Republican Savior."[11] Rubio was one of eight Republican senators to join with Senate Democrats to draft the immigration bill. In headline after headline, Breitbart painted Rubio as cosmopolitan, corrupt, and incompetent.[12]

---

10 Hannity has desperately tried to erase this moment from history.
11 I am not saying this is why *Time* is no longer relevant, but I am also not *not* saying it.
12 Even a racist squirrel finds a nut every once in a while.

These attacks took a toll. After only a few months, Rubio walked away from his own bill. The message had been sent and received: the only path to the Republican nomination was a nativist one. Even after the defeat of the immigration reform bill and the successful transformation of Rubio into an avatar for political cowardice, Bannon and Breitbart continued to torture the senator.

In the 2016 campaign, Breitbart acted as an adjunct of the Trump campaign. Emails leaked to the Southern Poverty Law Center from a disgruntled Breitbart editor were evidence that Trump aide Stephen Miller repeatedly used Breitbart as a dumping ground for negative information on Rubio. Trump and Breitbart were so close in fact that Bannon left the publication to chair Trump's campaign for the stretch run against Hillary Clinton. This deal was reportedly brokered by the Mercers.

Even without Bannon, Breitbart continued to be a major factor in the election, flooding the internet with an array of false, but damaging, information about Clinton. As Jane Mayer wrote in the *New Yorker* in 2017, "The site played a key role in undermining Hillary Clinton; by tracking which negative stories about her got the most clicks and 'likes,' the editors helped identify which story lines and phrases were the most potent weapons against her. Breitbart News has been a remarkable success: according to ComScore, a company that measures online traffic, the site attracted 19.2 million unique visitors in October."

This is not the role media outlets typically play. Even ideological ones do not act as an arm of a political campaign. They may push a point of view or a narrative or advocate for a policy, but Breitbart was in cahoots with Trump's campaign. Breitbart's work on behalf of Trump was rewarded. The Trump White House, run in part by Bannon in his new role of chief strategist (which is definitely *not* a fake title made up to deal with male-inadequacy issues), treated Breitbart as a party organ, the *Pravda* to Trump's Stalin.

Two Breitbart staffers were hired for prominent White House roles. Hardline anti-immigration advocate Julia Hahn joined the communications team. Hahn had ties to prominent white supremacists and a penchant for approvingly referencing neo-Nazi literature in her writing. Despite being a multimillionaire heiress, she masqueraded as a populist.

More alarmingly, Sebastian Gorka was hired as deputy assistant to the president, working on national security issues, with access to some of the nation's most classified intelligence. Gorka was an editor at Breitbart with ties to far-right extremists in eastern Europe. In 2014, he infamously wrote a story about the Muslim Brotherhood overrunning the National Cathedral in Washington, DC. If you don't remember the attack happening, it's because it didn't. Islamophobic conspiracy theories were Gorka's bread and butter. Speaking of conspiracy theories, one of Gorka's alleged first acts in his brief White House tenure consisted of compiling an intelligence dossier on a secret network of former Obama officials trying to undermine Trump's foreign policy. The group was dubbed the Echo Chamber. In the dossier, many of my Crooked Media cohorts and I were identified by name, dubbed "Obama loyalists who are probably among those coordinating the daily/weekly battle rhythm." Ben Rhodes, the former Obama deputy national security adviser and cohost of the podcast *Pod Save the World*, was identified as the "brains behind the this operation to undermine" Trump's presidency.[13]

To this day, I still can't believe Gorka uncovered our secret plan.[14]

The danger of handing control of large portions of a White House

---

13 As if he needed any help.
14 (There was no such plan. Gorka is a fucking idiot.)

messaging operation to a right-wing rag with white-supremacist tendencies and a penchant for conspiracy theories became evident quickly. The Bannon acolytes who ran Breitbart were satisfied simply to reprint the frequently typo-ridden releases from the White House Press Office.[15] Worse, Bannon leveraged Breitbart as a weapon against his internal rivals for White House power, regularly publishing attacks on Jared Kushner, Ivanka Trump, and other "globalists"[16] standing in the way of the MAGA agenda. Bannon was eventually fired for a host of misdeeds and disloyalties and for general incompetence. Hindsight is twenty-twenty, but handing one of the most important White House jobs to a guy who previously ran a racist blog turned out to be a mistake—a little like hiring sports columnist Skip Bayless to run the NBA. Everyone in the Republican Party, including the Mercers, severed ties with Bannon, who spent the remaining years of the Trump presidency traveling the world looking for wealthy authoritarians from whom to siphon money and hosting a poorly filmed internet talk show.

Breitbart is the most successful of the billionaire-funded right-wing media endeavors. It is the proof of concept that ensured that wealthy special interests would continue to invest in media properties to push their politics. But it is also far from alone.

Around the time of the Mercers' initial investment in Breitbart, there was a flurry of similar investments in right-wing media properties.

---

15 I know I am quasi-infamous for Twitter typos. If you don't know what I'm talking about, please don't look it up.
16 A very unsubtle and anti-Semitic term.

A Who's Who of the Vast Right-wing Conspiracy

The Daily Caller, a less successful, equally bigoted version of Breitbart, was started by the infamous Tucker Carlson prior to his becoming the belle of the resurgent white nationalist ball. However, Carlson was able to create the website only because Foster Friess, a wealthy Wall Street investor and Republican mega-donor, gave him three million dollars in start-up capital. To give you a sense of Friess's less-than-progressive mind-set, he spent millions to elect Rick Santorum, a homophobic bigot famous for retrograde thinking.[17] During an interview on MSNBC about President Obama's decision to include coverage for contraception in the Affordable Care Act, Friess said, "this contraceptive thing, my gosh, it's so—it's such—inexpensive, you know, back in my days, they used Bayer Aspirin for contraception. The gals put it between their knees, and it wasn't that costly."[18]

The Daily Caller is no stranger to controversy. In 2017, it ran a story headlined "Here's a Reel of Cars Plowing Through Protesters Trying to Block the Road." The story became grimly prophetic when activist Heather Heyer was killed in this exact fashion during the counterprotest to a neo-Nazi march in Charlottesville, Virginia, only a few months later. But the rage bait and anti-immigrant fearmongering were only part of their fuckery. Like most wealthy conservatives, Friess, who died in 2021, had a huge financial stake in preventing a transition from fossil fuels to a green economy. Therefore, the Daily Caller stands at the forefront of publishing specious research to cast doubt on the existence of climate change. It once published a story (based on zero evidence) that Barack Obama's Environmental Protection Agency was planning to hire 230,000 people to regulate greenhouse gases. The

17 In addition to being perhaps the worst pundit in the history of CNN, Santorum once compared same-sex marriage to bestiality.
18 Definitely not how it works.

Daily Caller's reporting on climate change was so egregious that E&E News, an environmental publication, once wrote:

> The Daily Caller, for its part, has a long history of giving its readers the impression that climate science is largely a political fight, rather than a rigorous scientific inquiry. It regularly attacks mainstream news outlets for their reporting on climate science, instead amplifying conservative think tanks and skeptical Republicans and the small number of climate scientists with legitimate academic credentials. Its climate reporting focuses on doubt and highlights data that suggests climate concerns from the world's leading science agencies and organizations are incorrect.

Like Breitbart, the Daily Caller played a significant role in helping Trump get elected. Trump once referred to climate change as a "Chinese hoax," and one of his first acts as president was to walk away from the Paris Climate Accords—a boon for people, like Foster Friess, who profit off the destruction of the planet.

From a business perspective, Ben Shapiro's media empire, which includes the Daily Wire, a Facebook-based troll farm masquerading as a news site, might be the most successful. Shapiro is a former Breitbart editor and media darling who grew to fame debating liberals on college campuses. He is the host of a podcast and commands a massive presence on Facebook. When I say massive, I mean several times larger than that of the *New York Times* or CNN.[19] Most of Shapiro's arguments cannot withstand thirty seconds of actual scrutiny, but he never admits he is wrong or evinces doubt. Perhaps his greatest talent

---

19 This little fact may best explain how Trump won and why Mark Zuckerberg is rocketing up the supervillain rankings.

is convincing the mainstream media that he is something other than a mediocre troll with extreme, bigoted views. Despite previously claiming that homosexuality was a mental illness and regularly mocking the trans community, Shapiro has been the subject of countless glowing profiles in publications like Vanity Fair. He was once asked to serve as guest editor of *Playbook*, Politico's flagship newsletter.[20] Shapiro's media empire exists only because wealthy Republicans viewed him as a vehicle for achieving their political goals. Dan Wilks, a Texas Republican who made billions in fracking, was an early investor in Shapiro. Someone who got rich from fracking would see it as in their interest to give a climate change skeptic like Shapiro a platform to spread his dangerous bullshit. Wilks also invested in PragerU, a conservative YouTube channel designed to radicalize American youth through conspiracy theories and false information.

The New New Right-wing Media Ecosystem

After the tragic murder of George Floyd, the rampant spread of anti-vaccine conspiracy theories, and the violent assault on the Capitol, Facebook and Twitter *finally* decided to aggressively enforce some of their own rules. I am not handing out any awards for courage here. These companies were doing the bare fucking minimum, and by the time they acted, the damage had largely been done. Some progress was made to stop the spread of hate speech and disinformation, but it would take time to clear up the mess. I imagine Mark Zuckerberg standing in the shell of a burned-out building touting his new approach to fire prevention.

Nonetheless, a crackdown on the spread of conspiracy theories and violations of the platforms' own rules regarding hate speech was

---

20 If this were all you knew about Politico, then you would know everything you needed to.

bad news for the right-wing media ecosystem. Their fledging business models and highly successful political strategies depended on conspiracy theories and hate speech. Who would've guessed? Keeping the Republican base at a fever pitch requires flooding the internet with racist agitprop, but some of the most successful racist agitprop producers were being banned from these platforms. Most notably, Trump himself was banned from Twitter and Facebook after the insurrection at the Capitol.

Have no fear, the right-wing billionaire class planned for this. In 2018, Rebekah Mercer was a founding investor in Parler, a social media network built in response to conservative complaints about Big Tech censorship. In short, Parler is the place you go after you get kicked off Twitter. Want to abuse people on social media? Go to Parler. Want to spout racist propaganda? Go to Parler. Is Facebook not enough of an angry, toxic cesspool for you? Go to Parler. Wanna self-identify as a white supremacist or an anti-Semite? Parler has your back! Think of Parler as the Mos Eisley Cantina in *Star Wars*, but with a high percentage of neo-Nazis. Nearly every Republican politician and MAGA media person of consequence is on Parler. At one point, Parler disappeared because Apple banned it from its App Store for all the same reasons these yahoos got banned from Twitter in the first place. After intense negotiations with Apple, Parler agreed to adopt some content moderation policies to remove hate speech and was allowed back online. The new version was described by some as "Parler PG." Its users, however, did not flock back. Being racist and misogynistic without shame or fear of reprisal was exactly the point. Once again, white nationalists, anti-Semites, and the most MAGA of assholes had nowhere to go to spout their views.

Enter Jason Miller, Trump's most odious and mediocre adviser. Miller, a middling Republican operative before jumping on the Trump train, was also one of the few Trumpists not forced into exile from polite society. I guess this is an achievement in Trump's circle, on par with the evolutionary abilities of the cockroach. Miller launched an alternative to Twitter called Gettr—with "alternative" meaning a sloppy facsimile of Twitter. Gettr even allowed users to import their old tweets, a useful feature for their desired user base (those banned from Twitter).

For weeks, Miller refused to disclose Gettr's funders. Trump? Peter Thiel, the Silicon Valley billionaire who bankrolls MAGA causes? The Mercers? Nope. The money behind Gettr comes from the family foundation of Guo Wengui, a fugitive Chinese billionaire who is close friends with Steve Bannon. Before the launch of Gettr, Guo was identified in a report by internet analysis company Graphika as the center of a massive disinformation network that pushed conspiracy theories about the US election, QAnon, and COVID-19.[21] At Bannon's behest, Guo, who fled to the United States to avoid prosecution in China, funded a number of right-wing disinformation efforts. In another moment that is also too on point to be true, Bannon was arrested while on Guo's yacht.[22]

The platform functioned as well you can probably imagine. In the first couple of weeks, hashtags using the N-word were often trending. Soon after its release, jihadists from ISIS began flooding Gettr with propaganda, including calls to violence against the West, videos of beheadings, and explicit pitches for Gettr users to take up arms. There was even a meme that showed Trump being executed while wearing an orange jumpsuit. An August 2021 Politico investigation found that more than 250 jihadi-related accounts were posting to the site. Trump

---

21 Basically, credentials as impressive as being press secretary in the Trump White House.
22 Like much of what happens in Trump world, this scene could have been ripped from an episode of *Arrested Development*.

minions face-planting in public is always amusing, but in all the online heckling at Miller's expense, a bigger significance was lost.

Gettr, like Parler, was specifically designed to cater to extremists, but Trump had shifted the Overton window (that is, the range of policies considered politically acceptable to the mainstream at any given time) so much that right-wing extremists were now viewed as only slightly right of the Republican mainstream. It should therefore have come as no surprise that extremists like ISIS would exploit a platform whose rules were written to enable extremist behavior.

It's easy for Democrats to laugh at this app. Except for a handful of reporters and Democrats monitoring these sites for professional purposes, there are only die-hard MAGA voters on Gettr and Parler. But—and this is the point Democrats too often miss—preaching to the choir is the point. Fox, Breitbart, the Daily Caller, and the rest are all part of a billionaire-funded effort to create a hermetically sealed (dis)information bubble. The goal is to control the flow of information to their voters. These social media platforms are the next turn of the wheel.

Skewing the Polls

There are innumerable examples of right-wing-billionaire-supported disinformation efforts, but there is one lesser-known but quite absurd example from 2020 that speaks to the deviousness and vast scope of the effort.

For as long as I have worked in politics, RealClearPolitics was a must-bookmark site for operatives, junkies, and reporters. The relatively spare website was a clearinghouse for political news and data. Prior to Politico, Axios, and other politics-centric sites, there were very few places to go for pages and pages of political news. RCP's most prominent feature was the RealClearPolitics polling average. This was not a complicated statistical model like Nate Silver's FiveThirtyEight or the *New York Times* needle that tortures Democrats every Election Night.[23] It was simply an average of all the available public polling. The RCP polling average was the go-to indicator of the state of the presidential election. Media outlets frequently cited it in their stories. Using the average of the polls, while far from perfect, helps negate overreacting to any single outlying poll. In a world of right-wing disinformation, purported liberal bias, clickbait, and conflict-driven political journalists, the RCP polling average was one place every serious person in politics trusted.

During the 2020 election, close watchers of the site started to notice something a little funky. The RCP polling average often favored Trump more than other measures. The once-reliable site started including a plethora of polls that did not meet industry standards. And all the junk polls were from pro-Trump publications and polling outfits. Yes, the polls in that race were quite wrong and very wrong in the Democrats' favor, but there is difference between being wrong and being intentionally deceptive.

Much like *Playboy*,[24] people didn't go to RealClearPolitics for the articles.[25] Those who happened to stumble upon them quickly noticed that something had changed there, too. Over the years, RealClearPolitics employed a handful of reporters covering the White House, Congress, and politics more broadly, but its bread and butter was aggregation. Its editors combed the internet for political articles and linked to them from the site. Now an increasing number of the curated

---

23 While the needle is a more accurate tool than political reporters counting yard signs and rally attendance, I still hate it.
24 If this terrible joke makes it into the book, it's evidence my publisher is on autopilot.
25 I sort of hate myself for this joke. Is it funny? Who knows, but I worry unfunny jokes have become my brand.

links were from hard-right pro-Trump outlets like the *Federalist*. The original reporting was no longer from journalists with backgrounds in traditional, neutral reporting. The staff was now mostly veterans of the disinformation machine or of the Republican Party itself.

It was well known that the site's founders, Tom Bevan and Ben McIntyre, were Republicans, but up to this point, their personal ideologies had not materially affected the editorial direction of the website. Something clearly had changed. Setting aside journalistic integrity, the founders had opted to follow the money.

A *New York Times* investigation revealed that RealClearPolitics received an influx of cash from right-wing billionaires Richard and Elizabeth Uihlein. The Uihleins are some of the biggest donors to far-right causes. Richard continued to support Alabama judge Roy Moore's Senate candidacy even after credible testimony had accused Moore of sexually assaulting minors. The *Times* also discovered close financial and organizational ties between RealClearPolitics and the *Federalist*, one of the most noxious sites on the internet. And BuzzFeed reported that the *Federalist* got its mail at the RealClearPolitics office in Chicago. The connections to the *Federalist*, a magazine so slavishly pro-Trump that even Sean Hannity would blush at its articles, is further evidence of the shift at RealClearPolitics.

After nearly every single media outlet on the planet had called the 2020 election for Joe Biden, RealClearPolitics continued to assert, against all available evidence and basic artithmetic, that the state of Pennsylvania was still too close to call. The absence of a call was being touted by Trump dead-enders as a reason for hope. It was a piece of evidence for those trying to overturn the election through extralegal and even violent means.

At the end of the day, does it really matter that Republican billionaires spent their money to rig a polling site in an election when all the polling was off? Probably not. It's small potatoes compared to what

Steve Bannon is doing with the Mercers' money. But it speaks to just how committed they are to winning the information war. There is no amount of money they won't spend to gain even the smallest edge. The hijacking of RealClearPolitics was another cog in the Big Lie machine of faux journalism.

8

Roger Ailes and the Evil Genius of
Faux Journalism

In 2015, just after Hillary Clinton launched her much-anticipated run for president, the *New York Times* published a blockbuster story about the soon-to-be candidate. In a breathless tone and with barely hidden glee, the story raised questions about connections between Clinton's actions as secretary of state and the financial interests of donors to the Clinton Foundation, the nonprofit she and her husband started at the end of his presidency. It featured prominently on the *Times* website and was promoted relentlessly on social media. In the eyes of the self-proclaimed "paper of record," this story was a big deal.

The *New York Times*'s source was *Clinton Cash: The Untold Story of How and Why Foreign Governments and Businesses Helped Make Bill and Hillary Rich*, a forthcoming book from a conservative author named Peter Schweizer. The accusations reported in the book were repeated without one iota of skepticism or original reporting by the *Times*. Here's just one example of what the *Times* regurgitated:

A free-trade agreement in Colombia that benefited a major foundation donor's natural resource investments in the South American nation, development projects in the aftermath of the Haitian earthquake in 2010, and more than $1 million in payments to Mr. Clinton by a Canadian bank and major shareholder in the Keystone XL oil pipeline around the time the project was being debated in the State Department.

At no point did the *Times* use its library of journalistic resources or experienced reporters to verify these claims or put them in context.

Conservative authors churn out books about the Clintons constantly. Long after Obama became president, Clinton books continued to make best seller lists and occupy right-wing media airtime. *Clinton Cash* wasn't even the first book released in anticipation of Hillary's second run for the presidency. Two books of similar pedigree, with similarly speciously sourced allegations, were released just months prior. The story struck many in Washington as odd. It was Clinton-related clickbait at its best and merely another example of what many Democrats believed to be the paper's long-running grudge against the Clintons. Buried in the seventh paragraph of the offending *New York Times* story about Hillary Clinton was this:

> *Clinton Cash* is potentially more unsettling, both because of its focused reporting and because major news organizations including the *Times, The Washington Post* and Fox News have exclusive agreements with the author to pursue the story lines found in the book.

The author of this paragraph seems unclear about the definition of the word *exclusive*; beyond that, arrangements like this are quite unusual.[1] Publishers often pitch newsy items to journalists with a promise of exclusivity, but I have never heard of a written agreement

---

1 As a general rule, if you are entering into an agreement with Fox News, you are probably doing something you shouldn't.

with three separate news outlets. While Schweizer's conservative view-point was apparent, the origin of his work was not. In its cryptic mention of the agreement, the *New York Times* did not disclose several important facts about the origin of Schweizer's work. Schweizer was not some dogged reporter digging through financial records and FOIA requests. He had used researchers from an innocuously named think tank called the Government Accountability Institute. And who started the GAI? Our good (not) friend, Steve Bannon.[2]

And who funded it? Robert Mercer.

To put a finer point on it, the *New York Times*, as well as the *Washington Post*, went into a partnership with the chairman and the chief funder of Breitbart. The close relationship between GAI and Breitbart was evident, and Schweizer's connections to the racist rag were not made public when the agreement was struck.

As they tend to be, the higher-ups at the *Times* are closed-lipped about their decisions. Never forget that the attitude of old-school journalism is "transparency for thee, but none for me."[3] Maybe a Google search on Schweizer or GAI was too much work? Was a salacious story about the front-runner for president so alluring that none of the *i*'s were dotted or *t*'s crossed? Margaret Sullivan, the *Times*'s well-respected public editor at the time, interviewed Matt Purdy, an editor who worked on the story. Purdy dismissed all criticism, offered no self-reflection after getting in bed with a website as sordid as Breitbart, and ignored concerns about how such a bizarre and opaque agreement could impact the public's trust in the institution. According to Purdy, the arrangement was "no different than the way we treat information from any other source."

To be fair, I am not accusing the *Times* of anything other than

---

2 He's not really our friend—in case that wasn't clear.
3 The "reader is always wrong" must be in the *New York Times* staff handbook somewhere.

poor judgment with a sprinkling of overly exuberant anti-Clinton sentiment. I bring up this dark moment in *Times* history for two reasons. First, it should never be forgotten that major media outlets partnered with Donald Trump's future campaign manager and chief funder on a series of stories that built the foundation for the "Crooked Hillary" message and the "Lock her up" chants. Second, the *Clinton Cash* incident demonstrates why the conservative movement invested so much time and money into building up a disinformation system cloaked by journalism.

Like everything rotten in American media and politics, how we got here begins with Roger Ailes.

The Ailes Model

Conservative media was around long before Roger Ailes showed up. The existence of right-leaning publications dates back nearly a century.

In the first two thirds of the twentieth century, conservative political policies were often pushed into the shadows. This was particularly true of economic and domestic policies. The Great Depression was a test case that seemed impossible to erase from the American consciousness. Republican policies began the Great Depression, and Democratic policies ended it. Of course, it's more complicated than that,[4] but FDR's four terms followed by Truman's reelection demonstrates that the American public was convinced of this sentiment. Conservative publications like *Human Events* and *National Review* began the uphill climb of refurbishing the reputation of conservatism. These New York– and DC-based publications, staffed with writers with Ivy League credentials, gave conservatives a modicum of credibility that

---

4 But not that much more complicated.

belied the failed policies they advocated, adding a sheen of intellectualism to a discredited philosophy. The primary audience was cocktail party–attending elites and policy makers in Washington. These efforts were well within the tradition of ideological journalism.

I don't want to dismiss the gaslighting and McCarthyism endemic to these conservative[5] publications, but it wasn't until Roger Ailes came onto the scene that conservative media turned from intellectually dishonest opinion pieces to politically weaponized propaganda and disinformation.

The story of Roger Ailes's rise from political consultant to media titan and his fall to disgraced miscreant has been told many times over. Ailes is the subject of at least two biographies, a Showtime limited series with Russell Crowe, and an Adam McKay movie with John Lithgow playing the Fox executive. The best of these accounts is Gabe Sherman's *The Loudest Voice in the Room*, an assiduously reported book that documents Ailes's life and career. To understand the modern right-wing disinformation playbook, you must understand Roger Ailes. The MAGA megaphone from Fox to Breitbart and everything in between is built on Ailes's ideas. It uses his strategy. Every union between a strategist and a billionaire—Bannon and Mercer, Shapiro and Dan Wilks and *Federalist* trolls and the Uihleins—is the modern-day equivalent of what Ailes accomplished with Rupert Murdoch. There are several key moments from Ailes's career that shaped his approach to Fox News and led to the Big Lies that dominate American politics.

Despite spending the last several decades of his life as a media executive, Ailes started as a political consultant. He rose to power by helping Nixon win the presidency with an explicit appeal to white voters angry over civil rights. During his time working for Nixon, Ailes

---

5 Many of them are still around and still practicing McCarthyism and gaslighting.

was intimately involved in nascent efforts to build a right-wing propaganda operation. First, he worked on a purportedly independent documentary about the Vietnam War financed by a pro-Nixon political committee. The White House's intimate involvement in this project was to be hidden. As Sherman reports, the point of the documentary was to "rebut a CBS program critical of the Vietnam War." The project never saw the light of day, but it became a model for future tactics.

Using propaganda under the guise of independent, fair, and balanced reporting became a classic Ailes tactic. Ailes was so concerned about Sherman's book that he sought out Zev Chafets, a writer known for favorable profiles of conservative figures, to pen a countering biography to beat Sherman's to the shelves. During George W. Bush's disastrous Iraq War, Ailes turned Fox News into an updated version of the prowar documentary he worked on for Nixon. The worse things went in Iraq, the more prowar Fox became. Under Ailes's direction, Fox highlighted the (little) good news, gaslighted the (immense) bad news, and viciously attacked the patriotism of anyone who dared ask why America's response to 9/11 was invading a country not involved in that attack.[6]

Early in the Nixon administration, Ailes became intimately involved in a more ambitious project, one that would be the genesis for Fox News. An extensive memo titled "A Plan for Putting the GOP on TV News" began circulating among Nixon's top advisers. The plan, later dubbed the Capitol News Service, was a detailed, expensive proposal to film pro-Nixon television stories and then distribute them to local television stations through a complex system involving trucks and planes traveling thousands of miles to drop off the tapes.[7] A version of the memo with Ailes's comments was found by John Cook,

---

6 Ailes even provided political advice on the war to the Bush administration at the request of Dick Cheney.
7 Life before the internet was hard!

a reporter from *Gawker*, in the bowels of the Nixon Library. In his handwritten notes, Ailes called the plan "a very good idea" and then offered incredibly detailed feedback on how to expand the program and further disguise the partisan origins of the content. The goal was convincing people to watch "news" produced by Nixon aides without being able to differentiate it from "traditional news" produced by journalists. Sound familiar?

The memo also opens with an assessment of the public. "People are lazy. With television you just sit—watch—listen. The *thinking* is done for you." (Ailes underlined "thinking.") That is the core of why Ailes was so committed to moving into television "news" as a political strategy.

Ailes's toxic personality eventually led him to be fired as Nixon's image consultant prior to the 1972 election.[8] (Imagine being too toxic for the Nixon White House.) The firing ended up being Aile's good fortune, because he was gone long before Watergate. But as he was wont to do, he landed on his feet. In 1974, he leapt into journalism for the first time. Despite having zero experience in television news, he became the news director of a broadcast television network called Television News Incorporated. In essence, Ailes was implementing the Capitol News Service plan and road-testing strategies for Fox News. TVN, as it was known, was created by conservatives with the explicit purpose of being a conservative alternative to the existing three broadcast networks. The founder was Robert Reinhold Pauley, a former ABC Radio executive, with far-right political views. Pauley supported Barry Goldwater for president and was a member of the John Birch Society. TVN was started with funding from Joseph Coors, the archconservative beer magnate. Jack Wilson, TVN's president,

---

8 Being too big an asshole for Richard Nixon is a true feat.

reportedly considered "Martin Luther King an avowed communist revolutionary."

TVN was around for a few years before Ailes came on board, but there were two ideas about the TVN experience that guided Ailes and informed the overall right-wing strategy. First, despite their deeply held conservative views, TVN's leadership claimed they had no ideological agenda. This faux neutrality was a precursor to Ailes's decision to relentlessly brand Fox's coverage as "fair and balanced."

Second, TVN was staffed by reporters who did not share the views of the leadership. The staff, including a cub reporter named Charles Gibson, were in a constant state of tension with Pauley, Wilson, and Ailes. They thought they had been hired to do news as it was commonly understood, not conservative propaganda. Numerous reports indicate that Wilson and Ailes repeatedly put their thumb on the scale. According to Sherman, Pauley asked prominent conservatives and former Nixon speechwriters Pat Buchanan and William Safire for advice on news coverage. TVN also employed Accuracy in Media, a right-wing think tank, to regularly review TVN stories to ensure they were adhering to the mission of the conservative founders. The constant tension boiled over into a scathing article in the *Columbia Journalism Review*. The article accused Ailes and others of political interference. TVN shut down soon after, but Ailes learned an important lesson. If you want to run a propaganda operation disguised as a news organization, make sure to hire reporters who share your mission (Brit Hume), who are too weak or too dumb to stand up to you (John Roberts), or too money-hungry to rock the boat (Bret Baier).

All these experiences taught Ailes that the path to conservative power ran through the news. After all, Ailes was a campaign ad maker by vocation. It would have been more lucrative for him to convince Joseph Coors or other wealthy Republicans to fund political ads marketing the Republican Party and its policies. But Ailes realized that conservative messaging packaged as news was exponentially more powerful than political ads or candidates' speeches. This idea led to Fox News and to the right-wing propaganda operation that threatens democracy and the planet today.

When you look at the rightward shift in the American political conversation since the advent of Fox News and the MAGA media's ability to elect and protect Trump, there is no question that Ailes was on to something—something insidious and powerful. And it is a model being replicated at a rapid rate across the media landscape.

Objectivity Laundering

Ailes had an incisive understanding of media culture and how to exploit it for partisan gain. There is nothing that old-school journalists value more than being perceived as objective, ideologically neutral observers of events. The notion that human beings can be objective and without personal or political bias is specious at best,[9] but for journalists, their value lay in the idea that they, unlike normal humans, could put aside their biases to call balls and strikes on the most important events, the equivalent of steady hands to a surgeon or a good ear to a composer.

When Ailes began playing with the idea of creating pseudo-journalistic partisan propaganda, the American public believed that the media was objective and could therefore be trusted. Gallup first started polling how much Americans trusted the media in 1972. In that first poll, 68 percent of those surveyed had a great or fair amount of trust in the media. Only 6 percent had no trust at all. Information delivered by someone who could be considered a journalist was more likely to be believed than a message from a politician or a political

---

9 Not to go all meta, but a bias for neutrality is still a bias.

party. Ailes was responsible for some of the most devastating attack ads in history, but because of Americans' inherent trust in newspeople, these ads' efficacy paled in comparison to the information that could be delivered on the news.[10]

If Ailes wanted to leverage the vaunted position the media held in American society, he had to adopt the mantle of objectivity. The idea that Fox News would be unbiased was absurd on its face. Murdoch was a well-known conservative who funded conservative media in Australia and the United Kingdom. Ailes was perhaps the country's preeminent Republican political operative. Their pitch to advertisers included reaching conservatives turned off by liberally biased mainstream media.

Despite the obvious ideological bias, Ailes claimed that Fox would be objective. He spent the press tour for the launch of the network attacking his soon-to-be competitors, calling them too biased to deliver news fairly or with objectivity. It added power and believability to his conservative messaging. Nicole Hemmer, a Columbia University research scholar and an expert on conservative media, uses the term *objectivity laundering* to describe these stealthy efforts to impart partisan messaging under the guise of traditionally objective journalism.

A brief peek under the hood of the Ailes/Murdoch operation revealed the actual purpose of Fox News. Many of the original staff came from Ailes's political consulting firm. Much of the energy of the new network was being funneled into opinion shows, shows hiring high-profile talent like Bill O'Reilly. Fox retains a fraction of the news staff of CNN or other broadcast networks, and it has almost no presence abroad.

This putative but patently absurd objectivity was an essential ingredient to Ailes's strategy, a necessary condition of being in good

10 How quaint.

standing with the rest of the media. Previous conservative media efforts failed to move the needle outside Georgetown and the Upper East Side because they self-identified as ideological journalism. Fox News would be different. It would be "fair and balanced."

In his typical brazen fashion, Ailes asserted that to believe Fox was subjective was evidence of your own liberal bias.[11] This absurd tautology worked, because it exploited an element of the media mind-set that Ailes and generations of conservatives helped create: the media's fear of its own liberal bias.

Fraternity of Reporters

Early in the Obama presidency, we got fed up with Fox News and decided to do something about it. Our concern was less about what was happening on Fox and more about how mainstream outlets like the *New York Times* and the *Washington Post* were regurgitating the right-wing bile spewing from Fox blowhards like Glenn Beck. Ailes and Fox were setting the agenda and putting us on the defensive. It was hard for Democrats to sell the president's accomplishments and push for his agenda when we were constantly responding to conspiracy theories and marginalia.

Before too long, we decided to fight back by calling out Fox's BS and no longer abiding by the obvious fiction that the network was fair and balanced. There were mixed levels of enthusiasm about this idea within the Obama White House. The president was fed up and ready to push back. Some of the more seasoned pros in the White House were pretty skeptical of taking on America's number one cable network. Not I. "We can't take this lying down," I said in a meeting on

---

11 A Trumpian logic pretzel—the proof that I am right is that you think I am wrong.

the Fox strategy. "If we don't push back, no one will do it for us. Honestly, fuck these people."

While I was definitely too young, too hotheaded, and trying too hard to prove to the president that I was tough enough for the West Wing, I was relatively sanguine about our chances of changing Fox's behavior. Still, I thought we could at least stop other outlets from regurgitating the BS from Murdoch's network.

It seemed like an open-and-shut case. Fox was not journalism as the term was traditionally understood. It was clearly a partisan operation with a simple purpose: to hurt Obama and help Republicans. Fox was also constantly trashing the rest of the media, calling them liberally biased and enthralled with Obama, while ridiculing their competitors for subpar ratings. Off the record, many of the White House reporters complained to us about having to cover these Fox-generated controversies. Even some of the Fox reporters complained about their bosses and sheepishly claimed that nothing could be done. The orders came from the top, and reporters' ability to push back was limited or completely nonexistent.

Our fight against Fox was launched with a double-barreled assault. We conducted a series of interviews wherein Obama White House officials like senior adviser David Axelrod and chief of staff Rahm Emanuel took to the Sunday shows to call out Fox for not being a news organization. In 2020, this is the most obvious statement in the world, but in 2009, it was quite controversial and led to a torrent of media coverage.

I didn't expect the rest of the press to side with us, but I was sure they wouldn't side with Fox. I was wrong.

Jake Tapper, then a White House correspondent for ABC News, confronted Robert Gibbs, the White House press secretary, during the daily briefing: "It's escaped none of our notice that the White House has decided in the last few weeks to declare one of our sister organizations 'not a news organization' and to tell the rest of us not to treat them like a news organization. Can you explain why it's appropriate for the White House to decide that a news organization is not one?"

A sister organization? A right-wing propaganda network run by Republican operatives with little to no standards was being defended by the very people Fox had been created to undermine.

And when the White House tried to exclude Fox from a series of interviews with a Treasury Department official being conducted with a shared camera, the rest of the networks refused to do the interview.

In my naïveté and impulsive anger, I misunderstood a key part of the culture of journalism. Traditionally, journalists abide by a creed similar to NATO's: an attack on one is an attack on all. Journalists like Tapper, who take their jobs and their integrity incredibly seriously, leapt to the defense of Fox because other media outlets might be competitors, but everyone else, including and especially the White House, was considered an adversary.

While this journalistic mutual defense pact might seem shortsighted in moments like these, I am sympathetic to the impulse. The freedom of the press is consistently under assault, and the ability to fight back depends on collective action. Sometimes those threats are relatively minor, like battles over access and press credentials. Other times, they involve efforts to criminally prosecute journalists or use the power of the state to prevent the publication of certain information.

Most journalists are inclined to side with one another over the people they cover. This is why Republican disinformation efforts have been so effective. It's the reason the *New York Times* can stumble into a partnership with Breitbart. Ailes knew that simply by self-identifying as a media outlet, Fox News would be welcomed into the community of journalists. Its obvious political agenda and farcical standards would be discounted. And when attacks came from

Democrats, Ailes knew that the media outlets Fox was trying to destroy would rush to its defense.

Mainstream journalists inherently took the stories pushed by Fox et al. more seriously than if they had come from the Republican Party or a Republican campaign. Information from a political entity was propaganda. Information from a media outlet was reporting to be followed up on.

In 2009, Clark Hoyt, one of Sullivan's predecessors as the public editor of the *New York Times*, wrote a column lamenting that the paper of record wasn't paying enough attention to Fox News. In response, the *Times* assigned an editor to monitor Fox and other right-wing media outlets for story ideas.[12] In his wildest dreams, Ailes couldn't have imagined that the *Times* would assign an editor to watch his network for ideas on how to cover a Democratic president he wanted to destroy. But it wasn't just the *Times* looking to Fox for story ideas. Marcus Brauchli, then executive editor of the *Washington Post*, challenged his reporters to pay closer attention to Fox and other conservative media outlets.

The *New York Times* would never go into a partnership with the RNC (or the DNC) on a major story about a presidential candidate, but it did so with Breitbart—even though Breitbart's ideological agenda is as clear as the RNC's.[13] The editor of the *Post* would never challenge his reporters to pay more attention to a political party's messaging, but a purely political operation dressed up in journalist's clothing[14] is granted immediate credibility and influence.

Since the early Obama days, more mainstream journalists were willing to call out Fox, Breitbart, and others for spreading

---

12 Definitely a violation of the Geneva Convention rules on torture.
13 Maybe even clearer.
14 Ill-fitting and perhaps pleated khakis, sensible but not stylish walking shoes, a boxy and stained blue blazer.

disinformation and conspiracy theories—most notably, Jake Tapper, now with CNN. But far too many people turn a blind eye to what the Right is doing and adhere to an outdated understanding of how the media environment works. This dangerous obliviousness continues to be the undoing of the last remaining shreds of traditional media's influence. At the risk of making a terribly unoriginal pun, they keep inviting the Fox into the henhouse and then wondering what happened to all their friends.[15]

---

15 There is something wrong with me. I can't stop.

II. HOW IT HAPPENED

9

Disinformation and the Destruction of Local News

My very first job on my very first presidential campaign was as northeast director of regional communications. This esoteric, inscrutable title meant I was the Gore for President campaign's liaison to all the local press from West Virginia[1] to the Canadian border. It was my job to build relationships with local reporters, ensure that the campaign got good press coverage on local television, and work with local campaign staff on a plan to dominate the local media.

I stumbled into this job by showing up at the campaign headquarters with a little bit of experience and just enough money to work for free at the exact moment the campaign needed volunteer staff. Even though I was quite young—as were the four other regional communications directors—this was an oddly crucial position in the campaign. Back in the days before Facebook, Twitter, and Politico, the local media was incredibly influential. Our campaign bent over backward to court local reporters. We timed our rallies so that they would happen live on the evening news. We invited the local press to cover the arrival of Air Force Two. The vice president did interviews with local

---

1 Yeah, I know West Virginia is not in the Northeast. I didn't draw the map, but the fact that our campaign considered the Mountain State to be in the same region as Vermont may explain why Al Gore was the first Democrat to lose West Virginia to a nonincumbent Republican since 1928.

press. There were even times when we invited local political reporters to travel on Air Force Two and interview Gore in flight.

Our campaign wasn't unique. George W. Bush's campaign was dedicating the same resources to influencing the local media. Bill Clinton's White House had a large operation focused on regional media, and President Clinton pioneered using satellite technology to do dozens of local television interviews in an hour without leaving the White House.

It was an article of faith in those days; while the national media was important, the local press was where campaigns were won and lost. This was for good reason. It's impossible to overstate how influential the local media was in the pre-internet era. Local television was by far the most watched and trusted news source for most Americans. Newspapers were thriving. The revenue from ads, subscriptions, and classifieds was more than enough for newspapers to hire a lot of reporters to cover lots of things and turn a pretty profit. Back in those days, newspapers did such good business that even midsize papers could afford to have a bureau in Washington, DC, to cover states' congressional delegations and the White House. Local political reporters and columnists were so influential that they could make or break a candidate—even a presidential candidate. Folks like David Yepsen of the *Des Moines Register*, Al Cross of the Louisville (Kentucky) *Courier-Journal*, Jon Ralston of the *Las Vegas Review-Journal*, and Carla Marinucci of the *San Francisco Chronicle* were titans to be courted and feared.

The power of local media was a huge reason every politician adhered to the aphorism "All politics is local." What you did in Washington was important, but you had to tend to the home fires. You showed your voters that you were doing what they had sent you there to do. This was the way to get elected and stay elected.

To anyone who started working in or paying attention to politics in the last decade, this all probably sounds insane. All politics is now national. The power and presence of local media has dramatically diminished. Local media has been gutted. Many towns no longer have a newspaper, and the few remaining local papers are a shell of their former selves, with almost no local reporters. Many younger Americans have fully cut the cord and no longer have access to local television news.[2]

Many see this as a simple but inevitable transition, like the move from radio to television and from flip phones to iPhones. But this change has had dramatic consequences for democracy. The decimation of local news is the primary reason that disinformation has become the Republican Party's dominant political strategy. With the loss of local news, an information and accountability vacuum was created and is now being ruthlessly exploited by the right wing to further dominate politics. Local news is now the latest and most dangerous front in the Republican war on truth.

What Happened?

Local news is dying a rapid death. Local television viewership has been declining steadily for more than a decade. The viewers who do remain are disproportionately older. According to a 2018 Pew study, eight in ten Americans over sixty-five get their news from TV compared with less than 20 percent of Americans ages eighteen to twenty-nine.[3]

According to a report from Penelope Muse Abernathy, a journalism scholar at the University of North Carolina–Chapel Hill, more than two thousand newspapers, a quarter of all newspapers, have gone out of business since 2004. Over that same period, half of all

---

2 Technically, they could buy over-the-air antennae to get their local news, but come on! Who would do that to see stories about crime, traffic, and dogs running on treadmills?
3 Truthfully, 20 percent seems high.

journalism jobs, mostly from local journalism, have disappeared. This is not a case of old print-first publications being forced out by cooler, nimbler digital outlets. Since 2018, the number of communities with no local news whatsoever has grown from 1,300 to 1,800.

The most experienced (and best-paid) reporters have been laid off, bought out, or outright fired. The amount of original reporting has shrunk to almost nothing. Vulture capitalist hedge funds are swooping in and buying up the news carrion, gutting their staff (and journalism) and harvesting them for parts (and profit).

Things are bad and getting worse. According to the 2021 annual Pew *State of the News Media* report, newspaper circulation is at an all-time low. In 1990, weekday newspaper circulation was approximately 63 million. In 2020, it was less than 25 million, including digital audiences.

There is no hope for the old model of local news to bounce back. Anyone who tells you otherwise is arranging deck chairs on the *Titanic*. If you want to blame someone for this, blame Al Gore for inventing the internet. And if that seems unfair, blame technological innovation. The last decade and a half saw the greatest transformation in how people got their information since the invention of the printing press. Think about it this way: When Barack Obama started running for president in 2007, the smartphone was not yet invented;[4] Facebook was primarily a way to stay in touch with college classmates;[5] Twitter was a niche platform for tech bros to tell one another what they had for lunch;[6] YouTube's most famous videos featured cats playing piano;[7] Snapchat, TikTok, and Instagram didn't exist; newspapers

---

4 The BlackBerry era!

5 As opposed to a way to stay in touch with fellow militia members.

6 As opposed to a way to express opinions about things you know little about.

7 As opposed to grifters convincing people to take horse deworming pills as a cure for COVID-19.

were powerful and profitable; network news anchors were trusted figures; and the Sunday Shows set the agenda for the week.

Changes in technology—notably, pocket-size super computers and ready access to high-speed internet—dramatically changed the landscape. Theoretically, the shift to digital should not have been so devastating for the news business. An economic model dependent on ads and subscriptions should have been easily transferred online. If you paid to have the news dropped on your doorstep, you would likely pay to read it on your phone or tablet. Car dealers and furniture stores that needed to reach customers weren't going to stop advertising simply because the internet had been invented. From the onset of the innovation era, there would be, as with the rest of the economy, disruptions, winners and losers, but the death of the news business was not a forgone conclusion.

The problems for newspapers were compounded by three things:

The first was one of the dumbest and most consequential business decisions in modern history, one that, in hindsight, is so confounding that it is impossible to imagine how anyone could have been that dense. When the internet first experienced mass adoption, nearly every news outlet in the country felt compelled to have an "internet strategy." Technology was changing, and of course, they should change with it. So, what did they do? They mostly put all the news on the internet for free. So, your choice was to pay to read it on a dead tree or to read it on your computer for free. And these news outlets wondered why people stopped subscribing. The ramifications of this decision are still felt to this day. Most media outlets now still give away a portion of their product. They offer ten or so free articles a month before putting up a paywall. While many people subscribe to many outlets because they are huge news consumers, want to support a struggling but important industry, or want to stick it to Trump and his "enemy of the people" rhetoric, most people don't pay for their news. They use their ten articles on one outlet before moving to another without ever smashing the Subscribe button.[8] To put a finer point on why this is such bad business, imagine if most coffee shops offered you five free coffees a month before you started paying. Most people would have their first five free coffees at one place and then get five more free coffees at the next place, and so on, until the end of the month. It is a truly insane way to run a business.

The second thing compounding newspapers' problems was the 2008 recession. At the exact moment when newspapers were most vulnerable, the financial crisis devastated the very businesses that made newspapers so profitable. People had less money to spend on cars, furniture, and other big-ticket items, which meant that retailers had less money to spend on ads in newspapers. Subscriptions had been declining for a while, but robust ad revenues had offset the problem. Once the financial crisis hit, though, the newspapers lost their belt *and* suspenders. The death spiral was in full effect.

The third and final thing compounding the problems for newspapers was the rise of digital advertising. When the economy finally recovered sufficiently for a rebound in the advertising market, the dollars didn't return to the newspapers. They went to Google and Facebook, the tech giants dominating digital ads. Why would a car dealer pay a premium for an ad in a print newspaper when they could pay Google less to target people in their area searching online for cars? Facebook offered tools to surgically select people in a given market who looked just like a business's typical customer. And unlike newspapers, the digital behemoths gave advertisers real-world feedback on how many people saw their ad, clicked on it, and bought their product because of it. This was not a close call. Going back to traditional newspaper ads would have been like using the Pony Express to deliver

---

8 If you know, you know.

your packages instead of FedEx. Relatedly, the internet also destroyed an equally lucrative but lesser-known part of the newspaper business: classifieds and personal ads. If you wanted to sell a used futon or rent a room, you paid a small fee to get your ad in the paper. If you wanted to meet someone outside the bar scene, you could buy an ad in the Personals section to try to find a match. In the pre-internet days, newspapers basically had a monopoly on these businesses. Then came Craigslist and dating apps, which were free or cheap and much more effective than newspapers.

In summary, newspapers had fewer subscribers, fewer advertisers, and had created a culture of free content.

Local television news is doing better than local newspapers, but that is like someone being more likable than Ted Cruz. It's a low freaking bar. Most people under thirty have never seen their local newscast. In fact, because they don't have cable, they don't even have access to the local news. It's not a part of their life and never will be.

There has been massive consolidation in the local television industry, with a handful of large corporations owning (and controlling) nearly all of the local news. These companies did not buy local television stations because they care passionately about journalism or were interested in strengthening a faltering pillar of democracy. They wanted to make money, and the best way to make money is to spend less money on journalism.

Why You Should Care

It's fair to ask: who cares if people get their news from a local newspaper or a national one, from a local TV station or national cable? It's still news, right?

The delivery mechanism shouldn't matter much, but in this case it does. Local news and national news are often very different, targeted at different audiences, and focused on different things. Historically, the local media played a very important, and different, role from that of their more famous, better-paid counterparts in the national media. A vibrant local news ecosystem is a bulwark against polarization. I spent much of my early career in politics working for Democrats representing red states. The only way these politicians could stay in office was by convincing a sizable number of Republicans and Republican-leaning voters that they were different from the caricature of the Democratic Party. Politicians relied on being omnipresent in local media, with lots of interviews from Washington to tell the folks back home what was being done for their issues. Appearances at ribbon-cutting ceremonies, fairs, and other community events ended up on the local news and on the front page of the local paper.

In 2002, when I was working to reelect Democratic senator Tim Johnson in very Republican South Dakota, our entire message was about how Johnson used his clout in Washington, DC, to deliver for South Dakota on nonpartisan issues. We highlighted the federal money Johnson had brought home to fund dams, libraries, roads, bike paths, and community centers. His big legislative achievements were aid for farmers suffering from a historic drought and money for South Dakota veterans. The Republicans wanted to paint Johnson as an out-of-touch liberal, but years of communicating in the local press about his South Dakota accomplishments and a campaign spent doing press conferences in front of those deliverables rendered this message moot.

Tim Johnson's local press–centric strategy could never work now. Many of the media outlets crucial to our strategy twenty years ago are long gone. Most of the rest are what media critic Margaret Sullivan calls "ghost newspapers," places where the name remains and where you can still buy a subscription, but where the staff and their ambitions are so diminished that they can no longer do the day-to-day reporting that allows citizens to make good decisions about candidates when they go to the polls to vote.

A hyper–local media strategy was also critical to Obama's victory in the 2008 Iowa Caucus. On paper, rural, lilywhite Iowa was a less-than-optimal fit for Barack Hussein Obama from the South Side of Chicago via Harvard, Honolulu, and Indonesia. The candidate's ability to connect with Iowans was further limited because he started the race as a huge celebrity, generating rock star-esque crowds. Presidential candidates usually begin Iowa as far Off-Broadway as possible, with small events at VFW halls, coffee shops, and in people's homes.[9] Obama's first event in Iowa drew a raucous crowd of seven thousand Iowans. The one-on-one, caucusgoer-by-caucusgoer approach typical of Iowa campaigns was a logistic impossibility. To address this challenge, our Iowa campaign staff[10] made sure that no candidate spent more time with the local media than Obama. After every event in a small Iowa town, the future president would sit down for an interview with the weekly newspapers that serviced communities too small to maintain a daily paper. These weeklies were the lifeblood of their community, and it was a big deal when Obama sat down with them. It was a gesture of respect to counter the rock star narrative Obama had to overcome.

This strategy would never work now. I would venture to guess that most of those Iowa papers are long gone. The people in those towns have no access to local news. If they pay any attention to politics, they probably get their political news from national outlets or, more likely,

---

9 A very popular Iowa campaign destination are Pizza Ranch restaurants. Pizza Ranch is a chain that targets towns too small for a Pizza Hut. Every Pizza Ranch has a party room in the back and serves a surprisingly delicious dessert pizza.

10 My *Pod Save America* cohost and former Obama Iowa press secretary Tommy Vietor was the mastermind of this strategy.

right-wing sites shared on Facebook by the people in their social media networks.

Less news, less focus on issues, and more division—this is no way to run a democracy. It is now nearly impossible for a politician to communicate directly with their constituents about anything other than the divisive cultural issues that dominate cable and Facebook. Most people these days have no idea who their congressperson is, let alone anything he or she actually has done or plans to do. Everyone is now a generic Democrat or Republican, which is why the number of Democrats representing Republican states, and vice versa, is down to a tiny, dwindling handful.

As if that weren't bad enough, the destruction of local media removed one of the last remaining checks on political corruption and exacerbated some of the worst trends in politics. There are no reporters from hometown papers in Washington, DC, keeping an eye on the congressional delegation. This is why, in 2018, Republicans actually reelected two sitting members of Congress who were under indictment for crimes committed while in office. A whole bunch of people went to the polls to send the indicted representatives back to Congress. Many voters had no idea, and most didn't care. Statehouse bureaus, which used to be the local equivalent of being in the White House Press Corps, are understaffed or empty. In short: no one is keeping an eye on the politicians, and the politicians have noticed. The Pew Foundation *State of the News Media* report I cited earlier asserted that the absence of local journalists means that "government officials conduct themselves with less integrity, efficiency, and effectiveness."

Not great, to say the least.

Filling the Vacuum

A few years ago, a clip started circulating around the internet. The video, compiled by Deadspin, the sports and news site, featured a

montage of different local news anchors repeating, with robotic preci-
sion, the exact same language about "fake news." It felt like something
ripped out of *1984* or a spoof from *The Daily Show*. When I first saw
it in the Crooked Media Slack, my first thought was *This can't be real,
right?* As someone who has hit the Retweet button too quickly and
spread misinformation more often than he would like,[11] I decided to
take a beat and do a little research.

The video was very, very real.

Each of these news anchors had something in common: they
worked for stations owned by Sinclair Broadcasting, one of the largest media conglomerates in the country. Sinclair owns more than 180
local television stations (the second most in the country) and has a
decidedly right-wing point of view. To ensure that their political
viewpoints make it on to the air, the owners of Sinclair take a very
hands-on approach to their stations. The video being circulated by
Deadspin was an example of what Sinclair calls "must-run" segments.
Every Sinclair-owned station is required to run these segments. Those
who refuse can be fired.

KOMO, a Seattle ABC affiliate owned by Sinclair, decided to take
a stand and released the script of the segment that led to the infamous
video.

Hi, I'm (A) _____, and I'm (B) _____. . .

(B) Our greatest responsibility is to serve our Northwest
communities. We are extremely proud of the quality, balanced
journalism that KOMO News produces.

(A) But we're concerned about the troubling trend of irresponsible, one-sided news stories plaguing our country. The

---

11 It happens to the best of us, right? Right?

sharing of biased and false news has become all too common on social media.

(B) More alarming, some media outlets publish these same fake stories...stories that just aren't true, without checking facts first.

(A) Unfortunately, some members of the media use their platforms to push their own personal bias and agenda to control "exactly what people think"...This is extremely dangerous to a democracy.

(B) At KOMO it's our responsibility to pursue and report the truth. We understand truth is neither politically "left nor right." Our commitment to factual reporting is the foundation of our credibility, now more than ever.

(A) But we are human and sometimes our reporting might fall short. If you believe our coverage is unfair, please reach out to us by going to KOMOnews.com and clicking on CONTENT CONCERNS. We value your comments. We will respond back to you.

(B) We work very hard to seek the truth and strive to be fair, balanced and factual...We consider it our honor, our privilege to responsibly deliver the news every day.

Sinclair forced hundreds of news anchors to spout out something consistent with Trump's "fake news" narrative. The timing of this message was strategic. Sinclair ran this segment at a particularly tough time for Trump, who was involved in yet another controversy over his submissive relationship to Russian president Vladimir Putin. The *Washington Post* had recently reported that despite Trump's advisers writing "Do Not Congratulate" at the top of the briefing they gave him prior to his meeting with Putin, what did Trump do? Slavishly congratulate Putin, of course.

The Sinclair segment was part of the larger Republican war on truth: convince people that they cannot trust any negative information about Republicans. Reporting something bad about Trump, therefore, became evidence of a media outlet's lack of credibility, not Trump's unfitness for office.

The "fake news" segment was just one example of Sinclair's disinformation efforts.

In 2017, Sinclair hired as its political director Boris Epshteyn, a Trump communications aide fired for incompetence.[12] Every station was required to run Epshteyn's pro-Trump commentary. Sinclair stations also aired a weekly show from Sharyl Attkisson, a noted conspiracy theorist and, uncoincidentally, one of Trump's favorite reporters.[13] Attkisson was fired from CBS for anti-Obama bias and for pushing antivax conspiracy theories.[14] She once accused the Obama administration of hacking her computer because the text on her screen began mysteriously disappearing before her eyes. Her claims made her a celebrity martyr of the Right. *She must be important, if Barack Obama was hacking her computer!* However, further analysis showed that the most likely culprit of the disappearing text was not a clumsy NSA staffer, but a stuck Delete key. More Ron Burgundy than Walter Cronkite.

In 2017, Sinclair anchors were forced to read a script that falsely claimed the FBI had a bias against Michael Flynn, Trump's first national security adviser, who pled guilty to multiple crimes. In 2020, numerous Sinclair stories raised false questions about the integrity of mail-in ballots. These stories helped create the context for the Big Lie and the insurrection at the US Capitol.

While Sinclair's actions have received a lot more attention in recent

---

12 How funny is that?
13 These two things are connected.
14 A Republican woman well ahead of her time.

years, their right-wing propaganda efforts are not new. After 9/11, Sinclair required its stations to read a script supporting George W. Bush. It also ordered them not to air an episode of *Nightline* in which Ted Koppel read aloud the names of the Americans killed in the Iraq War.

For all the caterwauling about the dangers of Fox News, Sinclair is a much bigger threat. The most-watched shows on Fox News get three to five million viewers a night. Most of their programming averages a million viewers. But, on a nightly basis, exponentially more people watch a Sinclair broadcast.

Most of the viewers who choose to watch Fox News do so because of its right-wing perspective. They seek out information that validates their existing worldview and explicitly avoid information that threatens that worldview. The vast majority of people who tune in to Sinclair broadcasting, however, have no idea their station is owned by far-right ideologues. They are sitting down to watch the news, learn about their community, maybe see what the weather is going to be like, and without knowing it, they are exposed to a bunch of right-wing talking points. Local television news remains the most trusted of all media sources,[15] so there is something particularly devious about using the local television anchor, with whom voters have a long-term relationship and great familiarity, to spread right-wing disinformation. The impact of Sinclair is not idle speculation from panicky Democrats.[16] A study by researchers at Emory University in 2019 discovered that "stations bought by Sinclair reduce coverage of local politics, increase national coverage and move the ideological tone of coverage in a conservative direction relative to other stations operating in the same market." Another study, published in 2021, found that voters living in markets with a Sinclair station approved of former president Barack

---

15 This is a very, very low bar.
16 Raises hand.

Obama at a lower rate than voters living in similar markets without a Sinclair station.[17]

There are limits to how big Sinclair can get. Television station ownership is regulated by the Federal Communications Commission. One entity cannot own more than two stations per market, and there is a 39 percent cap on how much market share it can accumulate. While the tools are outdated and the rules are relatively porous, there *are* rules, and people to enforce them.

In the run-up to the 2020 presidential election, something weird started happening in the critical battleground state of Michigan. Dozens of innocuously named news websites started popping up everywhere. There was the *Lansing Sun*, the *Ann Arbor Times*, the *Grand Rapids Reporter*, the *Detroit City Wire*, and the *Kalamazoo Times*. Given all the economic headwind, it had become pretty rare to see new local news sites, let alone dozens, launching at the same time. Had someone cracked the code and found a way to make money in local news? Had the digital cavalry finally arrived to replace the gone and gutted newspapers?

Not so much.

The content on these websites looked like local news stories, but upon closer review, it became clear the stories were not news at all. These right-wing propaganda sites were regurgitating content from conservative think tanks like the Mackinac Institute and the Heritage Foundation. They were pushing conspiracy theories about voter fraud, defending Trump from calls for impeachment, and producing other content designed to push the Republican point of view. The sites did not disclose their funding source or their ideological point of view.

For people scrolling through Facebook, where content from these

---

17 These yahoos love it when a plan comes together. (Props to anyone who gets that reference.)

sites was being promoted to Michiganders, there was absolutely no way to distinguish the *Lansing Sun* from the *Lansing State Journal*, the very real newspaper that originally discovered the existence of this new digital network.

The *Lansing State Journal* was eventually able to trace the Michigan sites back to a Republican activist and former TV reporter named Brian Timpone. In 2015, Timpone teamed up with Dan Proft, a conservative radio host and fellow Republican activist, to launch a group of local websites and newspapers in rural Illinois. The funding for these media outlets largely came from Dick Uihlein, the Republican billionaire donor who also funded the creation of Ben Shapiro's Daily Wire and other right-wing disinformation efforts. Timpone then took this model national, rapidly expanding the network to more than 1,300 sites across the country. Like the ones in Michigan, they have innocuous names and go out of their way to hide their ideological bent and their funding sources. The About page on many of the sites claims the site's goal is "to provide objective, data-driven information without political bias."

The financing for these sites is hidden in a web of interconnected and mysterious shell companies. The *New York Times* reported that at least eleven sites run by Timpone were funded by the U.S. Chamber of Commerce, which, like Timpone's sites, is an innocuously (and deceptively) named Republican advocacy organization. These sites make some money from digital ads, but the real source of income appears to be a system of "pay to play," whereby Republican political operatives, conservative think tanks, and others pay Timpone to publish articles of their choosing. Sometimes they submit the copy directly. In 2020, according to the *New York Times*, the *Maine Business Daily* was paid by a Republican operative with ties to Senate Republicans. Its prerogative was to write online articles critical of Democrat Sara Gideon, who happened to be running against Republican senator Susan Collins. Digital news sites face almost no regulation, require no disclosure, and can do almost anything they want.[18]

Timpone's network is by far the largest, and the most secretive with regard to its funding and agenda. It is not alone. The *Tennessee Star* started publishing online in 2017 and quickly gained traction in the state. While the person running the site describes it as "Breitbart for Tennessee," you would never know this from visiting the site. The intentions and financing are not disclosed. Most articles don't even have bylines, which prevents people from googling the reporters to discover their past work or employment history. In preparation for the 2020 election, the owners of the *Star* launched new publications in the swing states of Ohio and Minnesota that featured largely syndicated content from the Daily Caller. Trump's campaign repeatedly promoted content from these sites during his campaign, which helped him spread his message and put money in the pockets of the sites' owners by generating massive engagement and ad traffic.

To the average consumer, there is no way to distinguish between traditional local news and these sites. The latter are disinformation in its purest form. The vacuum created by the collapse of local newspapers is now being filled by right-wing propaganda more nefarious than anything found on Fox News or Breitbart. Locally based disinformation websites are the newest and least understood front in the war on truth.

In case you were wondering if Democrats were responding to this existential threat in kind, I have some bad news for you. There are

---

18 Just like Facebook.

more than 1,200 conservative local sites; at last count, there were eight Democratic ones.

Sinclair owns nearly 200 television stations. How many stations are owned by progressive activists? Zero. Not a single one.

If you wonder why Democrats continually get their asses kicked in the message wars, look no further.

10

Facebook: Too Big to Succeed

I made a lot of bad calls in 2016,[1] mistakes born out of a misplaced confidence that Donald Trump was destined for a historic ass-kicking in the election. But of all those bad calls, perhaps none was worse than agreeing to speak on a postelection panel in San Francisco hosted by a friend of mine the day after the election. When I got the invitation, I thought to myself, *Sure, I'll be exhausted, but how hard could it be to sit onstage for forty-five minutes and revel in Trump's defeat?* To be honest, my biggest concern was that I might be a wee bit hungover after celebrating Clinton's win and then getting up way too early to fly back to California from Washington, DC, where I had spent the week before the election doing political commentary for CNN.[2]

Explaining how and why Clinton lost to a group of shell-shocked Silicon Valley types was low on my list of concerns and was truly the last thing I wanted to do. I had yet to fully process how Trump had won or why I had been so wrong. Now I had to work through my emotions and explain my analysis onstage with approximately zero hours of sleep.

The event, held at a winery, was part of a regular series of get-togethers for people who work in public relations and marketing. The

---

1 The errors of 2016 are a recurring theme in all my writings.
2 Instead, I was hungover from drowning my sorrows and then not sleeping due to existential panic.

group was overwhelmingly Democratic but relatively uninvolved: lots of Democratic voters, but very few volunteers, folks who tend to read *TechCrunch* or Recode before Politico.[3] The location was perhaps the only fortuitous thing about the event: by the time my wife and I arrived, the bulk of the attendees were several glasses in. During the mix-and-mingle segment, there were tears and confusion and a lot of questions. I went for a walk around the block to figure out what I was going to say about an electoral outcome I had never once contemplated. I also wanted to avoid having to confront a bunch of people I had told not to "wet the bed" over the election. I didn't know if I could face them. I didn't know what to say.

I slid into the seat my wife had saved for me just as the first part of the program was beginning. The panel before mine was an interview and Q&A session with Elliot Schrage, Facebook's long-standing vice president of communications and policy. Schrage was one of Mark Zuckerberg's closest advisers. He came to Facebook from Google at the behest of Facebook COO Sheryl Sandberg and was involved in every consequential decision that Facebook made for many years. At the time of the 2016 election, Facebook was seen mostly as an unalloyed good and, at worst, as a harmless time suck. Schrage was unquestionably one of the most powerful people in Silicon Valley. Many of the attendees to the panel had worked for him at some point, and the rest were hoping to do so in the future. Most of the interview was about his career and his approach to management and communications. To learn from Schrage and his professional career was why a lot of the attendees had originally RSVP'd.

While totally appropriate for the venue and the agenda, the panel with Schrage was a conversation happening in an alternative universe, one where Trump hadn't just been elected president by exploiting

---

3 Frankly, it's hard to blame them.

gaping loopholes in Schrage's company's platform. Schrage's tips on professional development seemed beyond the point. To the great credit of the interviewer—a longtime Silicon Valley flack who had no journalistic obligations and a lot to lose by getting on Schrage's bad side— the final question was about whether Facebook and the prevalence of fake news on the platform had contributed to Trump's win.

It's impossible to imagine that a seasoned communications pro like Schrage had not prepared for this question, but he looked shocked nonetheless. How dare someone question Facebook and the infallibility of Mark Zuckerberg?

The immediate awkwardness permeated the room. The audience tensed up. To date, those who worked at Facebook had not been forced to reckon with the downsides to its disruption. There had been little to no backlash against its immense wealth and growing power. Facebook was untouchable then. You criticized it at your own peril.

This was about to change in a very big way.

The only person in the room who didn't see this coming was the one person whose job it was to see it. After a very pregnant pause, Schrage audibly guffawed and then arrogantly dismissed the idea that the world's largest media platform had played any role in the election outcome: "The idea that 'fake news' on Facebook could tip an election is, frankly, absurd."

My first thought was *This can't possibly be Facebook's public response to the conspiracy theories, fake news, and Russian interference that has clearly taken place.* Saying Facebook was not *solely* responsible would have been credible; saying it had *no* responsibility was laughable. An intern in the White House Press Office could have come up with a better response.

Maybe Schrage had partaken of too much of the free wine.

Nope.

A few days later, Mark Zuckerberg was appearing at a conference.

When asked about Facebook's role in the 2016 election, he adopted Schrage's tone of dismissive arrogance. Zuckerberg's words were eerily similar: "Personally I think the idea that fake news on Facebook—which is a very small amount of the content—influenced the election in any way is a pretty crazy idea."

When I look back on that postelection panel in San Francisco, I am struck by two things. First, I will never again agree to do a postelection panel. That is some really bad karma. Lesson learned.[4] Second, Facebook's response on that night is essentially still its response all these years later. And it has responded to the countless ensuing crises and revelations with the same arrogant dismissiveness.

After the panel was over, Schrage was warmly greeted by a group of people devastated by Trump's victory. There were hugs, laughter, and an exchange of contact information. This might have been the last night Facebook was seen as a positive force in society. The veil had been pierced. Never again would Facebook be the hero in any story.

Nick Clegg, the British politico who replaced Schrage at Facebook, would never be invited to such an event—and if he were, he would be afraid to show his face. A Facebook exec today headlining a gathering of Democrats would be like a Philip Morris exec appearing at a meeting of the American Cancer Society.

The idea that Facebook is really, really bad is now commonplace. American hatred for Facebook is a rare example of unity in a deeply divided country.[5] The United States is so polarized that the mere fact that Democrats hate something is a reason for Republicans to love it, and vice versa. Trump attacks the *New York Times*; Democrats

---

4 On Election Night 2020, Crooked Media's founders—former Obama speechwriters Jon Favreau and Jon Lovett and former Obama spokesperson Tommy Vietor—and I refused to do a Crooked livestream to discuss the results, a very correct decision. No one needed to see me as I slowly realized all the polling was off again.

5 The other topic Americans agree on: hating Mitch McConnell. Maybe there is hope for us yet!

subscribe in record numbers. Democrats boycott Fox News advertisers; Republicans buy their products to "own the libs." Not so with Facebook. Republicans and Democrats will disagree about taxes, health care, science (we're right), and everything else, but when it comes to Facebook, even the bitterest of enemies are willing to come together to chant "Facebook sucks!" A 2022 *Washington Post*-Schar School poll found that that 72 percent of Americans don't trust Facebook with their data.

Yes, everyone agrees that Facebook is bad, but not enough people understand *why*—and too many elected Democrats have no idea why Facebook is such a problem for our party and our country.

Facebook's MAGAlgorithm[6]

During the summer of 2020, Facebook gave Democrats something to cheer about. Well, technically, Facebook's Oversight Board did. This board acts as a self-appointed Supreme Court[7] of sorts. In the immediate aftermath of the January 6 insurrection, Facebook finally did the thing it had resisted for years: it suspended Donald Trump's account. Because Facebook is incapable of doing two good things in a row, though, it immediately offloaded the decision of whether to reinstate Trump at some point to its Oversight Board. I assume it did this to create distance between Zuckerberg and Sandberg and the decision, but it's not clear why Facebook expected people to treat a board created and funded by Facebook, with members appointed by Facebook, who serve at Facebook's discretion, as some sort of independent entity with credibility.

As the date for the Oversight Board's decision approached, most

---

6 I cannot believe it took me five years, hundreds of podcasts, thousands of tweets, and two drafts of this book to land on "MAGAlgorithm."
7 Having its own Supreme Court seems like a strong piece of evidence that Facebook has gotten too big and should be broken up.

Democrats assumed that Facebook would reinstate Trump. After all, the company had spent years bending over backwards to appease Trump and his base. Unlike Facebook, Twitter made its ban of Trump permanent. Twitter repeatedly pledged that nothing would cause the platform to reopen the case, including Trump's launching a 2024 presidential candidacy. Zuckerberg has repeatedly resisted making a similar declaration.

As a natural pessimist with a never-ending low-boil rage at Facebook, I was sure the company would do the wrong thing. No one ever went broke betting on Zuckerberg to do something bad for the world. I even woke early on the morning of the board's decision: I wanted to be prepared for an upcoming podcast and fire off a newsletter (and some tweets) lambasting Facebook. But the Oversight Board decided to continue Trump's suspension for the time being. In a surprisingly enjoyable twist, the board also tossed the decision right back in Zuckerberg's lap.

On Twitter, Democrats applauded the decision and expressed relief that Trump's banishment would continue. I was a hundred words into a newsletter about how this was a big blow to Trump and Trumpism when I got a Twitter alert that demonstrated the absolute hollowness of the victory.

A few years ago, Kevin Roose of the *New York Times* set up a Twitter account that every day tweets out the Facebook posts garnering the most engagement. This account is one of the most depressing things I read daily, but it was never more depressing than on this day. According to Roose's data, the top-performing links posts by U.S. Facebook pages in the last twenty-four hours were from:

1. Ben Shapiro
2. Ben Shapiro
3. Ben Shapiro
4. Fox News

5. ForAmerica
6. Dan Bongino
7. Sean Hannity
8. Dan Bongino
9. Fox News
10. *The Rachel Maddow Show*

That's when it hit me. Whether Donald Trump is on Facebook or not is beside the point. With or without him, his message dominates the platform. While Democrats were celebrating on Twitter, the Right was dominating Facebook. No matter his original intent, Mark Zuckerberg had built a pro-Trump platform. No matter what they tell themselves, the people working for Facebook are working to push Trumpism. Without Facebook, there is no Trump. Without Facebook, there is no January 6 insurrection. And if Trump is reelected president in 2024, it will be because of Facebook.

There are lots of theories trying to explain how a company run by Democrats became the strongest force for Trumpism the world has ever known. Greed? Incompetence? Fear of conservatives? Too many Republicans on staff? All these things are true to one degree or another, and each, in its own way, impacts the mostly poor decisions the company makes. But the real answer is something more concerning and less fixable.

It's the algorithm.

The Facebook algorithm decides what nearly three billion users see when they open the Facebook app or log on to the site. How it works is one of Silicon Valley's great secrets. But here is the shortest, most oversimplified version: Facebook does not show you everything your Facebook friends[8] post. Instead, the ever-evolving artificial intelligence–powered algorithm shows you the posts it believes you

---

8 "Friends."

are most likely to engage with based on the massive amounts of your personal data Facebook Hoovered up when you weren't paying attention. Facebook wants to show you engaging content because it wants to keep you on the platform for as long as possible in order to suck up more of your data and show you as many ads as possible.

While the details of the Facebook algorithm are among the most closely held secrets in the world, engagement is essentially the sum of shares, comments, and likes. More often, the content that generates engagement on Facebook is outrage bait; and outrage is the language of Trumpism. Trolling, unsubtle racist fearmongering, and conspiracy theories dominate the platform because they are shared and liked by people who agree with them and comment on them and because they are disliked by those outraged by them.

In the book *An Ugly Truth: Inside Facebook's Battle for Domination*,[9] authors Cecilia Kang and Sheera Frenkel offer a concise explanation of why Facebook operates this way:

> To achieve its record-setting growth, the company had continued building on its core technology, making business decisions based on how many hours of the day people spent on Facebook and how many times a day they returned. Facebook's algorithms didn't measure if the magnetic force pulling them back to Facebook was the habit of wishing a friend happy birthday, or a rabbit hole of conspiracies and misinformation.

In other words, Facebook values all engagement the same. Dislikes are the same as likes. Hate is valued as much as love. Calling something

---

9 This is a well-written, very revealing, and disturbing account of how Zuckerberg stumbled into world domination despite making a series of terrible decisions and surrounding himself with people too interested in being rich to tell him when he is wrong. Sounds almost Trumpian.

out as obviously racist or homophobic spreads the offending piece of content nonetheless. Fact-checking a conspiracy theory means more engagement and, therefore, more people exposed to the conspiracy. Damned if you do, damned if you don't. Heads, Mark Zuckerberg wins. Tails, America loses.

The Kevin Roose–generated tweet from the day of the Oversight Board decision is not an anomaly. Nearly every single day, right-wing content dominates the list. A National Public Radio analysis of data from NewsWhip found that, in May 2021, Ben Shapiro's Daily Wire "generated more Facebook engagement on its articles than the *New York Times*, the *Washington Post*, NBC News and CNN combined."

During the 2020 campaign, Roose wrote a very prophetic article, titled "What If Facebook Is the Real 'Silent Majority'?" It asked whether the dominance of Trump propaganda and right-wing disinformation on Facebook suggested the election might be much closer than the polls suggested. Here are just some data points Roose compiled to buttress his argument. In the month of August 2020:

- Facebook posts by Breitbart received nearly three times as many shares as the official pages of every Democratic senator combined.
- Conservative comedian and professional troll Terrence K. Williams averaged twice as many interactions per Facebook post in August as Joe Biden, the Democratic presidential nominee.

Are Republicans just better at Facebook? Maybe, but even the general lameness of some Democratic digital strategies is not enough to explain the disparity. Facebook's algorithm is overwhelmingly biased toward conservatives.

Given the scale of Facebook, even minor changes to the algorithm can have dramatic consequences. A few years ago, Facebook announced that it was focused on video and that the algorithm would promote posts containing videos over text, photos, and links. As the world's largest media platform by far, Facebook is the lifeblood of digital media companies. They depend on it for traffic. So, if Facebook wanted videos, the media companies had to pivot to video. Almost overnight, they shifted strategies, fired writers, and hired video people. Less than a year later, Facebook decided it didn't like videos that much anymore, changed the algorithm again, and left a bunch of media companies to go bankrupt.

Cool company, huh?

After getting shamed by the public, boycotted by advertisers, and hauled before congressional committees for its complicity in the 2016 Russian election interference effort, sketchy privacy policies, and general terribleness, Facebook decided to make a change. With great fanfare, the company announced that it was adjusting the algorithm to promote what it called "meaningful social interactions." In a blog post announcing the change, Facebook executive Adam Mosseri said:

> With this update, we will also prioritise posts that spark conversations and meaningful interactions between people. To do this, we will predict which posts you might want to interact with your friends about, and show these posts higher in feed. These are posts that inspire back-and-forth discussion in the comments and posts that you might want to share and react to—whether that's a post from a friend seeking advice, a friend asking for recommendations for a trip, or a news article or video prompting lots of discussion.

Seems harmless, right? Maybe the folks at Facebook had an epiphany and were no longer going to enrich themselves through division and hate. Nope.

Instead of making things on Facebook better, this change made them worse. Families and friends were interacting more, but instead of sharing life tips and baby photos, they were sharing conspiracy theories, violent content, and disinformation. According to documents released by Frances Haugen, a Facebook product manager turned whistleblower, the company's data team was aware of the problem and proposed specific changes to Zuckerberg, who resisted fixing the problem he had created. Zuckerberg has never explained why he did so. The answer may be found in another revelation from the trove of Haugen's documents.

Facebook decided to change its algorithm for the same reason it does anything: money.

The company had seen a drop in the amount of engagement on the platform. Less engagement meant less money. Facebook tracks the content you interact with in order to learn as much about your interests as possible. It then uses that information to target you with ads it sells to the highest bidder.

The repeated failure of Facebook to do anything about the disinformation is about much more than incompetence or avarice. For all its saccharine talk about connecting people, there is no version of the platform that doesn't work like this. Facebook's business model depends on sparking outrage and spreading disinformation. There's an old saying that if you aren't paying for the product, you *are* the product. In the end, Facebook does not a give a shit about you or me. We exist only to serve its actual customers: the advertisers addicted to the data Facebook extracts from our every interaction.

The problems with Facebook cannot be fixed because the problem *is* Facebook.

Bowing to Bad Faith and Listening to Bad Advice

If you really want to piss off Mark Zuckerberg, call Facebook a media company. Every time Facebook is accused of being a media company, Zuckerberg or one of his lieutenants doth protest too much. During congressional testimony in 2018, the Facebook CEO argued, "I consider us to be a technology company because the primary thing that we do is have engineers who write code and build product and services for other people... We do pay to help produce content," Zuckerberg said. "We build enterprise software. We build planes to help connect people, but I don't consider ourselves to be an aerospace company."

This may seem like one of those dumb debates, such as on whether a hot dog is a sandwich,[10] but it is actually a distinction of consequence. If Facebook were to be classified as a media company, this would open it up to a raft of regulations and a bunch of legal liability. The experts seem to agree that Facebook is not a media company in a narrow sense, but functionally, it is obviously a media company.

Facebook, like most media companies, pays people to write content, film videos, and make TV shows. Like most media companies, Facebook hosts the content it pays people to make on its site. As with media companies, users go to Facebook to see what's happening in the news. Facebook even broadcasted Major League Baseball games!

But here's the best piece of evidence that Facebook is a card-carrying member of the political media establishment: most of its problems come from bending over backward to appease bad-faith Republican critics. Much like the *New York Times* assigning an editor to watch Fox News to come up with ideas for the paper's Obama coverage, Facebook is so committed to disproving notions of liberal bias that it has become overwhelmingly biased toward conservatives.

---

10 It's not.

For many years, Mark Zuckerberg was close-ish with President Obama. He attended White House meetings, and hosted the president for an event at Facebook headquarters. He also founded and funded FWD.us, an organization pushing for immigration reform. Sheryl Sandberg was a staffer in Bill Clinton's administration, a regular on the Democratic fund-raising circuit, and on the shortlist to be Hillary Clinton's Treasury secretary.[11] Prior to 2016, Sandberg's and Zuckerberg's progressive credentials were never in doubt. Therefore, it was odd when Facebook hired Joel Kaplan, a former deputy chief of staff to George W. Bush, to run its Washington, DC–based government relations operation. There is a lot of Trump-inflected rose-colored nostalgia about the George W. Bush era of Republican politics. But just because Bush wasn't Trump, it doesn't mean he wasn't a hard-right ideologue. In addition to lying us into invading a country that hadn't attacked us on 9/11, Bush pushed a ton of far-right, deeply cruel policies that hurt this country. It should never be forgotten that he ran for reelection by campaigning on a disingenuous and unnecessary constitutional amendment declaring marriage to be between a man and a woman.[12]

It's unfair to hold Kaplan accountable for all the ills of the Bush administration, but he was a core part of that team. He was even a participant in the infamous "Brooks Brothers riot," when a group of Bush staffers shut down the counting of votes in Florida to try to tip a contested election to their boss.[13]

One would think that with a Democrat in the White House and Democratic control of the Senate, Facebook would want someone with ties to those folks, the ones calling the shots on issues of policy

---

11 Can you imagine those confirmation hearings?
12 Was that rant necessary? No. Was it cathartic? Yes. Reminding people that Trump didn't make the Republican Party abhorrent is my hobby. (Sad!)
13 The PG-13 prelude to the January 6 assault on the Capitol.

and regulation. But the Republicans had just taken control of the House of Representatives, and the dyed-in-the-wool Democrats in liberal Silicon Valley felt compelled to hire someone whom these new Republicans could trust. The hire was symbolic, not substantive. The House Republican majority had zero power to impact Facebook. They couldn't pass a law. Kaplan was a highly paid rebuttal to the talking point that Facebook was too liberal. Unfortunately for Facebook, and America, he became a powerful force in the company and an influential adviser to Zuckerberg, a political naïf. The Facebook government relations team was quickly staffed with former Republican operatives whose ties to congressional Republicans and the Trump White House would influence key decisions at key moments.

For most of its first ten years of existence, Facebook was largely ignored by the Right. Its influence wasn't sufficient to merit criticism, and tech companies like Apple, Google, and Facebook were largely embraced by policy makers in both parties. This ambivalence bordering on admiration was partly based on the fact that these companies were offering lucrative jobs to political staffers. The close—some would say too close—relationship between Facebook and the Obama White House did not go unnoticed. There was an undercurrent of anti-tech sentiment bubbling on the right. Steve Bannon and others saw an opportunity to take a populist anticorporate stand without angering the Republican donor base.

The dynamic shifted under the klieg lights of the 2016 election. In December 2015, Donald Trump's campaign posted to Facebook the video of his speech announcing his Muslim ban. People within the company flagged the post, stating that it was a clear violation of Facebook's anti–hate speech policy and that following the letter of the law would require the company to take the post down. While this decision was obvious, it was not easy. Taking down a post from a presidential candidate would have far-reaching ramifications. To be clear, at the time, there was no exception in the rules for politicians or famous people. Similar content posted by a typical user would have immediately been taken down. Internally, Facebook was divided on how to proceed. Concerned about the politics, Zuckerberg asked Joel Kaplan to weigh in.

As the most prominent Republican in a company largely run by Democrats, Kaplan reigned supreme. He was an all-knowing ambassador from a foreign land. There were people in the company who could push back on product changes or marketing strategies based on their experience, but there was no one in the Facebook C-suite with any connections to or experience in Republican politics.

And what was Kaplan's response?

"Don't poke the bear."

Trump's post stayed up in violation of the company's own rules and against the wishes of a lot of Facebook employees. Facebook made it clear that violating its own standards against hate speech was a price worth paying to maintain peace with the Right.

The fatal flaws in the "Don't poke the bear" strategy manifested themselves a few months later, when Gizmodo, a tech website, broke a blockbuster story claiming that Facebook was suppressing conservative topics and politicians from its Trending News section. In response to the rise of Twitter as the go-to place for breaking news, Facebook had created this section to highlight stories and topics that were getting a lot of engagement on the platform. Like many of Facebook's product features, this one was more imitation than innovation. The platform basically borrowed Twitter's Trending Topics feature. Facebook led everyone to believe that the topics said to be trending were picked algorithmically, but that wasn't true. The company had hired a series of news curators to wade through the data and then select which stories to link to. Republicans, many previously unaware that Gizmodo even existed, pounced. Trump, Fox News, and others jumped at the opportunity to play victim. They shed crocodile tears while screaming about liberal bias from Big Tech.

How Facebook handled this controversy presaged a series of decisions that set the stage for Trump's further dominance of the platform and for a growing backlash that ended in the #DeleteFacebook movement.

Facebook's response mimicked the worst instincts of a mainstream media entity absolutely terrified of being accused of liberal bias. It adopted a doomed-to-fail strategy of appeasement. It denied the allegations, but apologized anyway. Ultimately, when all the dust had settled, it was revealed that Facebook's human news curators were choosing to link to stories from traditional news sites like the *New York Times* and CNN, as opposed to right-wing sites like Breitbart and the Daily Caller. The decision was based on credibility as opposed to ideology.

Despite believing it had done nothing wrong, the company began a tour of self-flagellating and forgiveness begging. Proving its neutrality to Republicans became its top priority. Facebook instituted a program of political bias training (whatever that means), and Zuckerberg hosted a meeting with "influential conservatives." The meeting included Glenn Beck, the former Fox host who once accused Barack Obama of hating all white people; and Tucker Carlson, the Brooks Brothers–clad white nationalist who spewed racist anti-immigrant sentiments on a nightly basis. These are the people Facebook felt the need to appease. The idea that anyone would take the ranting and raving of a Beck or a Carlson as sincere is beyond me. Zuckerberg and Sandberg were clearly so self-conscious about their liberal beliefs that any and all conservative complaints had to be taken seriously, no matter how disingenuous or disgusting the complainer.

Republicans smelled blood. They asked for Zuckerberg's lunch money, and he emptied out his bank account. Facebook, it seemed, could be bullied into doing what the Right wanted. This is Big Tech's version of the balance-over-accuracy fallacy that has bedeviled the mainstream media. Time and again, Facebook chose not poking the bear over adhering to its own content-moderation policies, ensuring that the platform remained a toxic cesspool of right-wing misinformation and racist agitprop.

In response to the "fake news" debacle of the 2016 election, and in preparation for the 2020 election, Facebook announced a dedicated news tab on the platform that would feature journalism from a series of "trusted" partners. Among the participants were the outlets you would expect—the *New York Times*, *USA Today*, and the *Wall Street Journal*. But one outlet on the list stood out like a sore thumb: Breitbart. Yes, Facebook had included in its program of trusted media whose content it would promote to its billions of users a website that described itself as the "platform for the alt-right." In addition to being proudly racist and misogynistic, Breitbart was also infamous for shoddy journalism and promoting disinformation. Including the Republican National Committee Press Office as a trusted news partner would have been less ridiculous (and more honest). When asked in an interview why Breitbart had been included, the Facebook CEO said, "I think you want to have content that represents different perspectives, but doing so in a way that complies with the standards that we have."[14]

These incoherent, poorly prepared talking points aside, the reason for Breitbart's inclusion was obvious. If Facebook had not included a card-carrying member of the MAGA media, the Right would have screamed "liberal bias." As part of its program to combat disinformation, Facebook had felt compelled to include an infamous purveyor

---

14 If Breitbart meets your standards, you have no standards.

of disinformation. There are a few notable aspects to this decision. First, the people who run Facebook have the political and PR sense of sea cucumbers. Talk about leading with your chin. Second, Facebook, like many in the media, accepted the premise of the bad-faith conservative argument that all traditional media was inherently "left wing." Therefore, the *New York Times* or CNN must be "balanced" with the inclusion of an avowedly right-wing, pro-Trump media outlet. The bad-faith bullshit at the core of the whole thing is revealed with the *Wall Street Journal*'s not being considered sufficiently balancing by the Republicans. The *Journal* is owned Rupert Murdoch, and its conservative editorial board has been lacerating Democratic policies and promoting Republican ones for decades. But the *Journal*, unlike Breitbart, Fox, the Daily Caller, and others, hires real reporters and abides by traditional standards of journalism. It broke several big stories about Trump and, at times, was as tough on him as it was on Obama.[15]

As part of its post-2016 effort to promote "real" versus "fake" news, Facebook monitored these publications and others for false information. Violations earned strikes, and enough strikes warranted demotion or even suspension. This commonsense approach presented a problem for Facebook's strategy of appeasement. Guess which outlets kept getting flagged for misinformation? Yep, the right-wing outlets like Breitbart and the Daily Caller. And why did they keep getting flagged? Because they exist only to spread misinformation.

If Facebook followed its own rules—the rules touted as evidence of how seriously it took solving its 2016 problems—it would be forced to sanction a lot of right-wing media. Once again, Kaplan reportedly stepped in and made the strikes disappear, thus allowing these odious outlets to continue pushing their dangerous lies on the platform.

---

15 Its editorial page, however, is a slightly more erudite, polysyllabic version of Breitbart.

Zuckerberg was so concerned with being accused of bias by Trump and the Republicans that he rejected a recommendation from his own staff to ban Alex Jones, one of the most notorious conspiracy theorists in the world. Jones most famously pushed a conspiracy theory that the 2012 Sandy Hook massacre, which resulted in the deaths of twenty schoolchildren, was a hoax. Over the years, Jones continued directing abuse at the victims' grieving parents. Despite obvious rule violations, Zuckerberg resisted removing Jones. Kara Swisher, the celebrated tech journalist, pushed the Facebook CEO on his reluctance to take down Jones's notorious Infowars site. Zuckerberg responded with an answer that inadvertently revealed his naïveté and detached malevolence:

> The approach that we've taken to false news is not to say: You can't say something wrong on the internet. I think that that would be too extreme. Everyone gets things wrong, and if we were taking down people's accounts when they got a few things wrong. . . . I'm Jewish, and there's a set of people who deny that the Holocaust happened. I find that deeply offensive. But at the end of the day, I don't believe that our platform should take that down because I think there are things that different people get wrong.

Now, I imagine that no one on the highly paid Facebook communications staff put defending Holocaust deniers in his talking points, but Zuckerberg's response was, unfortunately, consistent with Facebook's approach to offensive content. Under tremendous pressure amid a media firestorm, the platform acted against Jones. But Facebook policies state that not only will dangerous individuals and organizations be removed from the platform, but praise for them will as well. Yet it refused to follow this rule and remove praise for Jones, someone it has acknowledged was a danger to its community. And why did Facebook fail to do this? Jones is, unsurprisingly, an ally of Donald Trump.[16] Reportedly, Trump called Jones the day after the 2016 election to thank him for helping put him in the White House. The Facebook pages posting praise of Jones and spreading his dangerous conspiracy theories are, of course, those run by right-wing politicians and media figures. Given a choice between following its own rules or poking the bear, Facebook left the bear alone.

Republicans quickly learned that Facebook would take these critiques seriously, so they doubled and tripled down. At every opportunity, right-wing grifters like Ted Cruz took to social media to complain about Big Tech shadow-banning them or demoting their content. If a post didn't go viral, it had to be the fault of liberal executives at Facebook or Twitter. Never mind the terrible writing, unfunny jokes, or general untruthful tediousness of a lot of right-wing content. Whenever Facebook was hauled before Congress, the Republicans would performatively hammer its executives for anticonservative bias while their own Facebook posts about Facebook's bias went viral.[17]

It didn't matter that the available evidence showed that Facebook's algorithm favored conservative content or that reporting showed that Facebook was more than willing to bend and break its rules to help right-wingers. Anyone who logged on to Facebook could see that it was a toxic swamp of Trumpist conspiracy theories. The Republicans were working the refs, and the refs were more than happy to be worked.

As a result of this less-than-brilliant strategy engineered by Kaplan and endorsed by Zuckerberg and Sandberg, Facebook burned bridges with all its allies on the left and gained no new ones on the right. Zuckerberg became a figure of comic villainy, equal parts evil

---

16 The Jones-Trump relationship is the opposite of "opposites attract."
17 And for being too tough on white nationalists. (Seriously!)

and incompetent. Sandberg was no longer a revered figure in polite society. There was an exodus of top staff. Working at Facebook is now the equivalent of having worked at Philip Morris in the 1980s.

And like Philip Morris, Facebook felt compelled to change its name, in a fruitless attempt to remove the stink from its soul. The company is now known as Meta, to signify its interest in doing to the metaverse what it has done this world.[18]

C.R.E.A.M.: Cash Rules Everything Around Mark[19]

If Facebook's "Don't poke the bear" strategy was born of a naïveté about politics and who and what the modern Republican Party is, that was far from the only motivation. Once Trump won, Republicans controlled the entire federal government, and Zuckerberg had a massive financial incentive to keep Trump happy. At any point, the Republicans in Congress could pass a bill repealing Section 230, the law protecting Facebook and other social media companies from liability. Trump's regulators could undertake antitrust actions against the company. To keep Trump happy, Zuckerberg stayed in close contact with the White House. He dined with Trump, and the two had secret meetings—undisclosed until Trump tweeted about them. The main interlocutor was Peter Thiel, a far-right Silicon Valley billionaire and longtime mentor to Zuckerberg. Thiel sat for years on the Facebook board of directors. At one point, Zuckerberg appealed to Trump's vanity by telling the president that he was "number one on Facebook." Trump, America's most insecure human, lapped it up and publicly boasted about it, once again embarrassing himself before the world.

---

18 Facebook/Meta made the change in the middle of my writing of this book. I could go back through and change all the Facebook references to Meta, but that feels like letting Zuck win.
19 Could also mean "Crypto Rules Everything Around Meta."

172 BATTLING THE BIG LIE

Appealing to Trump was about more than averting regulations and adverse laws to protect the overwhelmingly lucrative bottom line. The Facebook user base is significantly more Republican than that of any other social media platform. According to a 2021 Pew poll, nearly twice as many Democrats use Twitter as Republicans. Instagram users are more Democratic by 19 percent. But Facebook is split nearly evenly between Republicans and Democrats. Young people—who trend Democratic—have been fleeing the platform for years. It was Democrats who deleted Facebook in protest of the company's misdeeds. In the United States at least, Facebook (like the Republican Party) is facing an actuarial apocalypse. It simply cannot afford to anger the older Republicans using the platform.

The ultimate example of Facebook's failed and incoherent approach was Zuckerberg's policy for fact-checking politicians. Heading into the 2020 election, Facebook knew it had a looming problem. It had spent the previous three years touting its efforts to stop "fake news" and misinformation. But it also knew two things: Donald Trump and his campaign were going to be incredibly active on Facebook. The Trump campaign amassed a historic war chest[20] and was planning to spend tens of millions of dollars on Facebook. Trump was also a liar with a campaign full of liars and a track record of running false ads. If Facebook were to adhere to its own rhetoric, it would spend the entire election in a big public fight with Trump over which of his ads were false. This would be bad for business—it would put the company at further risk of regulatory scrutiny, anger the Republicans on the platform, and potentially cost Facebook millions in advertising revenue. In the larger scheme of things, political advertising is a drop in Facebook's giant bucket of revenue, but the company is relentlessly

---

20 In the end, most of this money ended up going into Donald Trump's pockets and into slush funds to pay hush money to various witnesses of various Trump transgressions.

greedy. You don't go from being a free website created to rate the attractiveness of Harvard coeds to a half-a-trillion-dollar company by leaving money on the table.

Presented with the choice between money and democracy, which do you think Zuckerberg chose?[21]

Zuckerberg came up with a solution that was equal parts ingenious and disingenuous. The Facebook communications team[22] previewed that Zuckerberg would be giving a major speech in Gaston Hall at Georgetown University, where many a president over the years had given major speeches. Giving a speech in Gaston is a signal to the political press to prick up their ears and listen. My old friend and Obama political guru David Axelrod used to say that most "big" speeches end up with the politician wheeling out a big cannon only to shoot out a little flag reading, "BAM."

This was not one of the instances.

Zuckerberg was outlining a new policy. Facebook would not fact-check politicians or political ads.

In a campaign between Joe Biden (or any other Democrat) and Donald Trump, who do we think would benefit from being given carte blanche to lie?[23]

This new policy had a dramatic impact on the election. The Facebook CEO was no longer an overly self-conscious liberal trying to avoid poking the bear. Instead, Facebook, under the counsel of the Republican-leaning policy team, decided to throw in with Trump and the MAGA world. The Democrats running for president were promising to look very seriously into breaking up Facebook and raising taxes on corporations and the wealthy. Trump's reelection meant a lower

---

21 Clearly a rhetorical question.
22 Aka willing enablers of everything bad.
23 Also rhetorical.

tax bill for Zuckerberg and the executives at Facebook, who had all become fabulously wealthy profiting off the destruction of democracy.

Despite Zuckerberg's suggestion otherwise, there is nothing unusual about fact-checking political ads. Local TV and radio stations often fact-check ads and pull ones they deem false. TV stations have a huge financial incentive not to anger the campaigns and, therefore, they tend to be quite permissive. Even though political campaigns have been advertising on the internet for more than ten years, Congress has been too broken (and too old!) to pass a relevant law with similar standards. Therefore, the choice was up to Zuckerberg, and he chose wrong.

Zuckerberg framed the decision as one of freedom of expression. He positioned himself as a defender of the First Amendment against an unspoken horde of woke cancel culture barbarians. People had a right to see what their leaders said—whether it was right or wrong, true or false, no matter how offensive. Facebook would have had an argument if the question had been all about what Trump (or other degenerate liars) were posting on their Facebook pages. In that situation, people can choose to see it or not. But that's not what Zuckerberg was talking about, nor what people were concerned about. Facebook ads are infinitely more powerful—and therefore, much, much more dangerous than television ads.

Smart political campaigns run television ads on shows watched by their target voters. Need to shore up your numbers with older voters? Run ads during *60 Minutes* and the local news. Looking for married women? Buy time on the Oprah Winfrey Network or HGTV. Men? ESPN. These decisions are imprecise and inefficient. But advertising on Facebook and other social media platforms is very different. Facebook has reams of data about you. The pages you have liked and commented on, whom you follow, what links you've clicked, and so on. But it is also tracking you all over the internet and on your phone. It knows more about you than your family. Facebook takes all this data and uses artificial intelligence to make alarmingly precise predictions about what you are interested in. It then sells this data to the highest bidder for the opportunity to target you with ads based on that information.

In other words, Facebook was allowing Trump and others to use its massive troves of data to target disinformation at the people with the greatest propensity to believe it. While Zuckerberg offered dishonest bromides about free speech and crocodile tears about censorship of Big Tech, he was simultaneously announcing a new policy of weaponizing disinformation for profit.

The Trump campaign took Facebook's policy as the green light that Facebook had intended it to be. Not long after, the campaign launched a multimillion-dollar barrage of false advertising that claimed that then-Vice President Biden had offered Ukraine a billion dollars in exchange for firing a prosecutor investigating a company his son Hunter was involved in. The ad was patently false. Trump's campaign knew the ad was false, and they knew Facebook would happily take their money.

To show the absurdity of Facebook's policy, Senator Elizabeth Warren's campaign cleverly purchased ads on the platform that falsely claimed Zuckerberg and Facebook had endorsed Trump's reelection. Facebook was forced to adhere to its own rules and keep the ads up.[24]

The pure dishonest audacity of Zuckerberg's Georgetown speech was notable as well. Without batting an eyelid, he completely rewrote history, claiming, with zero evidence, that Facebook had been born out of his heretofore-never-disclosed passionate opposition to the Iraq War. Facebook's origin story has been told nearly as many times as Batman's, but somehow, this cute little anecdote didn't make it into

---

24 Looking stupid goes down easier when you are worth billions.

the dozens of books written about the company. Nor was it in the Aaron Sorkin film about Facebook, *The Social Network*. Zuckerberg, who had spoken thousands of times before about how and why he created Facebook, had never once seen fit to divulge this secret. Imagine the amount of megalomaniacal narcissism it would take tell such an obvious lie without fear of repercussions.

It's also worth noting that journalist Max Chafkin reported in his book *The Contrarian: Peter Thiel and Silicon Valley's Pursuit of Power* that Zuckerberg and Trump cut a deal during a White House dinner attended by Jared Kushner, Thiel, and others. According to Chafkin, Thiel told people that Zuckerberg and Trump agreed that evening that if Facebook didn't fact-check Trump, the Trump administration would not impose regulations on the company. Everyone involved has denied this. I have a healthy skepticism of the report, but if there are three people on the face of the planet who do not deserve the benefit of the doubt, they are Mark Zuckerberg, Donald Trump, and Peter Thiel.[25] So, make your own judgment. Whether it was an explicit deal or an implicit one is largely immaterial. Facebook decided to align itself with an authoritarian white nationalist who stood against everything Zuckerberg and Sandberg claimed to support. And they did it for reasons of cowardice and avarice.

Full Heel Turn

Even after Trump was deplatformed, Facebook continued to be a cesspool of election and COVID-19 conspiracy theories. Even when Frances Haugen presented to Congress and the public hard evidence of the company's misdeeds, Facebook continued to dig in and deny the undeniable. Despite its role in the January 6 insurrection, in the

---

25 Probably in that order.

rapid spread of antivaccine conspiracy theories, and in stoking geno-
cidal attacks in Burma, the company continued to argue that the good
of Facebook outweighed the bad. None of this was its fault; its critics
were too envious or too stupid to understand the greatness of Zuckerberg's monster. Facebook leadership developed a victim complex that
was, well, Trumpian.

And how well did this strategy of appeasement fare for Facebook? Has the Right really embraced these Silicon Valley types turned
MAGA enthusiasts?

During a 2021 rally in Georgia, Donald Trump falsely alleged that
Zuckerberg had spent $45 million in Georgia to defeat him in 2020.[26]
And despite everything Facebook had done to help Trump, the crowd
chanted, "Lock him up. Lock him up!" As the crowd worked itself
into a frenzy over the prospect of incarcerating the boy wonder CEO,
Zuckerberg's BFF responded, "Well, they should be looking at that.
What is that all about?"

But before you feel sorry for Zuckerberg and the rest of the people at
Facebook, remember that, from Trump's election to just before his igno-
minious departure, the company's stock price more than doubled. Despite
making everything worse, becoming one of the least trusted, most hated
companies in the world, Facebook prospered—while we suffered.

Cool company.

---

26 Hmm, how's that lack of fact-checking working out for you?

11

Poking Holes in Facebook's Defenses

I live in the Bay Area. I know a lot of people who work at Facebook. Some are even old friends.[1] I wouldn't say they are super proud of their employer. In social settings, they tend to try to find ways to avoid saying where they work.

"I work in tech."

"I do tech communications."

"I work in Silicon Valley."

Oh, cool. Where do you work?

"Umm, Facebook."

Or, now: "Umm... Meta."[2]

Followed by a quick change of subject. Most people hate the company and think it's a danger to democracy.

Honestly, it's hard to blame the staff. No one wants to be harangued at their daughter's soccer game or while at the playground with their kids because of who signs their paycheck. During my time working for Barack Obama, I attended some weddings filled with anti-Obama guests and, while waiting in the buffet line, I went out of my way to avoid having a conversation about the purported tyranny of Obamacare.

---

1 Well, they are still *my* friends. It's an open question if I'm still *their* friend.
2 The name "Meta" is weird and awkward—which is how you know it was Mark Zuckerberg's idea.

My friends who work for Facebook[3] are not bad people. While I like to believe many of them could be happier and do less damage elsewhere, people's employment decisions are complicated. Whether it's Facebook or anywhere else, our country's backward social safety net links our retirement and health care to our job. The situation with tech companies is even more complicated because so much of many employees' compensation is tied up in stock grants. Depart your job one day before you fully vest, and you could leave 25 to 50 percent of your salary on the table. I know this sounds like I am defending the staff of Facebook; so, let me be clear: I have no patience or sympathy for the top executives, who have become millionaires several times over while wreaking havoc on the world, but I find it hard to declare a midlevel member of the communications or marketing team one of the great enemies of the world.

I digress. My point here is that, in private and public, Facebook has a series of defenses and justifications. It is not my concern how the Facebook employees I know respond to the critique. I'm more concerned with the lack of self-awareness Facebook executives use to defend the company in the press, in court, and in Congress. None of their defenses holds an ounce of water. Their position is so weak that the company can't muster a defense strong enough to sustain eleven seconds of scrutiny.

As laughable as their defenses are, they must be taken seriously. Facebook/Meta is one of the most powerful companies in the world. It has an army of lobbyists and perhaps the highest-paid PR staff in the world. More alarmingly, according to the *New York Times*, in 2021, Facebook launched something called Project Amplify, which would use Facebook's algorithm to show positive news about the company to its users. Sometimes quantity is more important than quality.

---

3 Get it?

No one at Facebook would ever agree to come on *Pod Save America*[4] to defend their company or explain its actions. Mark Zuckerberg, Sheryl Sandberg, and the rest of the Facebook leadership tend to hide behind their highly paid spokespeople. Other than a couple of encounters with tough interviewers like Kara Swisher, their only public interactions occur on friendly turf at tech conferences. And no former employee of Facebook, or anyone who has a yacht paid for by Facebook stock, will agree to defend the company in private or public. On the rare occasions when a Facebook executive has testified before Congress, their legislative interlocutors have been outclassed, embarrassed themselves with dumb questions based on laughably ignorant misunderstandings of the internet. In 2006, the now-late Alaska senator Ted Stevens called the internet a "series of tubes." Based on recent hearings, congressional questioners haven't learned very much in the years since.

Because of this, Facebook's defenses rarely face scrutiny or counterarguments. Many of their claims sound almost believable, in the Orwellian sense of "how can this not be true?" By intimidating politicians, persuading advertisers, and forestalling necessary regulation, Facebook can win the argument, and as long as it does, it will continue to operate without fear of consequences. I am not sure Democrats, or democracy, can survive that reality.

With that in mind, here is why everything Facebook and its apparatchiks say is total (but believable) bullshit.

---

4 Don't worry. When it comes to tough questions, I am not suggesting we are *60 Minutes* or Tim Russert–era *Meet the Press*.

Facebook Is Protecting Freedom of Speech

When Facebook is asked why it allows conspiracy theories, racist agit-prop, and generally hateful bile to run rampant on its platform, the answer is usually about how it has an obligation and a responsibility to defend freedom of speech. In his notoriously fallacious Georgetown speech, Mark Zuckerberg positioned Facebook as the defender of free speech in a world of cancel culture censors. After drawing parallels between the right-wing hate mongers on his platform and the civil rights movement, Zuckerberg went on to say, "We're at another crossroads. We can continue to stand for free expression, understanding its messiness, but believing that the long journey toward greater progress requires confronting ideas that challenge us. Or we can decide the cost is simply too great. I'm here today because I believe we must continue to stand for free expression."

Freedom of speech is good, right? Companies—especially global monopolies—censoring people does seem unconstitutional? Hmm, maybe Zuck has a point.

No, he doesn't.

For starters, the First Amendment and Facebook's content moderation decisions have exactly zero to do with each other. The First Amendment protects Americans from the government. But Facebook is a private company. There is no constitutional right to post on Facebook, just as there is no constitutional right to be interviewed on *Pod Save America*[5] or host the Oscars. Facebook can't keep you off the platforms for reasons based on your race or gender, but it is not obligated to post your conspiracy theories about the COVID-19 vaccine, microchips, Bill Gates, and a global cabal of pedophilic technocrats.

---

5 Yes, I am talking to you, PR people who send one hundred emails a week pitching obscure authors, unknown experts, and random entrepreneurs. My failure to acknowledge your email is not an invitation for you to send more.

Every user signing up for Facebook agrees to a set of terms and conditions about what can and can't be posted. For example, you can't sell weapons, post nude photos, or abuse people on Facebook. Hate speech and threats of violence are explicitly prohibited. Despite its recent claims to be free-speech fundamentalists, Facebook takes down such content all the time. But when it comes to powerful people the company doesn't want to upset, it cites free speech as a way to justify violating its own rules.

During the almost entirely peaceful uprising after the murder of George Floyd in the summer of 2020, Trump posted on Facebook, "Any difficulty and we will assume control but, when the looting starts, the shooting starts." Trump's comment was an allusion to an infamous violent threat from the Miami police chief in the 1960s—and a clear violation of Facebook's policies. Had this message been posted by anyone other than the president of the United States, it would have been removed instantly. If Facebook's leaders really cared about free speech, they would care about it for everyone, not just the people who hold the regulatory sword of Damocles over their highly profitable and incredibly sketchy company.

Second, when it claims to be a bulwark against censorship, Facebook doesn't tell the whole story. Zuckerberg's big defense for not fact-checking liars or removing dangerous content asks this: *Do you really want big companies like us to decide whose voice is heard? We know you don't trust us. Heck, we don't trust ourselves to make these decisions.* Except, like almost everything else Facebook says, this is a finely crafted lie.

Facebook makes millions of decisions every single day about which content is seen and which isn't. Content is exposed to millions or artificially suppressed based on what the company views as in its interest. And its interest is always financial. You can't claim to be a free-speech activist while using your AI-powered algorithm to make sure that some content is unseen by most of your users. "You have the right to free speech, but we will drown out what you say based on what makes us richer" isn't exactly what the First Amendment is all about.

Finally, Facebook is not some public forum in the spirit of Athenian democracy, where ideas are debated and arguments honed. It's a massive advertising company. Mark Zuckerberg isn't fighting for your right to speak; he is fighting for his right to profit off your words. Every post, like, and share is more money in his pocket. Every time you log on, Facebook learns more about you for the express purpose of selling that information to the highest bidder. The platform is a money-making machine—nothing more, nothing less. Frankly, the folks at Facebook would be less annoying if they dropped all the "connecting the world" BS and just embraced the fact they are in it to get really effing rich. I promise you that no one who works at Facebook gives two shits about your constitutional rights.

Facebook Is Not the Primary Cause of Polarization

After the *Wall Street Journal* ran a series of damning articles in 2021 based on internal Facebook documents, Nick Clegg, Facebook's top communications pro, wrote a 1,500-word rebuttal that included the following: "Social media has had a big impact on society in recent years, and Facebook is often a place where much of this debate plays out.... But what evidence there is simply does not support the idea that Facebook, or social media more generally, is the primary cause of polarization."

I'm sure Clegg, who is presumably paid millions a year, was quite proud of himself when he came up with this line. Like a lot of Facebook propaganda, it seems totally reasonable for a second or two—until you realize it's one of the dumbest things you have ever heard.

Of course, Facebook is not the primary cause of polarization.

No one said it was. Polarization was increasing in the United States long before Mark Zuckerberg stumbled onto his highly profitable democracy-destroying idea. Just because Facebook didn't create the problem of polarization doesn't mean it isn't making the problem much, much worse. Clegg is strenuously and unsubtly avoiding this question because Facebook's own research makes it clear that its platform contributes to growing anger and division in America. The protests at school board meetings over critical race theory? Organized on Facebook. Misinformation about COVID-19 vaccines? Spread on Facebook. The Big Lie and the violent assault on the US Capitol? Also Facebook.

Sure, It's Not Perfect, but on Balance, Facebook Is Good for the World

Not to be rude, but this idea is so stupid that it is barely worth entertaining. I will, however, make one point. If genocide in Burma, insurrections in the United States, and antivax conspiracy theories spreading around the world are a side effect of "connecting people," I will pass.

It's Not Facebook, It's the People on Facebook

After Frances Haugen, the Facebook whistleblower, accused her former employer of being complicit in the January 6 insurrection, Clegg called the allegation "ludicrous" and claimed that individuals, not Facebook, were responsible for what happened in Washington that day. The specific allegation from Haugen was that Facebook made a postelection change to its algorithm that elevated election-related conspiracy theories and empowered far-right Facebook groups to plan for the riot.

To be clear, Facebook admits it made this change, and it does not deny the change had this effect. It just thinks it doesn't deserve the blame.

Clegg is technically correct. Individuals *were* responsible for the insurrection. No one is saying they weren't. Many of those individuals have been charged with a crime; some have gone to prison. But just because those people bear responsibility doesn't mean Facebook escapes criticism.

What's so gross about this particular talking point is that it is ripped right from the National Rifle Association's playbook. After Americans (even young children) are killed in another senseless shooting, the NRA's favorite talking point is "Guns don't kill people. People do." For Clegg and the folks at Facebook, cribbing your talking points from one of the most deplorable organizations in modern American history should be a cause for shame. However, having the capacity for shame and working at Facebook may be mutually exclusive.

Why Are You Picking Only on Us?

Another classic Facebook defense is to point to the dystopian hellscape of the internet and say, "What about everyone else? Why are you picking only on us?" Hey, you, Dan Pfeiffer! Why did you write not one but two chapters in your book criticizing Facebook and write almost nothing about Twitter, YouTube, and TikTok?

This is the one time I will admit that Facebook's mercenary PR teams have a point. Social media writ large has a content-moderation problem. Algorithms are perverting our politics and poisoning our discourse. That's a problem much bigger than Facebook.

Twitter is filled with abuse. Numerous studies demonstrate the radicalizing effect of YouTube's algorithm. And TikTok, which in

2021 was the world's most-visited website, is rife with misinformation on COVID-19 and the 2020 election.[6]

Social media is one of those things that has positives, but huge downsides as well, and Congress has done nothing to protect the American public from those downsides—has passed almost no regulations, no rules, no laws. Instead, we rely on the goodwill of the companies themselves to protect society. That is truly insane and a stupid way to operate. What if there were no laws ensuring clean water and air and we just hoped corporations would voluntarily decide to pollute less (and make less money)?

So, I will stipulate that none of these companies is cloaked in glory. None of them is a hero. They are all rapacious capitalists chasing growth at all costs to justify their inflated stock valuations. But among this group…Facebook is *still* the worst, *still* the most deserving of scrutiny and concern.

First, in terms of scope, scale, and influence, nothing compares to Facebook. However, Facebook the company owns a lot more than Facebook the platform. It also owns Instagram, one of the fastest-growing apps in the world; and WhatsApp, the world's largest messaging service. Combined, these platforms have more than six billion users, all of them under the control of Mark Zuckerberg—who cannot be fired. Putting much of the world's digital communications infrastructure under the unified control of a reclusive man-child with megalomaniacal tendencies seems suboptimal to me.

It's technically true that more people in the U.S. watch YouTube than visit Facebook. A 2021 Pew Research Center study found that 81 percent of US adults use YouTube compared to 69 percent for Facebook. But Facebook is much more of a news source for Americans.

---

6 Disinformation set to the music of Will Smith is more entertaining, but no less dangerous, than other forms of messaging.

Thirty-six percent consider Facebook a regular source of news, and another 11 percent turn to Instagram for news. Only 22 percent consider YouTube a source of news. In an alarming finding, 70 percent of Facebook users visit the site every day, and nearly half visit it several times a day.

Political junkies and reporters are obsessed with Twitter. It's fair to say that it's an addiction for folks like me.[7] But as robust and consequential as what happens on Twitter feels, it is a conversation about which most Americans are blissfully unaware. Per the Pew study, only a quarter of Americans claim to use the platform. And while Twitter brands itself as a place for news, and while it's where reporters[8] go to break news, only 15 percent use it for news. Additionally, the Twitter conversation is even smaller than these numbers suggest. An earlier Pew study, from 2019, found that 80 percent of tweets were being sent by 10 percent of users. Twitter, for all its faults, is a small conversation dominated by an even smaller group. It pales in comparison to Facebook. Focusing one's criticism on Twitter at the expense of Facebook would be like trying to blow out a single candle before dealing with a raging inferno rapidly approaching your house.

TikTok is one to watch; it is growing at an unprecedented rate. And with that growth has come an explosion in disinformation. For example, in the summer of 2021, a hoax rapidly spread on TikTok that a certain day in December 2021 would be "National Shoot Up Your School Day." Users were challenged to go on shooting sprees at their schools. It appears that this was a very unfunny joke, but it spread like wildfire, causing panic among parents and forcing a number of schools to close, erring on the side of caution.

In addition to being bigger, Facebook is also worse than the rest

---

7 And to be honest, probably you, too.
8 And presidents who aren't banned from the platform.

of the social media companies. Time and again, it is the most resistant to taking action to protect users from hate, to standing up to powerful right-wing figures, and to stemming the flow of conspiracy theories. Even when it does act, its actions come later and with less punch than those of its competitors. Facebook resisted banning Alex Jones and his noxious Infowars site, and when it finally did, Zuckerberg was dragged kicking and screaming the whole way. Every other platform permanently banned Trump; Facebook suspended him only temporarily, and many observers fully expect the company to reinstate him if he runs for president again. The documents released by the whistleblower Haugen make clear that Facebook knew what it was doing was detrimental, but it kept doing it anyway.

So, that is why we are picking on you, Facebook. You are just the worst, and that's saying a lot.

12

The Media's Conservative Bias

The entire right-wing disinformation apparatus was built on a Big Lie told many years ago that persists to this day.

The idea that the media is biased against conservatives is the justification for the right-wing disinformation machine. The *Federalist*, Breitbart, and Sean Hannity are necessary, the thinking goes, to push back against the overwhelmingly liberal bias of the mainstream media. Almost as a condition of membership into the party, Republican politicians are required to blame their problems on "liberal bias." Struggling in the polls? Blame liberal bias. Failed to repeal Obamacare? Blame liberal bias. Got caught trying to extort a foreign country to interfere in an American election? Blame liberal bias. Got caught on a hot mic bragging about sexual assault with Billy Bush?[1] You guessed it. Blame liberal bias.

This strategy is deeply dishonest but devastatingly effective. The Right hammers this point home so relentlessly that everyone in politics believes it to be true. Reporters, editors, and publishers are so convinced of their own bias that they swerve out of their lane to adjust for it. Democrats are convinced that those in the media are our friends and teammates, and we are in shock every time a media outlet disappoints us. And Republican voters are so convinced of the bias that they

---

1 Ah, the famously liberal cousin of . . . [checks notes] George H. W. Bush.

might reflexively dismiss a *New York Times* article claiming that the sky is blue and the grass is green.[2]

The assumption of liberal bias is the driving force in political media. Nearly every decision and all strategies are centered on the idea. Either consciously or subconsciously, it infects all media coverage.

But here's the thing: It's all wrong. Dead wrong.

It is true that most reporters, editors, and publishers are more ideologically aligned with Democrats than Republicans. They believe in climate science, support marriage equality, and think making assault rifles easier to buy than cold medicine is probably a mistake.[3] Many live in New York City; Washington, DC; or Los Angeles, three of the bluest cities in America. We must acknowledge that the ideological background and geographic location of many in the media lends itself to unconscious bias in terms of what topics receive coverage and whose stories are told. Progressives unwilling to admit this make it easier for conservatives to sow distrust in the media ecosystem.

However, this is a far cry from the idea put forth by the Right that the media works in concert with Democrats or gives Democrats more favorable coverage than Republicans. After the massively disproportionate coverage of Hillary Clinton's email habits in the *New York Times* or the hours of free, unchecked airtime CNN and others gifted Trump rallies in 2016, it should be clear the media is not on the Democrats' side.[4]

But the problem is even worse than it looks. Despite the media being filled with Democratically aligned people working out of

---

2 To be fair, who knows what climate change will bring?
3 Crazy, I know.
4 To keep people watching the network, CNN used to show the empty lectern at Trump rallies hours before the candidate took the stage—like a sign on a highway reading, "Car Crash Ahead."

cities filled with Democrats for media outlets whose primary audience is Democrats, the political media is biased against liberals, not conservatives.

It's very possible, and perhaps likely, that at some point there was anticonservative bias in the mainstream media, but no more. The terrain has shifted. The mainstream media's cultural and institutional biases stack the deck against progressives.

Addicted to Conflict and Crisis

The mainstream media's dominant bias is not ideological, it's attitudinal. The media crave conflict over all else; they love a crisis. There's an old saying: "If it bleeds, it leads." This refers to the tendency of local television news to prioritize crime and traffic accidents over all other topics. In political news, clashes, showdowns, and circular firing squads get all the attention. After all, a functioning government is not sexy.[5]

Why might this dynamic benefit the Right? Well, with a small handful of exceptions over the years, the major conflict in politics comes down to this: Democrats are trying to make government work, and Republicans are using whatever power they have to break it. Coverage that Disproportionately focuses on the things that are broken versus the things that work benefits the antigovernment party.

This is an observation, not an indictment. I do believe that this tendency comes from a good place (in most cases). Ever since the days of Vietnam and Watergate, a huge chunk of the traditional media has seen its primary purpose as holding powerful interests accountable—rooting out malfeasance, waste, corruption, and incompetence. This tendency forces the media to focus on the bumps, not the road. While the search

---

5 Sorry, it isn't!

for accountability is well intentioned, it gives the public a misimpression of how smoothly the government often functions. The media coverage of President Obama's 2009 stimulus bill is a textbook example of how this dynamic provides the public with an inaccurate picture and needlessly undermines trust in government.

Obama took office in 2009 amid a cascading global financial crisis—the greatest since the Great Depression. In the early months of his presidency, our economic team woke every day worried that the banking system would crumble. There was palpable concern that Americans could go to the ATM and have no money come out. Stopping the Great Recession, as it was called, from becoming the Great Depression 2.0 was job number one for the new president. All other campaign promises and policy ideas were swept aside in favor of a massive stimulus package to stop the bleeding by quickly pumping money into the economy.

In the decade since this bill, a vigorous discussion has raged about the inadequacy of its size. But in the moment, it was a big, consequential response to a very big problem. The American Recovery and Reinvestment Act included nearly eight hundred billion dollars for infrastructure projects, loans for clean energy and climate change, and funding for cities and states that had their tax base gutted by an unemployment rate rapidly heading to double digits. During a financial crisis, speed is of the essence. A bill of this size and scope, operating at this tempo, had great potential for waste, abuse, and corruption. Once the money started to flow, many in the media leapt into their self-appointed (and fully appropriate) role as government watchdogs. The nightly news was awash in stories of potential waste.

Here's text from a 2009 ABC News story[6] typical of the coverage at the time:

---

6 Well over a decade later, I am still mad about this story. I can remember the smug, self-satisfied look on the reporter's face as he read verbatim the opposition research provided

Then there are the questionable projects. For instance, the Florida Department of Transportation wants to spend $3.4 million in stimulus money for a turtle tunnel. That's right, $3.4 million to help turtles cross under a highway. Each year, 1,035 turtles are killed on a half-mile stretch of highway north of Tallahassee, according to the Lake Jackson Ecopassage Alliance, a group advocating for the tunnel. They are hoping to use the stimulus dough to save the turtles.

Across the country in Montana, a border crossing that averages fewer than two passenger cars a day and two to three trucks a month is slated to get $15 million in stimulus funds for upgrades. One Utah sheriff's office wants to spend $25,000 in stimulus money for a new Harley-Davidson motorcycle.

To be clear, these were potential projects being requested through the normal and ethical course of business. This was something surely (and intentionally) lost on the viewer. Maybe a turtle tunnel is not your top priority.[7] It wasn't Barack Obama's, either; that project was denied.[8]

There was also a media firestorm over Solyndra, a solar panel manufacturer that received a $500 million loan guarantee as part of the Recovery Act. To hold the Obama administration account-able, reporters flocked to the California company raising the spec-ter of "crony capitalism" and connections between Obama donors and Solyndra investors. In the end, it was revealed that the program funding Solyndra and others had been created under the previous administration. President Bush's energy department was supportive of

---

to him by the Republicans. I could tell he was drafting his Pulitzer acceptance speech in his head.

7 Insert your Mitch McConnell joke of choice here.

8 I still feel the turtles got screwed. This is the one time the tortoise didn't win the race. (Sorry!)

Solyndra as a loan recipient, and the evidence showed that the loan was granted through the normal process, with no undue influence. It was a bad bet based on bad information from the company, nothing more, nothing less.

The tone and intensity of this type of press coverage had an impact. A 2010 CNN poll found that three in four Americans believed that at least half of the stimulus money was wasted. Only 42 percent of Americans supported the legislation, a drop of 12 points since the bill passed a year earlier.

But the news coverage gave the public a wholly incorrect impression. Obama's stimulus bill was one of the best-managed pieces of legislation in modern history. In 2011, when the bulk of the money was out the door, government auditors found that only 0.001 percent of the money had been wasted.

No one covered the stimulus closer than reporter Mike Grunwald. He even authored a book on the bill. In 2012, he wrote in the *Washington Post*:

> The stimulus was the biggest and most transformative energy bill in history, pouring an astonishing $90 billion into record expansions of every imaginable form of clean energy, from renewables to electric vehicles. It included $27 billion to computerize health care. Its Race to the Top was a landmark in education reform. Its high-speed rail program was the most ambitious transportation initiative since the interstates. It extended high-speed Internet to underserved communities, a modern twist on the New Deal's rural electrification, and modernized the New Deal–era unemployment insurance system. And much more... The stimulus will leave a different legacy: a down payment on a greener, more competitive economy with a healthier, better-educated, better-connected workforce.

There is nothing wrong with the media holding government accountable and exposing waste and abuse. Reporters shouldn't take government officials at their word; that's how we ended up invading a country that didn't attack us.[9] But there is something fundamentally wrong when the desire for accountability comes at the expense of accuracy. Liberals want to invest in government, and conservatives want to starve it. Media that focuses on governmental problems at the expense of government solutions is inherently pro-conservative. Reporters who read this will inevitably say that building trust in government is not their job. That's correct. But it is their job to convey information accurately.

If you believe that government is inherently incapable of functioning effectively and efficiently, you are not being objective. You are oppositional to a core premise of liberalism.

A Conservative Overcorrection

The major mainstream media outlets are *very* sensitive to the idea that they are biased toward liberal ideas. In theory, this sensitivity is a good thing. Having some self-awareness about your biases is essential. But—and this is a big but—the way traditional media outlets like the *New York Times* and others go about addressing those biases reveals that they do not fully understand the problem.

Mainstream media outlets have made an effort in recent years to hire journalists from conservative outlets to cover politics. CBS News reporter Robert Costa worked at the *National Review.* CNN's Kaitlan Collins was hired to the network from the Daily Caller, the digital media outlet founded by Tucker Carlson. Elaina Plott, a national political reporter at the *New York Times*, started in conservative media.

---

9 I am very committed to this anti–George W. Bush bit.

The list goes on and on. This ideological diversification of major newsrooms is not new, but the process sped up after everyone—raises hand—was caught off guard by the election of Trump. Editors and news executives believed their liberal cocoons prevented them from seeing what was really happening in America.[10] Therefore, conservative writers became a hot commodity among the "liberal" press. They were hired for their talent, but also their connections to the ascendant right-wing. With Trump calling the press "fake news" and the "enemy of the people," it was a way for distrusted outlets to regain some trust with the newly elected president. Ambassadors to MAGA Land could get in the door and speak the lingo.[11]

I don't bring up the conservative CVs of these reporters to impugn their objectivity. Far from it. No one who watched Kaitlan Collins go toe-to-toe with Trump and his aides could possibly think she is a secret pro-Trump mole. The ability of these reporters to hold a Republican president accountable—as they would a Democratic one—proves the point. If a journalist is personally liberal or conservative, they can still check their beliefs at the door and render fair coverage. However, the entire endeavor demonstrates that the blind spots and biases of the mainstream media are much more complex than "liberal versus conservative."

Hiring white conservatives to work alongside white liberals in big-city newsrooms demonstrates a dangerously limited understanding of diversity. Periodic safaris to diners frequented by a preponderance of MAGA hat–wearing customers is a demonstration of, not a response to, the elitism that plagues media. (I can imagine conservatives responding to that last sentence, *See, this proves our point. You liberal elites from liberal elite institutions simply can't fairly cover*

---

10 They weren't wrong, but their elite cocoons also prevent them from seeing what is happening to working people in the bluest parts of the country, too.
11 Not sure "speaking MAGA" is something to be super proud of, but that's just me.

conservatives. This is why we need Fox, Breitbart, etc.) But belief in liberal elitism in the media is bad-faith bullshit. There are as many conservative "elites" as liberal ones. Ted Cruz went to Harvard and clerked in the Supreme Court, and his wife is an executive at Goldman Sachs.[12] Donald Trump inherited what wealth he didn't steal. He went to Wharton and has a gold toilet in his house.[13] Performative populist and aspiring insurrectionist Josh Hawley went to law school at Yale. The C-suites of Fortune 500 companies, Wall Street banks, and hedge funds are filled with right-wingers. The notion of Republicans' being the "blue jeans party," as Cruz once claimed, is truly too absurd to take seriously.

As soon as Trump won, the media flocked to the rural and exurban counties of Wisconsin, Michigan, and Pennsylvania to conduct a forensic analysis of the white working-class voters who chose Obama in 2012 and Trump in 2016—once again, a subject worthy of exploration. But why weren't there more stories about the Black voters in Milwaukee and Philadelphia who didn't vote in an election with a bigot on the ballot? What about the Latino voters in Florida who moved into Trump's camp or stayed home? This narrow focus is the product of the narrow personal and professional experiences of an overwhelmingly white set of decision makers overcorrecting for alleged liberal bias.

The coverage of Trump's victory is a textbook example of how self-conscious journalists, petrified of offending conservatives, inadvertently end up enabling false right-wing narratives. Donald Trump is a racist who ran for president on a very specific campaign of white nationalism and racial grievance. Yet most media outlets and pundits insisted on arguing that Trump's win involved everything except

---

12 Cruz allegedly ratted out a poker game being played in his dorm to avoid paying what he owed. This is a total non sequitur but also a good reminder that he is an incorrigible asshole.

13 The fact-checkers claim the gold toilet thing is apocryphal, but I don't care.

race. There was an unwillingness to point out that nearly every single Republican Party leader and tens of millions of Republican voters backed a racist because they shared his racist views, supported his racist policies, or had a disturbing level of comfort with a racist wielding the power of the state. To do so would have been to risk accusations of liberal bias and offend potential subscribers and advertisers. Instead, the media attributed Trump's victory to "economic anxiety." I am mildly sympathetic[14] to the impulse to avoid grappling with the uncomfortable fact—that large swaths of the country are susceptible to a racist message. However, the economic anxiety thesis does not stand up to a nanosecond of scrutiny.

As Adam Serwer wrote in the *Atlantic*:

> Clinton defeated Trump handily among Americans making less than $50,000 a year. Among voters making more than that, the two candidates ran roughly even. The electorate, however, skews wealthier than the general population. Voters making less than $50,000, whom Clinton won by a proportion of 53 to 41, accounted for only 36 percent of the votes cast, while those making more than $50,000—whom Trump won by a single point—made up 64 percent. The most economically vulnerable Americans voted for Clinton overwhelmingly.... Trump won white voters at every level of class and income. He won workers, he won managers, he won owners, he won robber barons. This is not a working-class coalition; it is a nationalist one.

Refusing to call Donald Trump a racist or even identifying racial animus as a motivating force for his coalition is an abdication of one's duty to inform the public. Ignoring and refuting claims of racist policy

---

14 Only very mildly sympathetic. Grappling with uncomfortable is kinda the job.

only advantages conservatives in the information wars. Before Trump, Republicans used a dog whistle, instead of a bull horn, to appeal to the racial anxiety of their white base, out of fear that any overt racism would turn the majority of the electorate against them. Trump proved that those fears were unnecessary. With the election of Trump, the Republicans had their racist cake and ate it, too; and the media helped them do it.[15]

Given its role as the most powerful media outlet in the country, the *New York Times* is at the center of the conversation. Dean Baquet, the paper's executive editor, pushed back for years against tremendous internal and external pressure to use the word *racist* in reference to Trump. During a staff town hall meeting, the contents of which were ironically leaked to Ashley Feinberg of *Slate*, Baquet defended his policy of not using the word *racist* and his hesitancy to use the word *lie* in reporting about Trump:

> I used the word *lie* once during the presidential campaign, used it a couple times after that. And it was pretty clear it was a lie, and we were the first ones to use it. But I fear that if we used it 20 times, 10 times, first, it would lose its power. And secondly, I thought we would find ourselves in the uncomfortable position of deciding which comment by which politician fit the word *lie*. I feel the same way about the word *racist*.

The *Times* has done some of the most important journalism in the world. But, essentially, the paper doesn't want to use the word *lie*, because, the thinking there goes, the reporter can never know the speaker's (i.e., Trump's) intent. Though I understand the concern of desensitizing the public, if Baquet applied this standard of certainty

---

15 To be fair, a lot of Democrats did, too.

of intent to all *New York Times* reporting, the newspaper would be unable to function. A huge portion of political reporting depends on anonymous sources recounting conversations, meetings, and documents of which the reporter has no firsthand knowledge. Operating a major media outlet and fearing the accusation of liberal bias is like living in Seattle and being afraid of the rain. It's happening. You can't avoid it. You must deal with it.

The irony here is that the *Times* and other media outlets are angering the subscribers who pay their salary in order to appease the very people who profit, politically and financially, from their demise.

Gaming the System

The internet makes the Wild West look like an authoritarian society living under martial law. On the internet, there are no rules, no enforcers, little transparency, and less accountability.

The Republicans may "hate" the media. Their voters may distrust the media to the point of subjecting themselves to Laura Ingraham and Jeanine Pirro for hours a week. Republican politicians may refuse to be interviewed on mainstream shows, ignore questions from non-MAGA-friendly reporters, and threaten the media on Twitter. However, no one understands the institutional biases and fears of the traditional political press better than the American Right. They ruthlessly exploit those biases and game the system to spread their message through the press while simultaneously undermining it.

It's been happening for years. Most in the media are completely unaware of how bad they are being played. At this point, swerving from their lane to prove their bona fides to bad-faith critics has become instinctual.

After years of tough coverage on Donald Trump, the political press wanted, needed, to prove to Republicans and themselves that they weren't going to give Joe Biden a free pass. The problem for the press is that Joe Biden is not Donald Trump. Biden doesn't wake up every day and tweet offensive things. He abides by norms, strives to tell the truth, and isn't a walking conflict of interest. Being as tough on Biden as they were on Trump means creating controversies where there are none. This dynamic was perfectly encapsulated by a story run in the *New York Times* the day before Biden was even sworn in as president. Here was the headline and subhead from the "Paper of Record":

BIDEN HAS A PELOTON BIKE. THAT RAISES ISSUES AT THE WHITE HOUSE.
It doesn't exactly comport with his "regular Joe from Scranton" persona, but beyond the politics of it, the bike could present cybersecurity risks.

This article was rightly mocked, but it was emblematic of a dynamic that played out during the first year of Biden's presidency. It felt like some in the media had an annual quota of negative stories or scandals to report. Minor transgressions were treated like major scandals. Misstatements by Biden became equivalent to bald-faced lies from Trump. No one loves it when the politicians they support get tough coverage. I hated it when I worked for Barack Obama, and I hate it as a supporter of Joe Biden. Some in the press take these complaints as validation of their objectivity: *If both sides are angry, we must be doing something right.* With all due respect, that is idiocy.

Assessments of the tone and tenor of media coverage tend to be in the eye of the beholder. It can be difficult to separate legitimate complaints made in good faith from bad-faith working of the refs. But Dana Milbank of the *Washington Post* found some actual data demonstrating how badly the media has swerved out of its lane to appease its right-wing critics. Milbank asked an artificial intelligence company to analyze two hundred thousand articles and compare President Biden's coverage in 2021 with Donald Trump's coverage in 2020. The last year of Trump's presidency was one of the worst years politically and substantively for any president in history. Surely, his coverage was worse than Biden's.

It was not. As Milbank wrote:

In 2020, Trump presided over a worst-in-world pandemic response that caused hundreds of thousands of unnecessary deaths; held a superspreader event at the White House and got covid-19 himself; praised QAnon adherents; embraced violent white supremacists; waged a racist campaign against Black Lives Matter demonstrators; attempted to discredit mail-in voting; and refused to accept his defeat in a free and fair election, leading eventually to the violence of Jan. 6 and causing tens of millions to accept the "big lie," the worst of more than 30,000 he told in office.

And yet, Trump got press coverage as favorable as, or better than, Biden is getting today.

Do you really need any more evidence of how the media is biased and the Republicans have exploited those biases to spread Big Lies and drown out the truth?

13

Debunking the Dumbest Myth: Why MSNBC Is Not "Liberal Fox"

I am about to do something I don't normally do: defend cable television. Well, I am actually going to defend one particular cable channel as way of explaining why Fox News is a carbuncle on the body politic *and* why progressives are still getting our asses kicked in the information wars.

If you called out Fox News's bias to a Fox reporter's face when I worked in the Obama White House, they would stomp their feet in faux outrage while chanting "fair and balanced" and point to a snippet of some interview where Chris Wallace or Shep Smith did the bare minimum required as a journalist.[1]

The rest of the press would pretend to go along with this charade of neutrality. By the time Trump had been in office for years, even the willfully blind could no longer deny Fox's overwhelming pro-Trump bent. How does one argue "fair and balanced" reporting when on-air personalities are dialed into policy meetings in the Oval Office (Lou Dobbs) or advising Trump on military strikes (Tucker Carlson)?

Unable to deny the undeniable, Fox and defenders of the right-wing propaganda operations shifted tack. They now justify their behavior by claiming liberals have their own version of Fox.

---

1 Exception, rule. Blah, blah, blah.

Call it the "MSNBC defense."

This is a classic trope of the "both sides" Beltway types who want to sound smart, offend no one, and get invited to all the terrible cocktail parties the nation's capital has to offer.[2] People who use the MSNBC defense have clearly never watched either network (too busy attending the aforementioned cocktail parties).

The gist of this argument is that both networks air traditional news shows during the day but turn to opinion programming at night. In other words, Sean Hannity and Chris Hayes are opposite sides of the same coin. In addition to driving me personally insane, this notion is risible and dangerous. False equivalency is dangerous when it allows various stakeholders to avoid taking a stand against the right-wing's war on truth. If everyone does it, then no one can do anything about it. The Fox = MSNBC conversation is a proxy for the idea that liberals and conservatives engage in the same propaganda and disinformation strategies. This contention is insipid bullshit. Therefore, it is critical to underscore the real difference between MSNBC and Fox News.

The Deadly Consequences of Faux News

COVID-19 proved that there are life-or-death consequences to creating an environment where science is discounted and where the dumbest, most outrageous voices are elevated. To put it bluntly, Fox, the *Federalist*, and others in the right-wing media have killed their audience. By pushing antimask agitprop and sowing mistrust in vaccines, these outlets exposed millions to a deadly virus. A *Washington Post*/ABC News poll from the summer of 2021 revealed that 47 percent of Republicans were unlikely to get vaccinated despite the overwhelming scientific and societal arguments in favor of doing so.

---

2 Can you call it a party if Bret Baier's in attendance?

A study published in *The Canadian Journal of Political Science* documented this phenomenon. According to the research by Matt Motta, Dominik Stecula, and Christina Farhart, consumers of right-wing media were twice as likely to believe COVID-19 misinformation.[3]

It shouldn't require a bunch of political scientists doing research to prove that garbage in leads to garbage out, but this study and many others like it serve an important purpose. A lot of people like to believe that right-wing media is like professional wrestling: a big, fun farce where everyone "gets it." Many assert that right-wing news consumers and Fox News fans are in on the joke. Except, that's not how it plays out in the real world. Fox viewers take the disinformation seriously, refuse to get the vaccine, and die from COVID-19. Others take matters into their own hands and inject bleach, mail pipe bombs to the "enemies" of Fox and Trump, or show up at a Black Lives Matter protest in Kenosha brandishing an assault-style rifle.

MSNBC is functionally and culturally distinct from Fox News. For anyone willing to remove their "both sides" blinders and confront reality, here are a few stark differences.

Journalists versus Propagandists

On paper, the two networks have the same format: news during the day and opinion at night. However, that's where the similarities end. MSNBC, both its news and opinion sides, operates under traditional rules of journalism, with fact-checkers, editors, and accountability. MSNBC is an adjunct of NBC News, and for the most part, its reporting adheres to the standards for the nonideological parent network. At

---

3 This is one of those cases where you don't need a study to tell you something, but it's a helpful talking point with your Fox-curious relatives.

Fox, however, the editors are full partisans. In 2018, John Moody, one of the most senior Fox execs, responsible for the news side of the operation, was forced into retirement after writing an op-ed suggesting that the US Olympic Committee would like to change the Olympics motto from " 'Faster, Higher, Stronger' to 'Darker, Gayer, Different.' " Moody's sin, in the eyes of the higher-ups at Fox, was not being a bigoted asshole; it was being a bigoted asshole in public and lifting the very thin veil of faux objectivity for the "journalists" at his network.

The "news" side of Fox is a beard for the propaganda goals of the network. The journalists themselves are compromised by their own conservative beliefs. Witness Peter Doocy's questions at the White House briefing every day. The dim son of Steve Doocy, the even dimmer *Fox and Friends* host, heads to the White House every day to ask the White House press secretary questions essentially written by the Republican National Committee. While still at Fox, midday anchor Shep Smith periodically—and I can't emphasize "periodically" enough—fact-checked Trump and pushed back on the racist dreck[4] coming from Tucker Carlson and other Fox personalities. But instead of being hailed a totem of Fox's "fair and balanced" approach, Smith left the network because there was no appetite internally (or externally) for someone who said bad things about Trump or Trumpism. After losing one too many internal battles to Tucker Carlson, Chris Wallace also fled Fox, for CNN's streaming service.

The lineup at MSNBC is definitely anti-Trump, but it is not exclusively liberal and not pro-Democrat. The host of MSNBC's *Morning Joe* is not some fire-breathing progressive. The eponymous "Joe" is a former GOP congressman. While the show is decidedly anti-Trump, the ideological makeup of the conversation and the guests spans from somewhere on Joe Biden's right to somewhere on Mitt Romney's left.

---

4 *Dreck* is an underused word. I plan to change that.

Former Republican governor turned Biden supporter John Kasich is basically the median *Morning Joe* viewer. The daytime lineup at MSNBC includes some clear progressives, but it also includes Andrea Mitchell, a veteran foreign policy reporter famous for being tough on all comers regardless of party; Chuck Todd, the host of *Meet the Press* and a favorite punching bag of Resistance Twitter; and Nicole Wallace, who was George W. Bush's White House communications director.

Accuracy versus Allegiance

Reporting is a human enterprise, and humans make mistakes. Like any media outlet, MSNBC gets lots of stuff wrong. Some of the coverage of Trump and Russia was a little overenthusiastic, to say the least. The network over hyped a story about Trump's taxes. To be fair, most of its mistakes came from amplifying reports from other outlets without an appropriate degree of skepticism. MSNBC (and everyone else) got the big-picture story right: Russia did interfere in the 2016 election, Trump welcomed that interference, and many of the people around Trump lied about this collusion under oath. Yet sometimes its reporters have jumped on sketchy stories: for example, a report that Michael Cohen had secretly traveled to Prague. Still, when it has been wrong in its own reporting, MSNBC has acknowledged this and ceased distribution of the incorrect information. It isn't perfect, but no one is.

Fox, on the other hand, punishes people not for getting things wrong, but for telling uncomfortable truths. The political unit responsible for calling elections and conducting polling is the one place at Fox that is free from the influence of Ailes, Murdoch, and Trump et al. Whenever Fox publishes a poll that is good for Republicans or bad for Democrats, the Left chalks it up to its being a rigged enterprise like literally everything else the network does. But it's not. The Fox poll is one of the most reliable in the business. (I recognize this is faint praise after the polling mishaps of '16 and '20.) FiveThirtyEight gives the Fox poll an A rating. Few things stoked the ire of Trump more than when a Fox News poll gave him poor numbers.

Even among Fox haters like me, its Election Night calls on who has won which states and races have real credibility. In 2012, the network's political unit correctly called Ohio for Obama. Then embarrassed Karl Rove, the former Bush adviser and Fox contributor, when he tried to say on air that Romney could still win the state. So, it was a huge moment on Election Night 2020 when Fox called the state of Arizona for Biden. It was the first swing state to go to Biden, and its win interrupted a rapidly growing Democratic sense of 2016 déjà vu. According to a report from the *New York Times*, the Trump campaign flipped their lids when Fox called Arizona. Jared Kushner, Trump's dilettante son-in-law and top adviser, even called Rupert Murdoch and begged him to reverse the call. Instead, the network stuck to its guns and put Arnon Mishkin, the person responsible for the decision, on air to defend the call. Mishkin, a Democrat, aggressively pushed back against anyone questioning whether Biden would be declared the winner when the last votes in Arizona were counted. Trump and his supporters were enraged. In the coming weeks, they abandoned the network. Trump took to Twitter to encourage people to turn the channel from Fox to rival right-wing networks like OAN and Newsmax, and he stopped appearing on Fox shows or promoting their content on Twitter. Fox's ratings dropped precipitously in the aftermath of the election as Trump supporters went looking for a safer space to get their news.

In the end, Biden won Arizona. Mishkin and his team were correct. This was a rare moment of journalistic integrity for a network that had spent the previous four years debasing itself to appease the fickle and feckless president. And how did Fox respond? Did it promote Mishkin? Nope, it fired a bunch of his team to appease Trump. Not long after the ratings were back up, and Trump was once again on the air.

Hannity ≠ Maddow

The worst and most dangerous Fox/MSNBC false equivalency states that Sean Hannity and Rachel Maddow (or Tucker Carlson and Chris Hayes) are bizarro political doppelgangers. This is deeply unfair to Maddow (and Hayes), and it allows the proponents of this position to avoid confronting the deeply dangerous disinformation that flows on Fox every night. It is true that these are "opinion" shows. It is the anchors' job to talk about the news from their very clear ideological perspective. It's not hidden. The audience opts in to the experience. But having an opinion is not an excuse for spreading disinformation. Opinion hosts must be held accountable for the accuracy of what they say. Once again, MSNBC and its hosts are not perfect. They make mistakes; we all do. But they do not try to misinform their audience for either ratings or public gain. Maddow and Hayes are very smart, very serious, and very substantive people. Neither of them would intentionally mislead, but if they did, they would have to retract their words and face reprimand from their higher-ups.

The prime-time/opinion lineup at Fox is an unfettered fount of conspiracy theories. On a nightly basis, Sean Hannity, Tucker Carlson, Laura Ingraham, and the rest of the participants are what my *Pod Save America* cohost Jon Lovett once called "the White Nationalist Variety Hour." These disciples of conspiracy push disinformation designed to dupe and enrage their listeners. The examples are truly endless. It happens every single night and has for years. It was Fox News hosts who popularized the idea of the "war on Christmas," a completely false notion that anti-Christian liberals were passing laws punishing people for saying "Merry Christmas."[5] In 2016, Hannity and others repeatedly promoted a conspiracy theory that the shooting death of Seth Rich, a Democratic National Committee staffer in Washington, DC, was part of a plot to cover up something about Hillary Clinton's emails. Hannity smeared Rich despite zero evidence and pleas from Rich's grieving family.

The same pattern played out after the 2020 election as Fox opinion hosts spread the false and repeatedly debunked conspiracy theory that Dominion Voting Systems had stolen the election for Joe Biden. The Dominion conspiracy theory was a central part of the Big Lie. According to its proponents, the voting machine software created by Dominion and used in more than twenty states was not only hacked but was specifically *designed* to be hacked. And what kind of company would design its software to be hacked? A Chinese company with ties to George Soros and Hugo Chávez, of course. Except, Dominion is not a Chinese company, George Soros was not involved in the machines' manufacture, and Hugo Chávez died in 2013.[6] Eventually, the Fox personalities stopped talking about the Dominion conspiracy theory.

Did a network fact-checker step in? Did Ingraham et al. take fifteen seconds to google the facts? Were the hosts overcome with shame? Nope. Dominion sued Fox News for $1.6 billion. Even for the famously profitable network, $1.6 billion was a large enough sum to force Fox News to stop lying—about this one subject at least.

---

5 Winning fake wars and losing real ones is a hallmark of Republican presidents.
6 Or maybe he faked his death in order to dedicate more time to hacking voting machines.

Fox is getting worse, not better. Upstarts like OAN and Newsmax have taken the Fox model and made it crazier and less responsible. And here's the most disturbing thing: there is a market for "crazier than Fox." These networks were able to siphon off some of Fox's audience, and now they are in a race to the bottom.

14

Message versus Megaphone: The Real Reason Dems Suck at Messaging

In my many years working in politics, I have attended hundreds, if not thousands, of fund-raising events. A fund-raising trip is a tour of the twin plagues of economic inequality and money in politics. These events are held at huge brownstones on the Upper East Side, giant tech-funded mansions in Silicon Valley, ancestral estates in the Berkshires, and homes overlooking the ocean in Malibu and the Hamptons. Each of these venues would be worthy of its own episode of *Million Dollar Listing*. However, I rarely toured these totems to wealth (inherited and "earned"). At these hoity-toity events in people's homes, there is usually a room for the politician's staff. These "hold rooms," often servants' quarters or pool houses, are removed from the action. In New York City apartments, they are often spare bedrooms or kids' rooms with custom bunk beds. During presidential events, the hold room would be crowded with military aides, doctors, and the traveling government-in-waiting, in case a crisis broke out while the president was away from the White House.

At these events, senior campaign staff are encouraged to mix and mingle with the guests. There is only so much of the candidate to go around, and the organizers want the donors to feel they've gotten their money's worth of access. But, much to the chagrin of the fund-raising staff for the Democratic National Committee and the Obama campaign, I did everything to avoid the mix-and-mingle obligation. As soon as I arrived with President Obama or the myriad other politicians whom I've traveled with over the years, I would head directly to the hold room to hide out.The primary impetus for my self-imposed exile was my aversion to small talk.[1] But I also hid to avoid something I called "the Question," an inevitable feature of any conversation with any group of Democratic donors.

It didn't matter if Democrats had won or lost the most recent election. The Question comes in many forms, but it always boils down to some version of: Why do Democrats suck at messaging? The Question was usually, but not always, asked politely. Sometimes it came with a series of ideas. Politics is one of those endeavors where everyone thinks they are qualified to have an opinion. And the people successful enough to write checks big enough to attend these events are generally not the sort of people who experience self-doubt.

For much of my time in the White House, I was anonymous in face and name to all but the most attuned political observers. But in a crowd of well-heeled donors, I had all the markings of a staffer: a little too young, a bit haggard, with the dark circles that are imprinted under the eyes after a year of working White House hours.[2]

Eventually, as I stood in a corner hoping the server with the pigs in a blanket would come by, someone would invariably wander over to me and ask,[3] "Are you on the White House Staff?"

"I am."

---

1 I am genetically incapable of doing it well or without perspiring through my suit.
2 It took me one year to get the dark circles and three years for them to go away. Three years after I left the White House, my first child was born.
3 Food is weirdly hard to come by on a presidential trip. The schedule is built around the president's getting sustenance, not the rest of us. Despite the absence of food, I still managed to gain five to seven pounds on every trip.

"What do you do?"

"I'm President Obama's communications director."

"Oh good. I was hoping to run into you. I have some thoughts…"
And we were off to the races.

I never had a great answer for them—or, at least, I never had an answer they found satisfactory. And their "thoughts" usually amounted to their pretending that their experience making a fortune selling mail-order underwear, betting against the housing market, or producing a hit sitcom made them qualified to do my job.[4]

Political donors are not the only ones obsessed with "the Question." Pundits and the political press are constantly haranguing Democrats for their messaging mistakes. One liberal writer of several well-reviewed presidential histories called me often during Obama's first term to lecture me on why Obama didn't yet have a version of FDR's New Deal or LBJ's Great Society. The subtext of these conversations was that great slogans make great presidents.[5] Much of Progressive Twitter is filled with lamentations about some failure or missed messaging opportunity. There was a running joke in the Obama White House that you needed a master's in economics to discuss economic policy and a doctorate in public health to offer health care ideas, but everyone believed that reading the newspaper made them qualified to opine on messaging strategy.[6]

My own fragile self-esteem and awkwardness aside, I hate trying

---

4 The apotheosis of this behavior was former Starbucks CEO Howard Schultz, who requested a lunch with Obama so he could hector him for an hour on how to strike a bipartisan budget deal—because legislative wrangling is just like marketing Caramel Macchiatos.

5 I very much enjoyed calling this person after Obama won reelection by 126 electoral votes to ask how many more he thought Obama would have won by with a slogan.

6 This is not dissimilar to every sports fan thinking he can coach better than his favorite NBA team's coach because he plays a mean game of *NBA2K* on his PlayStation 5.

to answer the Question. Not only are there no easy answers, it's the wrong question.

Republicans are winning the message war, but not for the reasons these donors, the media, or 90 percent of the folks on Twitter believe. And there are steps we must take to change this very annoying dynamic.

In this more mature, less defensive phase of my life, I've stopped hiding from the Question (and the questioners). Instead, I've found a more accessible, equally dissatisfying way to address the actual problem without absolving the party (or myself) of mistakes and missed opportunities. But before I get to the Democrats, I am going to use authorial privilege to talk about why Republicans suck at messaging.[7]

Republicans Suck, Too

When donors, activists, and media folks ask why Democrats suck at messaging, they are really asking why Republicans are so much better at it.

There is an old saying in Washington: "The only people who believe Republican talking points are Democrats." This inherent sense that Republicans are better at politics than Democrats has survived as a feature of my party's psychology for decades. Democrats love to imbue our opposition with strategic evil genius. Roger Ailes, Lee Atwater, and Karl Rove are famous mostly because Democrats have hyperinflated their roles to explain away our losses.

There is no doubt Republicans are winning the messaging war, but are they winning because they are better messengers?

Democrats love to complain about the messaging chops of their

---

7 I know you (or your local library) paid for this book, but I wrote it.

congressional leadership team, but have you watched the Republicans? During every appearance, Kevin McCarthy looks like he just woke up from a nap and can't figure out where he is or what he is doing. Mitch McConnell, one of the worst communicators in modern political history, sounds like he is reading *The Almanac of American Politics* with a mouthful of marbles. And no one exemplifies the adage of "less is more" more than Ted Cruz, an amalgamation of the five most annoying people you went to high school with.[8] Arkansas senator Tom Cotton makes Jared Kushner look like a magnetic personality. Turn on Fox News, and you'll find a parade of awkward, angry white men doing bad impressions of Donald Trump.

Even Trump, the supposed master media manipulator, has the discipline and strategic thinking of a coked-up Tasmanian devil. Just look at his Twitter feed from the end of the 2020 campaign.[9] Instead of using his biggest platform to drive home a positive argument for his reelection and a negative message against Biden, Trump engaged in a scattershot Festivus-style airing of grievances against members of his own party, the media, and random celebrities.

This dynamic is in part why the founders of the Lincoln Project became huge celebrities among the Resistance Twitter/MSNBC crowd. The former political consultants, all Republican Never Trumpers, were able to siphon tens of millions of dollars from willing progressives hoping to sample some of that Republican messaging magic. The Lincoln Project was touted as tougher, faster, and smarter than those mealy-mouthed Democratic ad makers whom Democrats love to hate. Though, at no point have folks asked, "If the Lincoln Project is so good, why did so many of its founders keep losing presidential

---

8 Think about it. It makes perfect sense.
9 Technically you can't do that because he is banned from Twitter, but you get my point, right?

elections to Democrats?"[10] Nor has anyone stopped to wonder if an ad that appealed to highly engaged, very online liberals in California or New York would really be effective with disenchanted Republicans in Ohio and Iowa.

During the 2020 campaign, questions about the effectiveness of the Lincoln Project were dismissed by many as ad envy. However, once the campaign was over, a Democratic group released a study that showed that the ads from the Lincoln Project were largely ineffective. In fact, the study found an inverse relationship between efficacy and engagement on Twitter.

This is not to say that Republicans have no messaging attributes. They have perfected a strategy of social media trolling that tricks angry liberals into inadvertently spreading their message. The Right has effectively created a narrative about Democrats and has stuck to it. "Make America Great Again" is one of the most successful political branding efforts in history. But on the whole, Republicans, as much as they are winning elections despite getting fewer votes, seem to be winning the messaging war in spite of themselves.

Marketing the Big Tent

Back in 2003, I was working for Senate minority leader Tom Daschle. This was a tough time to be a Democrat. We had just lost the Senate majority in a brutal campaign cycle that included Republicans running ads comparing Democrats to Osama bin Laden for not being sufficiently supportive of President George W. Bush's post-9/11 agenda. Bush's numbers were through the roof, and the United States had just entered a war against a country that did not attack us on September 11, 2001. The party was staring down the barrel of a divisive primary

---

10 Only one Republican has won the popular vote since the late 1980s.

for the right to run against a popular wartime president. The situation was, as they say, not great.

For the Democratic senators under Daschle's leadership, it was a time to regroup and get back on offense. As the folks putatively in charge of the ideological and generational mish-mash of senators, our office initiated a process for a unified caucus message. Our group included moderate Democrats representing deeply red farm states and liberal Democrats from New York and California. In the caucus was a former Dixiecrat and a former First Lady. The ideological divisions were deep. A significant group of Democratic senators broke with the party to back Bush's war in Iraq and his 2001 tax cuts for the rich. These divisions were, of course, insoluble, but the party needed a slogan to rally around. We needed order to unify our disparate views. Daschle's staff knew this task wouldn't be easy, but as with every senatorial task, we would tackle this one over lunch.

Every week, senators from both parties would gather to discuss party business and legislative strategy over lunch. The weekly caucus lunch,[11] a "do not miss" event and the only time the senators sat down with their fellow party members, was a centerpiece of the Senate schedule and important for keeping everyone on the same page. I periodically attended this lunch when I worked in the Senate, and a number of times when I worked in the White House, to make presentations on strategy and messaging. The central topic of discussion in most caucus lunches was the mediocre menu. There was a jockeying for seats. During the presentations, the audience of mostly very old people constantly interrupted the presenters to make some quasi-related point with senatorial expanse or to ask them to speak louder.

11 The Republicans call them conference lunches because they think the word *caucus* suggests too much support for democracy. Seriously! Can someone say "Giant warning sign"?

The awkwardness of each encounter was off-putting and amusing. The vibe was that of a Dunder Mifflin Scranton conference room staff meeting.

As you can imagine, finding agreement with regard to Democratic messaging among this group of hard-of-hearing people unfamiliar with self-doubt did not go well. Democrats from red states, where Bush was sure to win in 2004, objected to anti-Bush messages. Supporters of the Iraq War opposed an effort to focus on the Bush administration's mismanagement of the war effort. Those wealthy few who had voted for the Bush tax cuts were against a populist economic critique. And the populists wouldn't sign off on a message of moderate growth. The discussion would go in circles, with no end in sight.

Group projects never work, and they definitely never work when every participant has a veto and no participant has the ability to override that veto. The decision on messaging wasn't resolved in one lunch or even two. After weeks of discussion, the senators eventually lined up behind the thrilling and incisive slogan "Better Together." In the end, the only thing the party could agree on was something so inoffensive that it meant nothing, the political messaging equivalent of plain yogurt.

The post-9/11, pre-Obama-era Democratic Party was in particularly dire straits. We weren't sure how to be against Bush but not the troops. We were constantly on our heels and had a policymaking hangover from eight years of Clintonian small ball. The strategic miasma of that era would be embodied by John Kerry's declaring, on the 2004 campaign trail, that with regard to the funding for the Iraq War, he was for it before he was against it.

It is tempting to view this messaging mess as a relic of a bygone era. Yet, nearly two decades later, the challenge persists. A series of focus groups conducted in the first few months of the Biden presidency found that voters were unable to identify what the Democratic

Party stood for. Two electoral landslide victories for Obama, a huge popular-vote win for President Biden, and four years of resistance to Trump—and the Democrats still have a brand problem. This is more than a failure by party leaders and activists to settle on a narrative.

The Democratic Party is more diverse (ideologically, demographically, and geographically) than the Republicans. This diversity is our strength, but it poses a central and seemingly insurmountable challenge to creating positive messages for the party. How does one compose a pithy slogan or a tweet-length narrative to accurately and appealingly describe a coalition so broad that it extends from Joe Manchin to Alexandria Ocasio-Cortez?[12] It's the difference between being asked to come up with a brand for one television network like HBO or ESPN and being asked to brand "television" more broadly. What compelling slogan would be inclusive of every channel, from Bravo to CNBC?

Frankly, the messaging and branding task is more challenging for Democrats than it is for Republicans. The geographic disparities in the Senate and the Electoral College mean that Democrats must turn out liberal-base voters and appeal to voters much more conservative than the median Democratic voter. Democrats have to sell a wider array of products to a wider array of people.

The Republican coalition is narrower. It's more ideologically homogenous and as white as a field of lilies. The Electoral College is biased toward Republican states, and the Senate gives small rural states like Wyoming the same number of votes as California and New York. To succeed, Republicans need only appeal to their base and little else, which allows for a simpler message.

---

12 Here's hoping Manchin hasn't bolted the party and given the Senate to the Republicans by the time this book comes out.

I'm sure you are reading this and thinking, *Shit is hard all over. Figure it out.*

You're not wrong. Democrats must do better. *I* must do better. But understanding the challenge helps explain how we got to this point.

For all the party's messaging mishaps, there are some facts running counter to the prevailing narrative that Republicans are messaging maestros. First, Democrats have won the popular vote in all but one presidential election[13] since 1988. Second, the Democratic Party's approval rating, while nothing to write home about, has been consistently higher than the Republican Party's for many years. Finally, the Democratic position on immigration, taxes, reproductive freedom, minimum wage, civil rights, voting rights, and climate change is more popular than the Republican position.

These facts help explain why Republicans and their billionaire supporters invest so much time and energy in building a disinformation apparatus that can overcome the opinions of the majority of Americans. Hence, the megaphone problem.

Megaphone versus Message

Democratic messaging is not perfect;[14] far from it. It's often too wonky and wordy, an Ezra Klein[15] column distilled into a paragraph of focus-grouped verbal apple sauce. Our party leaders are all over seventy, and none of them rose to the pinnacle of party leadership based on their communication chops. They are generationally disconnected from the party's base, but the problem isn't their age. It's that each has

---

13 The one time the GOP won the popular vote was in the presidential election right after the cursed messaging meetings I've just mentioned.
14 This sentence is a nominee for understatement of the year.
15 Ezra, this is a compliment!

spent more than half their years serving in Congress, where authentic human speaking goes to die.

Let's say, hypothetically, that all these problems were solved, that Democrats got better messages and messengers, the talking points were as sharp as talking points could be, and cable news was flooded with the best people saying the best things. It would help, but it still wouldn't matter much.

Imagine two armies doing battle. One of those armies is equipped with tanks and stealth bombers. The other shows up to the battle wielding pocketknives. Of course, Team Pocketknife gets its ass kicked. After the battle, it returns home, and the first question from the gathered townsfolk is "Why didn't you have a better strategy?"

Did the Team Pocketknife have the best plan? Maybe, maybe not. Ultimately, no one—whether Patton, von Clausewitz, or Captain America—could devise a plan for a pocketknife to beat a tank. Instead of drawing up a better battle plan, Team Pocketknife needed to focus its energy on figuring out how to get some tanks.[16]

In the context of political communications, this is the message-versus-megaphone problem. Democrats spend 99 percent of their time worrying about *what* they should say and only 1 percent figuring out how to get people to *hear* what they are saying.

The Republicans have a cable television network whose sole raison d'être is to attack Democrats and promote pro-GOP talking points. The conservative media dwarfs the progressive media in size and scope. And even then, it's an apples-to-oranges comparison. The bulk of the media on the right is an adjunct of the party apparatus; during the Trump presidency it was state-adjacent propaganda—*Pravda*, but with plausible deniability.

Much of the media on the left is focused on holding Democrats

---

16 Thank you for bearing with me on that tortured metaphor.

accountable and/or moving the party's agenda in a more progressive direction. This is, of course, an admirable and necessary task, but it doesn't do much to help Democratic candidates and causes win the messaging battle against Republicans come election time.

Facebook, the biggest, most important media outlet in the world, aggressively promotes conservative content. Democrats are out-gunned. We have fewer outlets with less reach. What we say is being drowned out. Sure, we need a better message, but first we need to get a bigger megaphone.

In the early months of the Biden presidency, James Carville, the legendary Democratic strategist, had some complaints about the Dem-ocratic strategy. Carville helped elect Bill Clinton in 1992 and became a national celebrity due to his political success and his marriage to a Republican operative working on the Bush campaign. Books were written and movies were made about him. He even starred in an HBO series (directed by Steven Soderbergh) based loosely on his life.[17] In recent years, when he has seen the party faltering, Carville has made a habit of periodically popping up in the media to offer some very blunt advice to Democrats. The advice he delivers, filled with Cajun collo-quialisms, is often correct.

On this occasion, he took a call from Sean Illing, a reporter at Vox, and unloaded on the Democratic Party. The part of the inter-view that made headlines was Carville's claim that the Democrats had a "wokeness" problem, a statement perfectly engineered to dominate Fox News for a week. Another part of the Carville interview, how-ever, demonstrates what Democrats still don't understand about their media deficit:

---

17 I found this so wild that I had to google it to confirm it wasn't a fever dream.

Two of the most consequential political events in recent memory happened on the same day in January: the insurrection at the US Capitol and the Democrats winning those two seats in Georgia. Can't overstate that.

But the Democrats can't fuck it up. They have to make the Republicans own that insurrection every day. They have to pound it. They have to call bookers on cable news shows. They have to get people to write op-eds. There will be all kinds of investigations and stories dripping out for God knows how long, and the Democrats should spend every day tying all of it to the Republican Party. They can't sit back and wait for it to happen.

Hell, just imagine if it was a bunch of nonwhite people who stormed the Capitol. Imagine how Republicans would exploit that and make every news cycle about how the Dems are responsible for it. Every political debate would be about that. The Republicans would bludgeon the Democrats with it forever. So, whatever you think Republicans would do to us in that scenario, that's exactly what the hell we need to do to them.

Carville is correct: Republicans are getting away with literal attempted murder. Within months of the insurrection, the cause of the event had been whitewashed, history rewritten, and blame shifted away from the leaders of the Republican Party.

But Carville's prescription is wrong. Putting aside the amusing suggestion that Democrats write more op-eds, a mode of communication that lost relevance with the death of the physical newspaper, doing all the things Carville suggests won't solve the problem. We should, of course, do them. I am not arguing that we throw in the towel just because we don't have a Fox equivalent. But the problem isn't strategic; it's structural.

This is a tough concept for the punditocracy (aka Twitter) to come to terms with. Political analysis is obsessed with style, strategy, and optics at the expense of structural forces. Politics is covered like drama, elevating the actions and decisions of individuals. The choices made by candidates and campaign advisers, the thinking goes, are what determine success or failure. This faux-Greek drama needs a narrative arc and a hero's journey. Every election cycle has an Icarus.

But campaigns are not won or lost on a single decision or a killer ad. Presidencies are not defined by a slogan. There is a harder, less entertaining, but much more informative way to understand politics: focus less on the personalities and more on the structural impediments to progress. Democrats have a much smaller megaphone, and our message is getting drowned out.

Republicans dictate the terms of the conversation in American politics and have done so for much of the twenty-first century. Democrats aren't doing everything right, but we also must recognize that doing everything right is still insufficient. Until more Democrats figure this out, we will remain trapped in the doom loop. During every campaign cycle, our strategy is defense.

So, how do we build a bigger, better megaphone?

III. WHAT WE DO ABOUT IT

———

15

The High Stakes of the Battle against the Big Lie

Let's do a thought exercise. It's Election Night 2024. For the third election in a row, it all comes down to Wisconsin. This campaign is a rematch of 2020. President Biden is once again running against Donald Trump, who has somehow avoided prison for his sundry crimes.

If Democrats were still capable of feeling good about elections, we would be feeling pretty good on this night. President Biden has run a strong campaign. The economy is roaring. Unemployment is under 4 percent. Wages are up. Costs are down. The Biden Economic Plan has ushered in a new era of prosperity. Heck, some commentators are calling it "the new New Deal."[1] The Democratic Senate has even passed a voting rights bill that unwound the rash of voter suppression laws passed by Republicans in the wake of the 2020 election.[2]

The pandemic is in the rearview mirror. America's oft-delayed return to normalcy is in full swing. We are once again gathering indoors, going to concerts, and generally socializing without fear of contracting a potentially deadly disease. Masks are worn only on Halloween, during surgeries, and by hockey goalies. Sure, we have to get a

---

1 Creativity is not a prerequisite for being a political commentator.
2 In case you were wondering, in this scenario, after the one-billionth tweet from the public, Joe Manchin changed his mind about everything and adopted Bernie Sanders's agenda.

COVID-19 booster every six months, but Republicans and Democrats agree that this is a small price to pay. To use a term from political science, Americans are in a great fucking mood.

All Americans except Trump, that is. The campaign hasn't gone well for him. He refused to participate in any of the presidential debates because the Biden campaign wouldn't agree to any of his chosen moderators.[3] Trump's choice of podcaster Joe Rogan as vice-presidential candidate has not turned out to be the political masterstroke *Politico Playbook* believed. Many Americans are skeptical that the former host of *Fear Factor*, a man who made a living encouraging contestants to eat live cockroaches on television, should be a heartbeat away from the presidency. (In this hypothetical, Trump is still a famously unhealthy man with a penchant for McDonald's and Diet Cokes by the case.) And the Republican National Committee's decision to host the party's convention in authoritarian Budapest was not the messaging bonanza for which Trump hoped.

Biden is a clear favorite for reelection against the twice-impeached, two-time loser of the popular vote, but there are, of course, obstacles. The Electoral College dramatically favors the Republicans. Although Biden is widely expected to exceed his 2020 popular vote margin, the election will once again come down to a couple of states whose populations are just a little bit more MAGA than the rest of the nation. This is worrisome for so many reasons—not the least of which is the fact that the safeguards that prevented Trump from stealing the 2020 election are no longer in place. The Republicans now control the House and the Senate. Also, the brave election officials who were the bulwark against the Big Lie the last time around have all been purged. In their place now is a coterie of conspiracy-believing opportunists, not-so-well-hidden MAGA sleeper cells waiting for the signal to overturn the election.

---

3 Tucker Carlson, Sean Hannity, Diamond, Silk, Jeanine Pirro, Jim Jordan, or a hologram of Rush Limbaugh.

Election Nights have taken on a familiar, but painful rhythm. The redder, rural counties report first, and then Democrats wait with broken glass in our stomachs for the big cities and the mail ballots to come in. We listen to every word uttered by Steve Kornacki and read every tweet by a nerd named Nate, straining for threads of hope. Are there enough votes left to overcome Trump's lead? In 2016, there weren't. In 2020, there were. In 2024, there is real optimism that not only will Biden win, but he will win by a margin large enough to render the inevitable Big Lie 2.0 moot.

As we wait with an underlying dread for the votes to be counted—we are Democrats, after all—there is some evidence that 2024 will be the election we hoped for in 2016 and 2020, the electoral ass-whipping that Trump so richly deserves. Based on early returns, it appears the MAGA base has not turned out at anywhere near the level of the previous campaigns.

With most of the other battleground states decided, Wisconsin will be the one deciding the next president of the United States. As we wait and wait for the votes in the Democratic strongholds of Milwaukee and Madison to come in, CNN and MSNBC fill airtime with blabbering pundits and pointless interviews.

Democrats are either dismissive or blithely unaware of what is happening in the right-wing media ecosystem.

Seven in ten Republicans still believe Trump was the actual winner of the 2020 election, but that was an incredibly close election, conducted in the middle of a once-in-a-century pandemic. If Biden wins by more this time, the Big Lie will fall on deaf ears.

On CNN, just as Rick Santorum is confirming his status as America's dumbest pundit on one of those eight-person goat rodeos masquerading as roundtables, Wolf Blitzer interrupts him for a "KEY RACE UPDATE":[4]

---

4 These updates can mean anything from the election has been decided to Jake Tapper needs a bathroom break.

"With a new batch of votes from Milwaukee and Madison," Blitzer says, "Joe Biden has now taken a one-hundred-fifty-thousand-vote lead in the key state of Wisconsin, and CNN is prepared to declare that Joe Biden has been reelected president of the United States."

A bigger popular-vote win, larger margins in the battleground states—surely any effort to sow distrust in the integrity of the election, let alone *overturn* the election, will be a fool's errand. Republicans may not believe in science, but they have to believe in math, right?

Nope.

While we are all listening to the dulcet tones of David Axelrod on CNN or geeking out on Kornacki's knack for back-of-the-envelope math on MSNBC, over on Fox, a different conversation is happening. There, it is all conspiracy mongering and nonstop reporting about specious claims of imaginary voter fraud. The same folks who lied about 2020 are lying about 2024. Even though Mark and Sheryl repeatedly promised to do better, Facebook has once again been chock-full of disinformation about mail-in ballots and the integrity of the electoral process. There were stories about dead people who registered to vote, about boxes of mail-in ballots found outside a Smoothie King. Each of these unproven, out-of-context allegations has been shared thousands, if not millions, of times. Trump has echoed these false claims on the stump and in his Gettr posts.[5]

After the other networks call the election for Joe Biden, Fox refuses, based on the same trumped-up bullshit it has been peddling for months. And as Joe Biden is giving his victory speech in front of a raucous COVID-19-free crowd in Wilmington, Delaware, Trump calls into Fox, which is refusing to air Biden's speech.

"The Fake News is at it again," he says. "I won this election, and the Democrat mayors, the elites, and illegals are trying to steal it. It's

---

5 He is still banned from Twitter.

mail fraud and fake votes. We have to take our country back. The Big Lie is Sleepy Joe won. Many people are saying that Sleepy Joe's friends in China tapped the machines."

It makes no sense. This is the ranting of a sad, deranged man, but that hardly matters. People tune in, and Trump's MAGA base buys every word.

Using a smuggled phone, Steve Bannon starts a Facebook Live stream on Dan Bongino's page from the toilet of the federal penitentiary that has been his home for the previous eighteen months and will be for the next seven years:[6] "It's time for real Americans to stand up and take our country back," Bannon says. "Every Republican has a duty to stop the steal by any means necessary."

A meme with Trump's face superimposed over the famous "By Any Means Necessary" photo of Malcolm X begins to make the rounds on social media.

At first, Republican officials are dismissive of Trump's claims. They make promises to honor the election. In a sign of good faith, Mitch McConnell heads to the White House for a photo op with Biden.[7]

The blowhards on Fox go bananas. Tucker Carlson calls on his viewers to protest the Vichy Republicans unwilling to fight. Protestors show up at GOP offices. A new poll by Crooked Media—by 2024, Crooked is the premier polling unit in American media[8]—shows that eight in ten Republicans believe the election was stolen.

Not long after, Rudy Giuliani is called to testify before the hastily convened Special Congressional Committee on Voter Fraud. The former New York City mayor, arriving with crates of affidavits from

---

6 Don Jr. is in the cell next to his, but he couldn't remember the passcode to his phone.
7 Also in attendance is Deputy Chief of Staff Liz Cheney, who had lost her primary 90–10 two years prior.
8 Hey, it's my thought exercise. I can do what I want.

supposed "witnesses" who claim voter fraud, spins an incredible and not-so-sober tale of foreign election interference that has all the logical consistency of QAnon. One by one, the Republican leaders announce that they will not vote to certify the election.

The Republican governor of Wisconsin announces that his own hastily formed commission, this one helmed by former Trump aide Stephen Miller, has found sufficient evidence of foul play. Therefore, he will not certify the election. Instead, the Wisconsin state legislature will send a slate of electors who intend to cast their votes for Trump. Michigan and Pennsylvania quickly follow suit, denying Biden the requisite 270 electoral votes. Despite no real evidence of malfeasance and a larger margin of victory, another Big Lie takes hold—this time, faster and with more force.

America faces its greatest political crisis in history. The person who won the popular vote and the Electoral College will be denied the presidency.

This is what we are facing. The clock is ticking. The consequences are real. The threats are growing.

I will be deadly honest with you: I don't have all the answers. There are no easy solutions, and addressing the disinformation will take time we don't have. But just because we as a society can't solve the whole problem, it doesn't mean we can't do better, fight harder, and think smarter. If we don't, we are doomed. With that in mind, I have put together a series of ideas about what to do—a plan for Democrats, the media, and every one of us to take up arms in the battle against the Big Lie.

16

Get on a War Footing and Win Hearts and Minds

A week or so after Barack Obama's 2008 victory, a few of us were hanging around the now-empty, no-longer-bustling campaign head-quarters. During the previous year, I spent fifteen hours a day in this place. It was brimming with people and excitement. Now it was quiet—like when ESPN goes live in a deserted football stadium long after a victory in a big game. The remnants of the Election Night cele-brations were strewn across people's desks. Empty champagne bottles filled the wastebins. Copies of the *Chicago Tribune* announcing the news of Obama's win were on every desk.

The ostensible purpose of the gathering was to discuss what should happen to Obama's political apparatus now that the campaign was over and he was headed to the White House—what to do with the massive email list, how to keep our volunteer army engaged, and where various aides should go to work within the party apparatus we now controlled. Just because one campaign had ended, it didn't mean we shouldn't start thinking about the next one.

At one point, the conversation turned to our communications and digital success in that campaign. Now, we were admittedly a little high on our supply at this moment, but the 2008 Obama campaign did change the game with innovative internet strategies and new ways of communicating with voters. We were proud of what we had done and were batting around how to bring that same approach to the staid and outdated White House communications operation.[1] One of the hallmarks of our campaign was using the (now-rudimentary) tools of the period to communicate directly with our supporters.

Obama had announced his intention to explore a run for president in a video posted on the campaign website, not in a media interview. The announcement of his selection of Joe Biden as vice president was sent out in a text message to supporters, not in a press release. When the national political press was writing us off because they couldn't fathom the notion of someone not named Clinton winning the Democratic nomination, David Plouffe, the campaign manager, began sending videos and memos to our supporters via email to explain why Obama was going to win.[2] At one point in the campaign, we commissioned a short-form documentary[3] about John McCain's involvement in the Keating Five scandal. The press wouldn't cover the story, so we did. The Obama operation had the email list and Facebook presence to reach millions of people directly without having to go through the filter of the traditional media.

Could we do the same thing in the White House? And how would it look?

It was at this point that I made a suggestion that brought the meeting to a screeching halt: "What if we created our own newscast?"

Everyone laughed.

I laughed, too, albeit a bit awkwardly. "I'm kidding, but not really. Think about it. Just a weekly or even nightly take on what Barack— umm, I mean the president-elect—is doing for our people.[4] They are

---

1 Some would say (correctly) too proud.
2 Plouffe was right; the pundits were wrong.
3 We were Quibi (more successfully) before Quibi.
4 It took a lot of us some real time to switch from calling him "Barack." Even the president-elect still answered his phone "Hey, it's Barack" before he remembered he was now the most powerful person in the world.

used to hearing directly from us, especially when the press is kicking our ass."

A few folks were intrigued. On one level, it made a lot of sense. It was an extension of what had worked so well in the campaign. Was it that different from the Plouffe videos? Why wouldn't we press our advantage? Why would we cede the narrative to a press corps who didn't believe in Obama in the first place?[5] In our mind, very few people who wrote and talked about politics for a living "got" Obama or what his movement was all about. There was some real appeal to having a regular, direct communications channel with our voters.

The flirtation with the idea of our own newscast was brief. A wiser, more Washington-savvy meeting attendee shot it down. "The press would go fucking bananas. They will call it propaganda, and they will be right. Starting off the presidency with a pissing match with the press is a very bad idea." Others quickly joined in the condemnation.

I retreated, playing it off as if my idea had been offered in jest.

The folks who shot me down were correct to do so. The press *would* have gone bananas. Somewhat notoriously, Bill Clinton's presidency got off on the wrong foot because his administration picked a dumb and pointless fight with the press on his first day in office. The Clinton staff closed a door that prevented the White House Press Corps from wandering up to the suite of offices known as "Upper Press," where the White House press secretary works. This offense was seen (absurdly) as an assault on their First Amendment rights. The White House press responded the only way they knew how and wrote a ton of shitty stories about the new administration. That was a headache Obama didn't need as he was entering office with the worst economy since the height of the Great Depression.

---

5 It seems insane now, but much of the political press was patronizingly dismissive of Obama's chances in 2008. Check the tapes.

My idea for a partisan "newscast" may have been misguided, but my reasoning wasn't. I believed then, and I believe even more now, that political communications is not public relations. It's not press management. It's information warfare. And if you want to win a war, you need to be on a war footing. Republicans understand this. Too many Democrats don't.

I wanted a direct channel to our supporters because President George W. Bush had one with Fox News when he was in the White House. I am not sure Bush would have won reelection without Fox News propagandizing his failed war in Iraq. Rupert Murdoch and Roger Ailes used their network to bludgeon anyone and everyone who dared point out the folly of invading the wrong country as a response to 9/11.[6] After what we went through in the campaign, dealing with Fox, the birthers, and Sarah Palin's conspiracy theories, I knew Obama would be fighting with one hand tied behind his back as he tried to clean up the giant mess left by his predecessor.

The other side was preparing to wage war on the first Black president, and we were unwilling to fight fire with fire.

Approaching communications from a war footing is more than adopting the apocalyptic rhetoric of the Right or the military cosplay of folks like the Republican members of Congress who brandish assault rifles in their Christmas card photos. Adopting a war footing means understanding not only that the rules of the game have changed, but that there are no rules. We need to be more aggressive in our strategies and tactics. We don't have to fight as dirty as the Right, but we must fight as hard.

Democrats—me included—are so afraid of being called propagandists that we are unwilling to tell our story on our terms. A major

---

6 Ailes even sent a political strategy memo to Bush adviser Karl Rove after the September 11 attacks.

part of every war is the battle for hearts and minds. This is why Demo-crats must be willing to adopt strategies we previously avoided out of fear of being called propaganda promoters.

Is There Such a Thing as Good Propaganda?

As a wise coworker pointed out many years ago, people have a real knee-jerk reaction to the word *propaganda*, and there is a good reason for that.

The first and most common use of propaganda is by authoritarian states. Historically, propaganda is associated with Nazism and with the Soviet Union. A classic example is *Pravda*, the Soviet newspaper largely controlled by the government. This paper kept up a steady stream of pro-Soviet, anti-American messaging during the Cold War. In an extreme instance, North Korea touts a village near the Demili-tarized Zone to illustrate the prosperity and generosity of the govern-ment. According to the state, this village is a socialist utopia with child care, public schooling, and a collective farm. *See? North Korea isn't so bad.* Except, the village is reportedly fake. It is a literal Potemkin vil-lage. No one lives there. It exists only to disinform.

Resistance to this sort of propaganda is a point of pride in liberal democracies like the United States, where the constitutionally pro-tected free press is supposed to be a bulwark against state-sponsored information campaigns. Propaganda is commonly misunderstood as inherently un-American. It's also a safe rule in life to avoid any and all things associated with Adolf Hitler, Joseph Stalin, or Kim Jong-un.

The second and more recent use of the term *propaganda* is very specific to Trump. The term has been thrown around by people like me to describe Fox News and the pro-Trump, reality-bending hagi-ography of most of the conservative media in recent years. We used the term because we knew it would get attention, spark a backlash from the traditional press against Fox et al., and allude to the obvious authoritarian leanings of the new regime. The new president was undertaking an unprecedented and particularly unsubtle approach to messaging, one that needed to be called out. The people who lied for Trump—whether they were Fox hosts, his numerous White House press secretaries, MAGA media grifters, or Republican members of Congress[7]—were called propagandists. I am (very) hesitant to dig through my Twitter feed from 2017 to 2020, but I am sure I called these people out on multiple occasions.[8]

Unlike his authoritarian idols, President Trump did not control Fox in the way Stalin controlled *Pravda*. In fact, the Fox-Trump relationship was a Möbius strip. It was impossible to know who was influencing whom. Fox, along with its audience, was relentlessly pro-Trump, and Trump was equally relentless in his desire for the approbation of the network, its personalities, and its audience. "Disinformation" or Trump's favorite "fake news" is probably a more accurate way to describe what is happening. I eventually landed on "state-adjacent propaganda." Alas, the main problem with Fox is not the propaganda, but the racist disinformation designed to deceive and divide the country to keep power in the hands of extremely wealthy people like the Murdoch family, the Trumps, and all the faux populists who dominate the network and the rest of right-wing media.

The Kim Jong-un/Rupert Murdoch brand of propaganda is what causes Democrats to blanch. *Why in God's name would we want to be associated with such people and their despicable tactics?* That's a narrow view. Propaganda is simply messaging designed to persuade. The "Keep Calm and Carry On" posters employed by the British during World War II were propaganda. Propaganda includes the Rosie

---

7 And basically, all of them *did* lie.
8 Frankly, I should just delete that shit. My typo-ridden tweets are not exactly records that need to be preserved for history.

the Riveter character used to encourage American women to enter the workforce during the same period. The famous "HOPE" poster encouraging people to join Obama's grassroots movement was propaganda. Heck, every episode of *Pod Save America* is a form of propaganda. As is every campaign ad, tweet, and press release.

Ultimately, propaganda is just content designed to persuade.

Why are Democrats afraid to wholeheartedly embrace any and every strategy to persuade people? If the reason is that we are too sensitive to criticism from Republicans and the media, then we are ill-suited for twenty-first-century politics.

Not Fox Lite

Ultimately, I am arguing for Democrats to employ a more aggressive and direct form of communication with our voters. *Our* story, on *our* terms, told through *our* channels—everything from using the progressive media, to distributing content created by campaigns and politicians, and to doing more advertising.

Here's what I am *not* arguing for: doing what the Right does. I don't want Democrats to adopt disinformation, division, or diversion as a political strategy. I don't want Democrats to lie, declare war on the media,[9] or flood Facebook with false memes. Democrats don't need grievance politics or our own versions of Tucker Carlson[10] and Ben Shapiro.[11] Those strategies and people are gross and immoral. Our side can and should be better than that.

But even if we put the "When they go low, we go high" idealism aside, simply adopting the Republican playbook wouldn't work for three reasons:

---

9 Well, maybe some media.
10 The archetype of the preppy faux populist.
11 An "actual size shown" internet troll.

First, Democratic voters maintain a very diverse media diet, one heavily indexed on the traditional media reporting facts. You can't create an alternative reality for your voters to live in if they keep visiting actual reality. This is one of the few contexts in the age of disinformation where facts may still matter.

Second, Democrats cannot win the Electoral College, the Senate, or the gerrymandered House on the strength of our base alone. Republicans can. Therefore, we need different political strategies and different messaging operations to reach our electoral coalition. Democrats need independents, who, by definition, would live outside any information bubble we created. We also need people who pay less attention to politics than the average Fox News viewer or *Pod Save America* listener—once again, a cohort of voters that is hard to reach through purely ideological media, people who would never seek out this media and who would be repelled by it if they found it organically.

Third and finally, anger and fear are excellent motivators for partisans. They drive people to the polls and turns voters into volunteers and volunteers into donors. Anger and fear are the currency of the right-wing media. Turn on Fox News or open Facebook at any time of any day, and you will find it chock-full of ranting, raving, and fearmongering. But fear and anger are not effective strategies for engaging the less-than-politically engaged. In fact, the anger and fighting are often a reason these people aren't interested in politics.

This is about more than taste or morality. The Republican playbook won't work not just because our target voters are less likely to ingest the BS without question. For reasons of pure efficacy, progressive messaging must look different from the conservative tripe clogging the airwaves and social media feeds. We need to be better. There is simply no other option.

What "Better" Looks Like

In addition to being less tacky and not racist, what makes progressive propaganda different from the Right's methods? In our efforts to win hearts and minds, Democrats should apply a two-part test:

First, what we say must be true, and not just kind of true or mostly true. It must be damn true, with the facts flyspecked within an inch of their lives. This is not about morality or nobility—although we should aspire to be both noble and moral.[12] It is a question of efficacy. Our goal is to persuade, not deceive, and persuasion requires trust. Politicians suffer from a trust deficit. The American people have a well-worn cynicism when it comes to politics. They assume that all politicians lie for a living. And as I've just articulated, Democrats have a political imperative to reach out to the people most cynical about politics and most distrustful of politicians. If we lie, we lose.

The second part of the test is transparency. This is where my ill-fated newscast idea ran into trouble. Progressive propaganda needs to be clearly labeled as such, with none of the "fair and balanced" bullshit that has made Fox so dangerous. It's tempting merely to find a billionaire to buy up a bunch of local television stations and run a similar play as Sinclair News. And it might even work in the short term, but it would be devastating to the Democratic coalition in the long term. Democrats have to prove to voters that we are better than Republicans. If we are seen as equally disingenuous but with a better policy agenda, we will fail. Transparency is our friend. That means wearing our biases on our sleeves. I like to think that *Pod Save America* is fair, but we sure as hell aren't balanced, at least not when it comes to Republicans. We are open about our goal of stopping Trumpism in its

---

12 Nobility and morality should be reason enough, but this is politics, not *Downton Abbey*.

tracks. This kind of transparency builds trust. Given that Republicans generally run on an agenda of stopping things from happening and that Democrats run on an agenda of doing things, trust matters more to us than it does to them.

The Press Problem

Think of our message as our product and of the voters as our customers. Our success as a political party depends on getting our product to those customers in the best condition possible. But unlike Amazon or Papa John's, we can't deliver the product. We rely on someone else to provide distribution. In this very tortured, overly long business analogy, that distribution comes from the mainstream media. The problem for Democrats is that while the media are not a direct competitor like Republicans, they have no incentive to deliver said product in good condition. Instead, it is in their interest to alter that product in certain ways that benefit them. Imagine if a cookie company used an anchovy distributor to deliver its cookies, but the anchovy folks put anchovies on all the cookies before giving them to the customer because adding anchovies was good for *their* business. The media have no interest in delivering Democratic messaging to voters the way we want it heard. As is their right, they put that messaging through their own filter, optimizing what is good for their business and brand. And often, if not always, what is good for the media is the exact opposite of what is good for Democrats.

Take the example of Joe Biden's efforts to pass historic jobs and family legislation in 2021. As with any legislative process (particularly one involving Democrats), it was a protracted mess. Centrist Democrats like Senators Kyrsten Sinema and Joe Manchin held things up and took an ax to some of the most popular and necessary provisions.

Representatives from California, New York, and New Jersey banded together to demand a tax break for wealthy homeowners that undermined the message of the bill. But despite the best efforts of these troublemakers, Biden's agenda remained quite popular. According to multiple polls, majorities of Americans—including a decent number of working-class Trump supporters—supported the provisions of the bill. But those polls also showed that most people didn't have the faintest clue what was in the bill. Even the most politically engaged Democrats would fail a pop quiz about the Biden legislative agenda. These are folks in the ninety-fifth percentile of news consumers. They watch *Rachel Maddow*, read the *New York Times*, and make breakfast while listening to *The Daily*.[13] And they still don't know what the Democratic Party desperately wants them to know.

Politicians often complain that the media doesn't cover their agenda and actions, that too many of their efforts are like the tree falling in the proverbial woods. This was not one of those times. There was no shortage of coverage on the efforts to pass the bill. Every twist and turn of the legislation received intense scrutiny. But the coverage focused on everything but the bill's substance. It was about personalities and process, conflict and congressional wrangling. There was little focus on how the various provisions would impact people's lives. This is not because the media is dumb, lazy, or mean. It's not because they hate Democrats. Reporters reading this will point to the few stories that exhaustively detailed the impact of certain provisions, but such stories are the exception rather than the rule. They were few and far between, and more important, they received little promotion or attention because those types of stories don't drive traffic and subscriptions.

---

13 Don't blame me. One hundred percent of *Pod Save America* listeners would pass that quiz. Blame *The Daily*'s Michael Barbaro. His soothing voice puts people to sleep.

For reasons discussed earlier, it was also very important to the media that they not be seen as too favorable to Biden and the Democrats. The coup de grace was, on the day the House of Representatives was about to finally pass Biden's plan, the *New York Times* app featured the headline "Pelosi Predicts Thursday Vote on Biden's Ambitious Social Policy Bill."

Honestly, WTF does that mean? You could conduct a decade of market research and not come up with a less appealing, less informative headline for a transformative piece of legislation than "ambitious social policy bill." It's certainly not obvious from this headline that the bill included the largest and most important investment to arrest climate change in history. Nor did it tell anyone that the House was passing a bill to provide universal pre-K and subsidized child care for millions of Americans. Or that insulin prices would now be capped at thirty-five dollars a month.

The *New York Times* had no incentive to use Biden's branding or to describe favorably what was in the bills. They put anchovies on the cookie because they are in the anchovy business.

The Republicans do not have this problem. They do not rely on the mainstream press to deliver their message. They have a wholly owned means of distribution. As Alex Pareene aptly described it in *The New Republic*:

> Conservatives, on the other hand, simply tell their supporters whatever message they wish to convey through their expansive and organized propaganda networks. It is important to note that the official Republican Party does not lead this process. In fact, the party at this point is led by the propaganda network (parts of which are in turn captured by their increasingly rabid audiences). Conservatives can argue about whether this development has been "good" for those in the party actually

interested in conservative policy goals. But no one can really deny the political success of the operation. It has kept the GOP relevant—and kept conservatives solidly in control of the party—even when actual conservative governance has regularly led to catastrophe, scandal, and failure.

This is why we are losing the messaging wars. Republicans have a way to communicate with their voters on their terms, and we don't.

I don't make this recommendation lightly. There is something fundamentally uncomfortable about an argument that can be shorthanded into "Former Obama Aide Calls for Dems to Build Propaganda Machine." I can already hear the ensuing caterwauling as I write this.

"Democrats Declare War on the Media"

"Democrats Adopt the Tactics of Trump"

"Progressive Propaganda Portends End of American Democracy"

And I get it. I really do. I wish we could go back in time and return to a world where the traditional media had the credibility and the reach to call balls and strikes. And maybe I am helping to speed our descent down the slippery slope, but the true threat to liberal democracy is not progressive propaganda. It's the people fighting for democracy surrendering to an authoritarian movement because we were too cowardly to fight back.

It's really that simple.

17

A Modern Model of Journalism

It would be easy to read this book and believe that I hate journalism and journalists, that I am rooting for their failure so as to usher in a new era of progressive advocacy journalism. I am sure people see my views as self-interested politically and financially. I am, after all, a cohost of a progressive podcast and the author of a progressive newsletter,[1] not to mention this book. This is all true and fair, but I want to set the record straight.

Contrary to my tweets and, at times, scathing criticism, I don't want journalism to go away. I don't want anyone to lose their job. I don't hate traditional journalism or journalists.[2] In fact, I think the decline in the credibility and viability of the press is directly related to our democracy being on life support. I don't want to replace the traditional media. I simply want a progressive echo chamber to balance out the right-wing version that is destroying our country and the planet.

My fear is that a combination of technological changes and anachronistic thinking will destroy what remains of the traditional media. If that happens, an important guardrail will have been removed, and the financially and politically powerful will be able to operate without fear of accountability.

---

1 I think this is where I am supposed to ask you to subscribe to *The Message Box*.
2 Okay, there are few journalists I do hate.

I believe that, absent significant change, the role of the media will continue to deteriorate. Before too long, there will be no fourth estate, no one to hold the powerful accountable. All media will be what Politico once described itself as: "ESPN for politics."

Don't get me wrong, the *New York Times*, *Wall Street Journal*, and *Washington Post* will still exist. CNN will continue to appear on cable and have a well-trafficked website. These media titans will probably even thrive financially as the industry consolidates and they get better at monetizing their audience. But their influence and audience will diminish. The media will become nothing more than narrators or play-by-play commentators. This would be a huge loss for the country. Our politics would worsen. The public would be less informed. And our democracy would be hanging on by a thread.

After January 6 and the Republican Party's embrace of Trumpism, election conspiracy theories, and brazen antidemocratic rhetoric, there is a growing sense that the media is enabling this dangerous behavior by adhering to an outdated model of journalism. Some outlets have adjusted their coverage, but most haven't. By favoring balance over accuracy to avoid any perception of bias, the media is inadvertently minimizing deeply dangerous behavior. It is normalizing something very abnormal. It is fiddling while Rome burns. Given that dozens of reporters were also put at risk by the assault on the Capitol, their nonchalance is bizarre. A free and fair media depends on a healthy democracy, but it seems that the desire for perceived objectivity trumps[3] self-preservation.

Little Reach, Less Credibility

By repeatedly lying and rejecting norms, Trump already demonstrated the impotence of traditional media accountability. Take the example

---

3 I am going to beat this pun into the ground.

of his tax returns. For decades, presidents and presidential candidates released their tax returns to the public. There is no law or regulation that requires such transparency. Most candidates don't want to do it: it's a pain in the ass logistically, and it usually leads to a raft of bad coverage about their income, investments, and charitable contributions (or lack thereof). Some politicians genuinely believe in transparency and happily release their tax returns, but most would prefer to do anything other than voluntarily submit to a financial colonoscopy for the voters.

Until Trump, every major candidate in the moden era released their tax returns because they feared the political consequences of not doing so. Reporters, columnists, and editorial boards across the media spectrum are united on very little besides the importance of transparency.[4] Failure to release tax returns would result in a spate of brutal press coverage that would drown out the politician's message and convince voters the politician was hiding something nefarious.

In 2012, Mitt Romney initially resisted releasing his tax returns. The former private equity executive made a lot of money and went to great lengths to avoid paying taxes on that wealth. Understandably, Romney was concerned that the public would not appreciate the fact that he had stashed a bunch of his money in a Swiss bank account while promising to cut taxes for the wealthy and raise them on working-class people.[5] But Romney's initial refusal to release his tax returns led to such brutal press coverage that he ultimately decided to give in. Admitting to having a Swiss bank account was less politically painful than getting beaten by the media.

In 2016, Trump did what Romney couldn't. He refused to release

---

4 Notably, they do not believe that transparency applies to *their* decision making, but more on that later.

5 The same working-class people Romney laid off when his vulturous hedge fund bought companies and mined them for parts.

his tax returns, concocting an absurd story about a mysterious audit preventing their release. The media made an issue of it for a while. The Clinton campaign tried to fan the flames, but our collective attention span was too short. Before too long, the focus moved on to other Trumpian outrages and disproportionate coverage of Hillary Clinton's email protocols. It wasn't just attention deficit disorder. The feeding frenzy was halfhearted because the media assumed Trump was going to lose. But Trump didn't lose, and he didn't pay the political price Romney did for his failure to release his tax returns. Once in office, Trump continued to thumb his nose at the media and the Democratic desire for his returns. When House Democrats issued a subpoena for his taxes, Trump thumbed his nose at them, too. There were bad articles and bad editorials about Trump's lack of transparency. There was plenty of harrumphing on cable and Twitter about the shattering of norms, but it didn't matter. Trump did not feel an ounce of political pressure. Yes, Trump is/was protected by the right-wing media. Yes, he is a moron who has only a passing relationship with what is in his best interests. Yes, he is self-destructive, which suggests his subconscious hates him as much as the rest of us. But that doesn't mean he is immune to political pressure.

And just to drive the point home, the *New York Times* eventually got ahold of Trump's tax returns and published a blockbuster story about his malfeasance, crooked accounting, and potential criminal liability. And…nothing happened. No one really cared that much. Sure, some liberal blue checkmarks on Twitter tweeted about it. Rachel Maddow made it the focus of her show. *Pod Save America* had a field day. But nothing really changed. It was a blip. Nothing more. This story exemplifies the waning media influence. A Pulitzer-worthy scoop about a sitting president in the paper of record failed to drive coverage.

For huge swaths of the electorate, the fact that the *New York*

Times reported the story was all they needed to know in order to disavow it. Trump and the right-wing media had worked so hard to discredit the *Times*, CNN, and the rest of liberal media that nothing they reported could be taken seriously.

In a 2017 study, the American Press Institute ran a series of experiments in which they showed the participants articles shared by people they trusted and others shared by people they distrusted. Some of the articles were from credible nonpartisan media outlets like the Associated Press. Others were completely made up and filled with factual errors. The findings were proof positive that the Republicans had won the war on the press:

> The sharer tends to have a greater significance on attitudes than the news organization that reported the article in the first place. The reporting source still matters, according to the experiment, just not as much as who shared the article. For instance, when the story is passed on by a trusted figure and the article is attributed to the AP, 52 percent of people think the article got the facts right. When the article is still attributed to the AP but the person passing it on is less trusted, only 32 percent say the facts were right.

Think about it this way. With one tweet or Facebook post, a right-wing media grifter like Dan Bongino or one of Trump's corrupt, dumb children can shred the credibility that a news organization spent decades building. With one push of the Share button, despite all the previous Pulitzers won and blockbuster stories written, a news organization's authority evaporated. To be clear, this phenomenon does not exist only on the right.

There's no question that Trump was good for the media financially. He was a one-man stimulus package for the once-struggling industry. Ratings and Web traffic went up, and subscriptions exploded at the national newspapers. Media executives could hardly hide their glee at the Trump-driven spike in revenue. Les Moonves, the president of CBS, was even quoted in 2016 saying of Trump's campaign, "It may not be good for America, but it's damn good for CBS." Trump hated the traditional press, but he was also their best friend. The relationship was not lost on the public.

Trump's candidacy may have made the media barons richer, but it was a Pyrrhic victory to say the least.

Losing the Left

While progressives continue to consume traditional media and financially prop up the industry, there is growing skepticism and downright anger toward the media. It has always been the Republican playbook to beat up the media. During a Republican primary, attacks on the press are nearly as frequent as those on Democrats. The media is a convenient foil for Republican candidates trying to demonstrate their conservative bona fides. For the first time in my political career, attacking the press is good politics for Democrats.

During the 2020 Democratic presidential primary, Bernie Sanders repeatedly attacked the "corporate and billionaire-owned media" and even went so far as to attribute negative coverage about his campaign to his anticorporate and antibillionaire rhetoric. During a 2019 rally in New Hampshire, Sanders said, "I talk about [Amazon's taxes] all of the time. . . . And then I wonder why the *Washington Post*, which is owned by Jeff Bezos, who owns Amazon, doesn't write particularly good articles about me. I don't know why."

The media went insane over this attack. Editorials were written. Cable hosts delivered monologues lamenting Sanders's remarks. But Democratic voters cheered. And if they didn't cheer, they certainly didn't complain. Sanders is 100 percent correct about the corporate media problem. That major media outlets are increasingly owned by the world's largest corporations and wealthiest individuals creates a conflict of interest and an inability or unwillingness to hold the wealthy accountable. Truthfully, there is no evidence that Bezos's ownership of the *Washington Post* played a role in their coverage decisions. Accuracy aside, the fact that a Democratic candidate was now energizing his supporters by attacking the press was notable, especially after four years of Democrats reflexively defending the media out of opposition to Trump.

Sanders's attack didn't come out of nowhere. Democratic anger toward the political press has been growing for years. The 2016 election was the precipitating event. Democratic activists are still furious about how the election was covered. It began with CNN and other media outlets becoming addicted to the boost in ratings Trump brought. The Sunday shows were so desperate to have Trump on that they let him call in by phone, something rarely offered to any other guest, including sitting presidents. It's hard to think of worse television than watching a still photo of a caller for minutes on end, but the shows were willing to do it just to taste some of that Trump ratings magic.

The reaction to the absurd abundance of Trump coverage was not just whining from Democrats. Trump's opponents in the Republican primary repeatedly complained about the way the press, including Fox, covered Trump.[6]

It wasn't just the slobbering over Trump. Many Democrats are still livid over how Hillary Clinton was covered in that campaign. There was an inherent and particularly unsubtle misogyny in the coverage of

---

6 These Republicans were correct about the coverage, but that doesn't change the fact that they ran some of the worst campaigns in political history. That some of these people still work in politics is stunning.

the first woman to lead a major-party ticket. Qualities that would be celebrated in a man were derided in Clinton: her laugh, her voice, her appearance, her clothes. And with the media's absurdly disproportionate coverage of Hillary Clinton's decision to use a private email server, Democrats correctly believed that in treating a relatively minor issue as a major scandal, the media helped elect Donald Trump.

The anger grew throughout the Trump years and exploded during the 2020 Democratic primary, when a historically diverse field was covered through the prism of racist and misogynistic tropes. Supporters of Elizabeth Warren and Kamala Harris were rightfully livid about how their candidates were covered. Moments after Warren announced her candidacy to great fanfare in front of an enthusiastic crowd, Politico[7] posted an article with the headline "Warren Battles the Ghosts of Hillary." The article outlined sexist trope after sexist trope and questioned whether Warren was likable enough to be elected president.

"Electability" discussions dominated the primary because defeating Trump was the top priority for Democrats. This was a fair topic for discussion, but the undertones of all the electability coverage was that only a white man could beat Trump, an unproven assertion that disadvantaged Harris, Warren, Amy Klobuchar, Cory Booker, Julian Castro, and others.

In 2020, the advocacy organization Times Up conducted a study of Harris's press coverage after she was named to the ticket as the vice-presidential nominee. According to its report, a quarter of her coverage included racist and sexist stereotyping and tropes.

The anger has turned to rage since the 2020 election.

But don't take my admittedly biased word for it. Andrew Taylor has covered Congress for decades. He was one of the most respected journalists ever to walk the halls of the Capitol. When I worked on

---

7 When looking for an example of really shitty press coverage, simply google "Politico."

the Hill, Taylor was the singular voice to trust on budget issues. He could spot an accounting gimmick from a million miles away, and he understood the appropriations process better than 99 percent of staffers and 100 percent of senators. He was also in the Capitol on January 6, 2020. What he saw that day, and how people responded to it, changed his life. Not long after, Taylor left journalism and did an interview with Margaret Sullivan of the *Washington Post* laying out his reasons for quitting: "The rules of objective journalism require you to present facts to tell a true story, but the objective-journalism version of events can often obscure the reality of what's really going on." He explained to Sullivan that, as he sees it, "The typical practices of putting everything that happens in the context of normal behavior, of giving 'both sides' an almost equal say and of describing events in a neutral tone have an overall damaging effect. Put simply: 'It sanitizes things.'"

If the old model doesn't work, what would a new one look like?

A Modern Model of Advocacy Journalism

Reporters hate it when nonreporters offer thoughts on the media. There is a tendency to circle the wagons and dismiss the criticism as self-interested griping from people who don't know how things work. I get it. Political operatives hate second-guessing and nitpicking from pundits and media types who have never worked on a campaign or in the White House. No one who hasn't walked in your shoes or done your job can truly understand how hard it is. But sometimes an outside perspective can be helpful. I spent years working on the other side trying to get the press to do what I wanted—to ask the questions and cover the stories that benefited my candidate. I read everything they wrote and watched every broadcast to learn as much as I could, because that was my job. I spun, pitched, and dished for years. I like to think that I know what works and what doesn't and which loopholes to exploit for maximal political benefit.

Anyone who fears for our democracy has a stake in the media. And I am very, very worried about our democracy. So, now I am operating much like the spy who came in from the cold, as a double agent. The enemy of my enemy is now my friend.

I hope my friends (and less-than-friends) in the media[8] will see these suggestions for a modern model of journalism as the good-faith offerings of someone who has spent twenty years working with the press:[9]

- **Recalibrate Objectivity.** The most important change the media can make is to recognize that accuracy and balance are two irreconcilable values. If the goal is to appear balanced or objective, a media outlet will ultimately fail consumers. The foundation of traditional journalism is the idea that objectivity is equivalent to credibility. The entire model assumes that consumers want an unbiased rendering of current events. And anything that could cause someone to question this is an existential threat to the entire enterprise. This is why the *New York Times* and others go out of their way not to use the words *lie* and *racist* to describe racist liars. It's why the *Washington Post* reportedly wouldn't allow a reporter who survived sexual assault to cover any story involving #Metoo or sexual misconduct.[10] It's why so many reporters default to the "he said, she said" formulation, even on settled certainties like climate change. For a media outlet to pick a side in a debate, even when the facts are clearly on one side, causes some

---

8 If you work at Fox, you are my enemy. Sorry, but that's your choice.
9 And if they don't, I would point out that I am subscriber, viewer, and consumer, and the customer is always right or at least should be listened to.
10 Think about that one for a second.

readers to question that outlet's prized objectivity. But there are two problems with the objectivity model of journalism.

First, the idea that any person or publication could be completely objective is absurd. Every reporter, editor, and producer brings their own personal experiences and values to every story. Media outlets have their cultural mores and beliefs, which inform every decision about which stories to cover and how to cover them. Business decisions about what drives traffic, produces subscriptions, and brings in new audiences will always be a major influence on news decisions. Up until the inevitable moment when all reporters are replaced by AI-powered algorithms—the future that Zuck wants—all journalism will be subjective.

Second, no one buys the idea of "media objectivity" anymore. You can see this in the precipitous decline in the public's trust in media. And it's not just Republicans. Democrats are growing more skeptical of traditional media. By clinging to an idea of objectivity that is patently untrue and that no one believes, media outlets are rapidly eroding what remains of their credibility.

■ **An Advocacy Model.** It's worth noting that in the long history of the press, the last few decades of "objective" journalism are the exception, not the rule. Prior to the post–World War II period, many media outlets had very specific ideological agendas. Some pushed for specific parties or policies. Newspapers were weapons wielded by their wealthy owners—just as Fox News's Murdoch family uses the platform to promote their conservative agenda.[11] I believe the future of journalism looks more like this distant past. If objectivity as a concept is dead, then the only option is to reembrace the advocacy model. I am not arguing that the *New York Times* and the *Washington Post* become organs for

---

11 "Conservative" is doing a lot of work in this sentence.

the Democratic Party. While that would certainly be helpful in the near-term battle against an antidemocratic GOP, it would be bad for the country in the long run. But media outlets should be willing to aggressively and transparently advocate for certain values like democracy, truth, stopping the destruction of the planet, civil rights, and equality. An embrace of these values would be a return to the days of muckrakers like Upton Sinclair and Ida Tarbell and a departure from the current ethos of covering politics like sports.

At times, pushing for these values would cause the media to side with one party over the other. Most of the time, but not always, that party will be the Democratic Party. Adopting this model would require media outlets to choose accuracy over balance; to stop treating climate change as a subject for debate or Republican efforts to overturn elections as "normal" politics; to call a lie a lie and be explicit about racist appeals and white-supremacist ideology. This shouldn't be a dramatic shift. Many media outlets are already fierce advocates for press access to politicians. Hence, the numerous articles about how few press conferences presidents have done. These articles are the press using the only weapon they have to push for something they believe in. It would be great if they used that weapon for something of more consequence than greater access for employees of Comcast, the Walt Disney Corporation, and Amazon, though.[12]

■ **Build Immunity to the Big Lies.** Better, more impactful journalism begins with accepting the new reality about the role of the media and what it's covering. The old days are gone. The golden era of accountability journalism is over. There will be no

---

12 Was this overly harsh? Maybe. Was it a little unfair? Perhaps. Is corporate media a real problem? Definitely.

more Watergates or Bob Woodwards. Never again will there be a Walter Cronkite or an Edward R. Murrow to calm the nation. None of this is news[13] to the media. Every reporter is aware of this fact, but the problem is that executives have not adjusted their tools to reflect their new limited influence. Even though it's been years since the old tools had any impact, much of the media continues to rely on them.

Take the example of fact-checking. In recent years, media outlets have dedicated more and more resources to fact-checking politicians. The *Washington Post* has its Fact Checker column. CNN hired former *Toronto Star* reporter Daniel Dale to perform rapid-response fact-checks on Trump. For a while, fact-checking was an effective tool. If the fact-checkers called out a politician for putting too much spin on the ball, the politician usually stopped repeating the offending line. If the goal was accountability, public shaming was the mechanism. Barack Obama took fact-checking very seriously. He never wanted one inaccurate line to ruin the impact of a speech. Referring to the *Washington Post*'s fact-checking metric, Obama told his policy staff and crack research team to adopt a "no Pinocchios" approach to every speech.

Shame worked on Democrats more than Republicans. In 2010, PolitiFact deemed the Republican message stating that the Affordable Care Act was a "government takeover of health care" to be its "Lie of the Year." As far as I can tell, not a single Republican stopped repeating the takeover message. But when actual implementation of the ACA undermined the promise Obama had made to Americans that "If you like your plan, you can keep it," he stopped saying this and apologized.

---

13 These puns hurt me even more than they hurt you. Trust me.

Trump saw that the Republicans got away with thumbing their nose at the fact-checkers. *Why lie a little when you can lie a lot?* The media invested in more fact-checking, with the hope of shaming Trump, but claims from the "Amazon *Washington Post*," "Low ratings CNN," and "MSDNC" (Trump's cleverest nickname, in my opinion) that Trump was lying became proof positive of his truthfulness. The whole endeavor was a case study in failure. The fact-checkers not only failed to stop Trump from lying, but by calling out his lies, they inadvertently broadcast them farther and wider and validated his false statements to people predisposed to distrust the press.

Look, there's nothing wrong with calling out politicians on their lies. In fact, it would be great if more people fact-checked CEOs and Wall Street types. But if the goal of this is to curb lying and convince readers of the truth, the media's approach is failing miserably. The media's influence and power have shifted. Recognizing this new reality will help them invest time, energy, and reporting resources in areas that can impact the public debate (presuming that is still their goal).

- **Punish the Liars.** The first piece of advice I received when I got my first job as a spokesperson was simple and sacrosanct: don't lie. As an official mouthpiece for a politician, you can spin, dodge, and decline to answer, but you never, ever lie. If you do, your career will be over before it begins. The theory was that the reporter-flack relationship was a two-way street of trust. Reporters had to trust the information we gave them, and we had to trust that the information would be protected and used as promised. Trust was so important that reporters would rather go to prison than reveal their sources. I took the advice not to lie deadly seriously. I once couldn't sleep for weeks because I was caught off guard by a question and obfuscated in order to avoid revealing top-secret negotiations to normalize relations with Cuba. When the negotiations subsequently came to light, I was petrified that my ability to speak on behalf of President Obama would be irreparably damaged.[14]

As it turns out, I was wrong to worry. Trump and his aides lied to reporters nonstop for four years and faced no consequences whatsoever. Team Trump figured out early on that they could lie whenever they wanted, and the press would do nothing in response. The media's failure to act was born of a fear of perceived bias as well as a thirst for access to the people closest to the biggest story in town. Careers were made and broken based on the ability to get the right Trump adviser on the phone to spill the tea. Once again, this approach worked in the short term but did long-term damage to the press's reputation and credibility across the political spectrum.

It doesn't have to be this way. The press could become vocal advocates for the truth by:

□ Publicly outing anonymous sources who lie. The anonymity granted to sources would be conditional upon their telling the truth. If they are caught lying, they should be exposed as leakers and liars.

□ Refusing to invite known liars onto prestigious media platforms for interviews. To his credit, CNN's Jake Tapper already does this by refusing to have on politicians who promote the Big Lie about the 2020 election. (It's getting harder and harder for him to find Republicans for his show.)

□ Refusing to provide live coverage for politicians who repeatedly use their speeches to spread disinformation.

---

14 I got off with an overly generous slap on the wrist from the press, who understood the impossible position I was in.

During the Trump years, the cable networks would cover Trump live, but then bring on a fact-checker to call out the lies. This was admirable, but unfortunately there was a significant drop in audience between the speech and the fact-checking.[15] No one is saying don't cover the president, a presidential candidate, or a former president, but media outlets have an obligation to their audience not to air unfiltered lies in real time.

■ **Build Trust.** The attitude of most major media outlets in recent years has been "Transparency for thee, but not for me." Reporters demand to know anything and everything about the people they cover. No matter how much access is offered, the press will demand more. Refusing to detail internal meetings or personnel decisions is treated as an affront to press freedom. This tendency certainly annoyed me over the years, but even I have to admit it comes from a good (if sometimes disingenuous) place. The problem is not media outlets demanding transparency; it's their refusal to offer any window into their own decision-making process. Major revisions are made to online stories throughout the day without any explanation of why the change was made. When media outlets get something very wrong, there is little to no transparency of why they did so or what is being done to prevent similar errors from happening.

A few days before the 2016 presidential election, the *New York Times* blared an earth-shattering headline: "Investigating Donald Trump, F.B.I. Sees No Clear Link to Russia." The *Times* was reporting that, contrary to accusations by Democrats, the FBI had

---

15 In an ideal world, they could call out the lies in real time using the same technology employed by VH1 on its show *Pop Up Videos* back in the day. (Look it up, kiddos.)

concluded that there was no connection between Trump and Russia. The *Times* stated, "the hacking into Democratic emails, F.B.I. and intelligence officials now believe, was aimed at disrupting the presidential election rather than electing Mr. Trump." This story was a massive boon to the Trump campaign just as the paper was trumpeting FBI director Jim Comey's decision to briefly restart his investigation into Hillary Clinton's emails. The *Times* story absolved Trump of collusion with Russia. It was also 100 percent wrong. We now know, ironically enough from a different set of *New York Times* reporters, that the FBI was actively investigating direct connections and contact between the Trump campaign and Russian operatives.

In the five years since that incorrect story ran, the *New York Times* has never really explained what went wrong, who lied, or how the paper could have made such a grievous mistake at such an important time. I am sure there have been countless meetings and internal reviews at the *Times* offices, but it's been crickets for the public. This level of secrecy erodes trust in the media at a time when the media (and democracy) can least afford it. One easy step to increase transparency is the reinstatement of the ombudsman and public editor role. Readers/viewers need an advocate who can ask tough questions and force the powers that be to answer them. Such a step won't solve every problem, but it's a start. Jay Rosen, a professor at the New York University School of Journalism and a prominent media critic, argues that the new model of journalism should be founded on the idea of "reader trust." Under this approach, building that trust (as opposed to maintaining objectivity) should be the frame though which every decision is made. Rosen's model is a thoughtful solution to some very hard problems, but trust is impossible without transparency.

   ■ **Move Away from the Digital Ad Model.** This one is much, much easier said than done, but reducing dependence on digital advertising should be a priority for every media outlet. If the survival of your business depends on internet traffic, you are ceding control to the perverse incentives of the internet. In the bygone days of print, ads were priced based on the overall circulation of the publication. In the digital era, the amount of traffic to the article is directly connected to the media outlet's profits. Therefore, a dependence on digital ads inevitably leads to doubling down on stories that get traffic regardless of their journalistic value. This problem is exacerbated by the fact that Facebook is a major source of traffic for many outlets. This causes the media to rely on the same algorithm that promotes Ben Shapiro, Dan Bongino, and rampant conspiracy theories to meet their monthly revenue goals. It's easy to deride these esteemed journalistic institutions for engaging in clickbait journalism to drive traffic, but the media is a business with payrolls to meet. If they don't make money, they lay off their reporters and do less journalism. This creates a Faustian bargain—to do *any* journalism, you have to do a lot of shitty journalism. Moving away from the digital ad model and embracing a subscription/reader-supported model or inviting in a patron like Jeff Bezos, who is too rich to sweat the bottom line, would relieve some of this tension and ultimately offer a better product, one that will increase trust in the media.

I don't pretend any of these changes are easy. The mere fact that a political operative is pushing for more partisan media will be disqualifying in the eyes of the people who could make these changes. I hope these ideas will get as much of a hearing as performative Republican complaints about bias. The best future for media is one where progressives build up an echo chamber to compete with the MAGA megaphone *and* in which there is a robust, fair, vibrant, independent media to hold both sides to account.

That is not the path we are currently on.

18

Preaching to the Progressive Choir

In December 2016, I was sitting next to my wife on a plane from Washington, DC, to San Francisco, where we live. We were taxiing to the runway when my cell phone rang. I was about to turn it off, before the flight attendant could put me in FAA jail, when I saw that it was a call from the White House. Out of habit, I answered. It was Anita Breckenridge, President Obama's deputy chief of staff and longest-serving adviser. She was calling to invite me to a meeting at the White House.

"POTUS wants to get everyone together to talk about what happened in the election and where the party goes from here. He's pretty fired up."

"That's very good to hear. When is it?" I asked.

I considered this call good news. It's always gratifying to get invited to a meeting with the president, even years after leaving the White House. With Obama about to exit stage left just as Donald Trump was entering stage right, I, too, was deeply concerned about the future of the Democratic Party. I had been in the White House the day before, visiting old friends and dispensing career advice to my soon-to-be unemployed former colleagues. During the visit, I popped in to see the president and gently pushed him to get engaged with the political fallout from the disastrous election before leaving office. I wasn't the only one. David Axelrod and David Plouffe, his top political strategists, were making a similar pitch.

And then came the bad news.

"Tomorrow," Anita told me. "It's short notice, but you know how he gets when gets fired up about something."

There was no chance I was going to miss this meeting, so I bought a last-minute ticket on the red-eye leaving that night. Then I went home, changed clothes, packed a bag, and headed back to the airport.

The meeting was well worth the travel. As I sat down around the big table in the Roosevelt Room, I realized that this was the last time this group of people was likely to get together in this setting. Many of the people around the table were the same ones at the very first meeting of our long-shot campaign nearly a decade prior. We had attended a million meetings and conference calls together over the years, been through the highest highs and the lowest lows. We were bonded together in service to a man and a cause we believed in deeply. Now much of what we had worked so hard for was at grave risk from a threat we didn't see coming or take seriously enough.

Part reunion, part therapy session, the meeting lasted for hours as we discussed what went wrong and what role the departing president and his team could play in righting the ship. Coming out of the meeting, we were assigned with bringing back to the president a "gap analysis" and a set of recommendations. My assignment naturally involved communications. I looked at the state of the party's messaging and communications operation and what role that had played in our defeats up and down the ballot in 2016. Call it propaganda, progressive media, or content creation—Democrats need more of it, because we are massively outgunned and simply cannot succeed in the current landscape.

Others looked at the state of Democratic data, fund-raising, and organizing. The goal was to see where we were lacking and what could be done about it. All of what we learned was combined in a memo for the president, who planned to share it with Nancy Pelosi and

Chuck Schumer, the senior elected officials in the party responsible for mounting the opposition to Donald Trump. While researching this book, I stumbled upon my submission to that memo. What I found was deeply depressing:

- A lesson of the 2016 election is that we were outgunned by the conservative noise machine. Trump was aided by the traditional GOP allies in talk radio and on Fox News, but also Breitbart and an army of conservative-leaning content creation and distribution sites that were amplifying his positive message and driving a negative message across social media.

- To fight Trump in the short term and win in the 2020 election, we need a donor network to fund progressive media outlets that push progressive content into the Facebook and Twitter ecosystem. These outlets should be both Geo, Demographic, and policy based.

It's been six years since that meeting in the White House, and the problems we identified in 2016 are much worse now. Very little progress has been made.

It's time to invest in a progressive propaganda operation that can go toe-to-toe with the Right. It seems utterly ridiculous now, but during Trump's presidency, there was a vigorous debate about whether disinformation and right-wing propaganda were a problem worth addressing. No one, to my knowledge, thought things were going great or that Fox et al. weren't a real problem. But the list of Democratic Party problems was long, and combating disinformation rarely rose to the top.

After the 2012 election, the Democratic Party fell behind the Republicans on technology and data, party infrastructure atrophied to an alarming degree, and new groups were needed to channel the rapidly growing "resistance." After an election dominated by disinformation and an attempted insurrection founded on obvious Big Lies, there is no longer a debate about the threat of right-wing disinformation. A lot of smart people are now thinking and talking about what to do about it. Even former President Obama made it a focus of his postpresidency, frequently meeting experts and technologists looking for ways to get back to a world where "Americans argue over solutions not facts." As the former president told Jeffrey Goldberg of *The Atlantic* in a 2020 interview, "If we do not have the capacity to distinguish what's true from what's false, then by definition the marketplace of ideas doesn't work. And by definition our democracy doesn't work. We are entering into an epistemological crisis."

The debate now is about how to address the threat.

The Billionaire Bailout Fallacy

One school of thought pushed by some very prominent, wealthy, and well-meaning advocates involves doubling down on the traditional media. These folks are pushing progressive billionaires to buy up struggling media properties with a particular focus on the rapidly disappearing local press. The way in which Jeff Bezos saved the *Washington Post* is the model. Prior to Bezos, the *Washington Post* was falling into irrelevance. Revenue was down, and many of the paper's best journalists were jumping ship to the *New York Times* and Politico. Every earnings report for the company led to more layoffs and a greater sense of impending doom. One of America's great journalistic institutions, the paper that famously took down a president, was in danger of becoming nothing more than a middling regional rag. The coup de grace was when the *New York Times* scooped the *Washington Post* on the revelation of its most deeply held secret: the identity of "Deep Throat," the mysterious source behind much of the *Post*'s biggest Watergate scoops. Also, President Obama didn't sit down for an interview with a *Washington Post* reporter in his first term. Many speculated that the paper was being snubbed due to its tough coverage, but the reality was more damning. The sad fact was that, in my estimation as the White House communications director, the paper wasn't worth Obama's time. That's how far the *Washington Post* had fallen.

Then Jeff Bezos swooped in, bought the paper, took it private, and used his deep pockets to hire some very talented people. The Amazon founder and aspiring astronaut is so rich that the bottom line of the paper was largely irrelevant to him. Bezos paid $250 million for the paper, which is basically spare change to someone who made $70 *billion* during the pandemic. A few years after the change in ownership, the *Washington Post* returned to national prominence and was producing some of the best journalism on the planet.

Bezos is certainly not a progressive by any definition of that word,[1] but his bailout of the *Washington Post* inspired his more progressive brethren in the billionaires' club to try something similar. Laurene Powell Jobs bought *The Atlantic*.[2] Saleforce CEO and longtime Obama donor Marc Benioff bought *Time* magazine. There were folks begging Michael Bloomberg to buy anything and everything, concerned people pleading with the very wealthy to save our doddering democracy one newspaper at a time. I am sympathetic to the idea. Democracy needs a vibrant media, particularly at the local level, and there does not seem to be anything resembling a viable business plan for this sort of media. Therefore, turning to what amounts to charity from people too rich to worry about making money may be the

---

1 His political philosophy seems to be a combination of rapacious capitalism and interstellar imperialism.
2 Her LLC also invested in Ozy, that faux-media Ponzi scheme that collapsed in 2021 after one *New York Times* story exposed it as a fraud.

only way to stem the tide. However, I fundamentally disagree with this approach to combating disinformation. Propping up the old media may be necessary, but it is insufficient. And if it's the primary strategy to win the war on truth, the good guys are going to lose.

First, while many in the traditional media apparatus atrophied and collapsed under pressure from changing economics, new technologies, and Mark Zuckerberg's greed, many have thrived. The addiction to news that many people developed during the careening crisis of the Trump era meant that even after Trump was banished, ratings and subscriptions were still at or above their pre-Trump baseline. The *New York Times*, a focal point of Trump's anti-media rhetoric, has never been more powerful. The self-described newspaper of record is now a multimedia powerhouse with podcasts, documentaries, and a television series. In terms of influence and financial success, it is without peer. During the Trump era, CNN and MSNBC grew in ratings and influence. Yet it was at this exact golden period for the media that right-wing disinformation flourished. If a thriving media failed to slow the spread of disinformation, I am not sure why people thought doubling down on that very same model would have a different impact.

Second, relying on the munificence of billionaires to save democracy presents all kinds of problems. The world has three major problems:[3] climate change, the rise of authoritarianism, and widening economic inequality. The very wealthy are at the center of all three. Even if we are relying on liberal billionaires, they are still billionaires. Handing control of the media to a small group of unaccountable, extremely wealthy individuals is a short-term solution that

---

3 Besides the pandemic, which I fucking hope is well over by the time you are reading this. I started writing this book nearly a year into the pandemic and finished it before normalcy returned.

we will look back on with regret. Just because we had media barons in the past, it doesn't mean we need to make that our future.

Finally, whether it's with Michael Bloomberg's pocket change or some other means, believing that better-funded traditional media is a viable solution demonstrates a misunderstanding of the disinformation problem. The right-wing is waging a war on truth. To win that war, we need to invest in people and organizations committed to fighting that war, not covering it. If the last decade is any indication, the traditional media has no interest in fighting back. Therefore, we need something new, something more aggressive. We need a progressive echo chamber, but how do we get there?

From Dem Debating Society to Messaging Machine

In these discussions, many believe the progressive media landscape is largely barren. This is true when you compare it to the massive apparatus on the right, but the idea that there is not a thriving progressive media ecosystem is wholly incorrect.

There are a number of decades-old liberal-leaning magazines like *Mother Jones*, *The American Prospect*, and *The Nation*. In the pre-internet era, these magazines played an important role in shaping the internal debate on the party's agenda and political strategy. Their influence began to fade as the internet-driven news cycle rendered most weekly and monthly publications less relevant and economically viable.[4] While it was a bumpy and precarious road, these publications made the shift to digital and continue to put out important writing through a combination of subscriptions and reader donations.

---

4 The low point of the era of the ideological magazine happened when the not-so-liberal *New Republic* doubled down on its support for the Iraq War by endorsing Joe Lieberman for the Democratic nomination in 2004, a decision nearly as poorly thought out and filled with hubris as the decision to invade Iraq.

During the latter half of the Obama years, a series of leftist media outlets rose up largely in opposition to the Democratic president. The two best-known examples are *The Young Turks*, a groundbreaking YouTube show, and the Intercept, the digital outlet founded by Glenn Greenwald. Farther under the radar but still influential was a series of outlets and media personalities that either leaned toward or were explicitly pushing for socialism. The surprisingly strong candidacy of Bernie Sanders brought this element to the fore and demonstrated that there was a large appetite for a bolder, more populist Democratic Party. For many, Hillary Clinton's loss to Trump was seen as a rebuke of her more moderate style of politics and evidence of the need to move left. This notion further fueled the rise of leftist media within the party.

Whether it's old-school folks or the new, more aggressive leftist sites, the main purpose of these outlets is to wage internal battles: to move the party left, back certain candidates, and punish others. After 2016, there was a huge push to get more Democrats to support Sanders's Medicare for All health care plan. When it was reported that former congressman Beto O'Rourke was considering a run for president, some in the pro-Sanders media saw him as a threat to their chosen candidate and started digging into O'Rourke's record, looking for inconsistencies and raising questions about his progressive credentials. When Pete Buttigieg, the moderate former mayor of South Bend, Indiana, shot up in the polls, he became the focus of their ire. Other outlets gave attention and support for progressive primary challengers like Alexandra Ocasio-Cortez.

I find this internal debate to be a good thing. There should be a vigorous debate within a party. It's healthy. If folks think one candidate is better on their issues, they should push aggressively for that candidate. If some in the party are advocating for a policy that is substantively or politically bad, it's good to have people in the media who will push back. I say this knowing that my former boss and my current views are often in the crosshairs of the leftist media. This is not to say that these fights are always conducted in the most constructive manner.[5] Far from it. Sometimes we are so busy fighting one another that we forget about the other, much more dangerous party.

The Republicans also have ideological media outlets focused on internal matters. Before Trump, *National Review* and others focused on moving the party rightward, advocating for conservative policies like more tax cuts and invading more countries and pushing back whenever a Republican contemplated helping people get food, shelter, or lifesaving health care.[6] Since Trump came on the scene, most of the conservative media have gone full MAGA. And therein lies the fundamental difference between the Right and the Left.

The Right-Wing media is an echo chamber, and progressive media is often a debating society. The Right is focused on defeating Democrats. The Left is focused on shaping our party, not beating the other party. If Democrats have any hope of winning the messaging battle, we need to invest in media properties that will take the fight to Republicans and communicate directly with the public on our terms.

That's why Jon Favreau, Jon Lovett, and Tommy Vietor made the risky but smart choice to start Crooked Media. It's easy to look at the company's current success and think that it was preordained, but that is far from the case. When they began talking about leaving the sport and pop culture website the Ringer, where *Keepin' It 1600*, our previous podcast, was hosted, and starting their own media company, most people told them it was a bad idea. Media is a tough business,

---

5 For example, spreading the rumor that Pete Buttigieg was a CIA-trained spy and then using a rat emoji to identify him was probably not constructive (or as clever as the people who did it thought it was).
6 This sounds like hyperbole, but is it?

and progressive media is an even tougher business. Remember Air America?[7]

But the election of Trump was a crisis, and it was a crisis that the existing media and messaging apparatus were incapable of meeting. My cohosts quit their jobs, invested their own money, hired a talented staff, and built a truly successful company that does good work and pumps out great content that entertains and inspires. Just as other Obama alumni and Democratic activists started grassroots organizations, super PACs, and ran for office, their impetus wasn't just defeating Trump. It was to address a political media that seemed almost designed to make people cynical and frustrated.

For *Pod Save America*, our working motto is "Where you can learn about the news and what you can do about the news." The latter part of that awkwardly constructed sentence is what differentiates Crooked from the mainstream media and from previous generations of progressive media. For all the attention the company has received in recent years, my sense is that most people in politics are largely unaware of the tremendous impact Crooked Media has had on American politics. In addition to touting the accomplishments of my friends and cohosts,[8] I want to highlight the work of this progressive media ecosystem designed to defeat Trumpism, fight disinformation, and elect Democrats.[9]

Crooked Media is changing the game in three specific ways:

1. **Mobilization:** *Pod Save America*, and Crooked Media, is an extension of and reaction to the podcast Jon Favreau, Jon Lovett, Tommy Vietor, and I hosted in 2016. *Keepin' It 1600* was an artifact of the age before Trump. The fact that four experienced

---

7 The fact that you don't proves my point.
8 Not to mention the people who sign my paychecks.
9 Which is the best way to defeat Trumpism and fight disinformation.

276 BATTLING THE BIG LIE

(read: old) political operatives were spending the presidential election hosting a podcast on a sports and entertainment network shows just how confident the world was that Trump was not a threat to win. This was a hobby. It was punditry—though, we hoped, funnier and definitely more profane—but it was different from those god-awful cable panels of nine washed-up hacks sitting at a table built for seven (and I say this as someone who was a paid cable pundit for years). We used our twice-weekly platform to encourage people to donate and volunteer, and we tried to explain what was happening on the campaign from the perspective of people who had been there and done that. But the tone was cocky, and dismissive of Trump, and the idea was that he could not possibly win. I have never been more wrong about anything in my life.

As we thought about where we went wrong and what we could do better next time, one major idea occurred to us. The audience was an opportunity! For reasons I still can't explain, hundreds of thousands of people were listening to our little podcast in 2016. The listeners were politically engaged Democrats,[10] but what if we could turn that audience into activists? It started with mobilizing people to fight to save the Affordable Care Act and become active in politics. In 2018, the political team at Crooked launched Vote Save America, a one-stop shop to learn about the candidates and issues on the ballot as well as a place to volunteer, donate, and register to vote. For the presidential election, they added an Adopt-a-State program to recruit people trapped in their homes to volunteer in six key battleground states. These efforts to mobilize the Crooked Media audience were more successful than anyone

---

10 Believe it or not, several members of Paul Ryan's staff listened to the podcast, which was probably their subconscious telling them I was right about Ryan being one of this century's great cowards.

possibly imagined in the days after Trump's shocking victory. In the 2020 election, 300,000 Crooked listeners signed up for Adopt-a-State. Those volunteers made 17 million phone calls and sent more than 8 million text messages. Our listeners also made more than half a million donations, raising $46 million to fund individual candidates, grassroots organizations, and lawyers to protect the vote. As someone who has been in politics for way too long, I cannot emphasize how stunned I was by these numbers. Many of the major Democratic presidential candidates raised less money than Crooked did in 2020. This level of volunteer recruitment exceeded almost every organization working in Democratic politics other than Joe Biden's campaign.

2. **News Curation:** In any given week, a lot of shit happens in politics. The media cannot and will not cover all of it. Important news falls by the wayside. How is the public to discern what is important and what isn't? What is worth worrying about and what isn't? For even the most sophisticated news consumer, weeding through all the content is impossible. Through podcasts, newsletters, and social media, Crooked can make sense of the news for its progressive-minded audience.

You may be asking—with good reason—who cares? Sure, news curation is a nice service, but how does a *TV Guide* for news and politics advance the cause? People's political views are shaped by what they see and read. Decisions about whom to support, how to vote, and even whether to vote are shaped by what people see in the news. The Democratic Party tends to outsource the job of informing its voters to media outlets that do not care if Democrats win or lose elections.[11] For the thousandth time, that is an insane

---

11 And some seem to be rooting for Democrats to lose so they can get another taste of those sweet Trump-era ratings.

way to run a political party. The media narrative on any given day is fickle. It doesn't paint the full picture or give people the information they need to make an informed choice. Also, for the thousandth time, that's not the media's job. Their focus is on conflict and controversy, not substance or impact.

Take President Biden's Build Back Better bill. The media covered it exhaustively. Every twist and turn was documented in dramatic fashion. Every utterance from Senators Joe Manchin and Kyrsten Sinema, the decisive votes, was treated like the delivery of the stone tablets from Mount Sinai. But after months and months of intense coverage of the legislative process, polls showed that even the most engaged Democrats didn't have a freaking clue what was in the bill or how it would impact their lives. There were people running around angry at Biden for not doing things he was actually doing. These people didn't know what the bill included because the media had no interest in telling them.

If the traditional media won't tell them, progressive media must. Crooked Media uses its platform to highlight stories that aren't getting enough attention and explain why some stories are just a distraction. And again, for the thousandth time, no one in the Crooked Media universe is creating "fake news" or spreading disinformation. This is not "Liberal Fox" or "Bizarro Breitbart." Crooked deals in factual, transparently biased information for the purpose of saving the country[12] from a dangerous Republican Party chock-full of MAGA yahoos.

3.   **Recruitment (On-ramp):** Not every *Pod Save America* listener is a Democrat. I know this because a handful of MAGA types listen to every podcast and then tweet profane commentary at me.[13]

---

12 Hence the very ironic name of the podcast.
13 Folks whose Twitter bios include some version of "Proud Father of 2 kids and 12 guns. Love the Sooners, fishing, and Christ. Proudly blocked by Alyssa Milano.

While data is hard to come by, I assume the overwhelming majority of its listeners lean Democratic. But not every Democratic-leaning listener is a voter, and not every voter is a volunteer, and not every volunteer is a donor to Democratic causes. Crooked Media strives to make the case for getting involved in politics. Some people don't have the faintest idea how to get involved. Others know how but are understandably nervous about the experience of phoning up strangers or knocking on their doors. The goal is to demystify and explain the value of these activities.

A lot of people will read this and say, "That's great, but aren't you just preaching to the choir?"

First, our party isn't currently preaching to the choir. The sermon in this tortured analogy is being delivered by the likes of *Meet the Press* host Chuck Todd and the authors of *Politico Playbook*.[14] The people listening to *Pod Save America*, *Pod Save the World*, *Pod Save the People*, and other explicitly political offerings are interested in politics.

Second, Crooked offers a lot of nonpolitical content, with podcasts and other videos focused on pop culture, sports, and reality television. Those audiences are not holistically political. And for the less political listeners of those shows, their decision to listen to a Crooked show creates what Crooked Media's chief content officer calls an "on-ramp" to politics. Those shows and their hosts promote the political content and opportunities for activism. There is nothing subversive. Politics isn't jammed down people's throats. No one is forced to do anything, but they are exposed to

---

#letsgobrandon, #F&ckFauci, #BidenDementia." Their tweets are all basically variations on telling Democrats to fuck off in graphic ways.
14 This is a bad thing FYI, in case the main thrust of the book thus far has been less than clear.

politics and activism in ways listeners of other sports and enter-tainment content never are.

There is nothing more difficult, or more important, than bringing people into the political process. By making politics fun and approachable, Crooked Media created a model that can (and should) be replicated.

Key Ingredients

A progressive media echo chamber cannot be built without financial and political support from the Democrats, top to bottom. It would be great if the progressive billionaires who fund much of the party infrastructure gave up their dreams of being modern-day Henry Luces and tried to become modern-day Rupert Murdochs, investing in the media ecosystem. But we can't wait for that. For all the reasons that we don't want billionaires owning all the local papers in America, we also don't want a progressive media operation entirely dependent on the munificence of a small handful of the very wealthy. Ultimately, we need a self-sustaining progressive media funded by either profitable businesses or nonprofits with a sustainable donor base. Both are pos-sible, but neither is easy.

And this is where you come in. It's time to stop begging the bil-lionaires to save us and start taking responsibility for saving ourselves. Democrats have a huge grassroots funding base that donates to can-didates up and down the ballots, as well as grassroots organizations like Swing Left and Stacey Abrams's Fair Fight. We need to continue supporting these candidates and groups, but we also need to subscribe to, patronize, and support progressive media. We need to share its content. The other side has done this for decades. We haven't, and it shows. A robust progressive media is as important as overflowing campaign coffers.

Crooked started with a great idea at the exact right time. The first episodes of *Pod Save America* dropped right as Trump was about to be sworn in and as millions of people were desperately looking for answers about what had happened and what was going to happen next. There was a tremendous appetite for politics and activism in that moment, and few places to turn. Re-creating that moment is impossible, but that doesn't mean building out progressive media is impossible. It can be done, but it's going to take work and support from everyone, from grassroots activists to the White House. This effort requires doing something that I do not recommend lightly: following Trump's example.

There is no more annoying genre of punditry than "What Democrats can learn from Republicans." And the most annoying version of that annoying genre is "What Democrats can learn from Trump."[15] Yet, here I am becoming what I hate. Still, I think this is the single instance where it makes sense. Trump was a shitty president. He is a shittier person. He is as dumb as a doornail and has the compassion of a banana slug.

But Trump was a massive boon to the right-wing media ecosystem. I rarely use the word *strategic* to describe Donald Trump's communications strategy. Everything he does is more instinctual than intellectual,[16] and his instincts are terrible. But the way he nurtured[17] and uplifted[18] the right-wing media was truly masterful. Trump used the power of the presidency, and his massive social media following, to give legitimacy and attention to the media outlets telling his story on his terms.[19] While in office, almost all the interviews Trump did

---

15 This is basically Politico's raison d'être.
16 A word I *never* use to describe Donald Trump.
17 Just to hammer this series of jokes into the ground, this is the first time "nurture" has been used in the same sentence as "Trump."
18 You know the joke by this point.
19 Hagiographic bullshit that would make Kim Jong-un blush.

were with right-wing media outlets. If there was a story Trump liked because it made him feel better about himself or buttressed his narrative, Trump used his Twitter account to share it with the world. If someone wrote a book that was good for him, he used Twitter and Facebook to ask his supporters to buy it. This often guaranteed that the book made the *New York Times* Best Seller list, which in turn guaranteed that the book was read by more people and the authors booked on more news shows.

I bet almost no one had heard about the *Federalist* before Trump was elected, but once its writers began creating MAGA fan fiction about the investigation into collusion between Russia and the Trump campaign, the former president made them a leading voice in the Republican Party. Once Trump laid his unusually small hands on their work, *Federalist* writers became frequent guests on Fox News. Republican members of Congress and MAGA personalities with large social media followings began sharing their content. All this attention led to more traffic, which led to more revenue, which allowed the *Federalist* to hire more writers to produce more content supporting Trump and the Republican Party.

Similarly, the attention Trump lavished on Fox was a boon to the network. Their ratings were up. Fox hosts became so influential within the party that Tucker Carlson is now considered a potential presidential candidate if Trump does not run in 2024.

The financial and political success of the pro-Trump media creates an incentive for folks to fall in line. If your bottom line depends on internet traffic, why wouldn't you start writing your pieces or crafting your tweets in service of getting a president with tens of millions of followers and a twitchy Twitter finger to share them? And what Trump giveth, he can taketh away. After Fox News ever so briefly decided to accept the reality that Joe Biden had won the election, Trump turned on the network, and his supporters followed suit. In the postelection period, Trump used his last remaining tweets to repeatedly attack Fox for disloyalty, and the network suffered its worst ratings in nearly twenty years.

Fox News's ratings dominance has been such that even calling the relationship among the three cable channels a "competition" is being overly generous to CNN and MSNBC. The right-wing network has had the most viewers at nearly every hour of the day for as long as I can remember. But after the kerfuffle with Trump, now they were in third place. The folks working at Fox are malevolent, but they aren't dumb. They immediately reengineered their programming to win back former President Trump and his fans: less news, more MAGA opinion. And the folks who accurately called the election were purged from the network. All of a sudden, the pushback against the Big Lie was nonexistent on Fox. Trump returned with a series of interviews after Rush Limbaugh passed away. Within months, Fox was back in the catbird seat atop the ratings.

It's safe to say that everyone in the Republican Party and the right-wing media learned their lesson. You are pro-Trump, or you are unemployed.

On the Democratic side, there is a hesitancy to embrace progressive media in the way Republicans embraced the right-wing media. You rarely see Democratic politicians actively promoting content from their media allies on their own social feeds. You rarely see them make news by sitting down for an interview with a progressive outlet. There continues to be an old-school public utility mentality in our party. Whenever Democrats have something important to say, they usually go to CNN, the *New York Times*, or one of the Sunday shows. As someone who hosts a progressive podcast and writes a progressive newsletter, I am obviously and perhaps irreparably biased on this

issue. But, with that in mind, I think the party is missing a huge opportunity to communicate with the public and build progressive power
over the long term.

There are three reasons Democratic politicians and operatives
don't embrace progressive media:

The first is muscle memory. Most Democratic leadership is old
enough to remember being excited about the advent of television.
Therefore, it's somewhat unreasonable to expect them to naturally
embrace podcasts, YouTube, and other internet-based media. They
rose to power in a different media world and never adjusted to the
newer, more ideological digital world. But it's not fair to blame it all
on age. Bernie Sanders, the octogenarian senator, has been a leader in
pushing progressive media and is a frequent guest on *Pod Save America*.[20] His campaign embraced direct communications with his voters
through livestreams, newsletters, and a podcast hosted by his staff.
The Sanders campaign even brought the hosts of the pro-Sanders left-
wing podcast *Chapo Trap House* to Iowa to campaign for him. Sanders is the exception to the rule because, as a political outsider, he was
never a favorite of the traditional media.

This leads to the second reason Democratic politicians don't
embrace progressive media: social pressure. The DC political establishment is an incestuous mix of media and politics. Every night, the
nation's capital is filled with book parties, soirees, charity balls, and
salons populated with politicians, lobbyists, and reporters. Other than
brief mentions in the gossip columns and *Politico Playbook*,[21] these
events are off the record, and the reporters and the people they cover
mix and mingle at them with no fear of the public ever knowing

---

20 Which I know drives a certain segment of his supporters insane.
21 Too often a gossip column delivered to your in-box.

what was said. These events are where sources are developed and reporter relationships are born. It is in these informal settings where a reporter might push for an interview or get a senator to agree to be on their show. While attendees sip wine and nibble on canapés, tidbits are shared and rumors spread. These relationships are not just transactional, and they are often quite meaningful, which makes politicians reluctant to do something to offend these media colleagues.

Ideological media and the newer digital outlets are a threat to the established order. In theory, an embrace of this new world would mean less influence and access for the press. With the rise of Trump and of his anti-press rhetoric, many Republican elected officials and politicos stopped going to these events. The few Republicans who do attend represent the tiny and diminishing Never Trump wing of the party. But this is about more than who attends which party. If Democrats move away from the establishment media, who will be left?

The third and final reason Democratic politicians avoid progressive media is fear of backlash. Similar to Sanders, Barack Obama didn't come up through the traditional political channels. He was younger and digitally savvier[22] than his predecessors and successors. This made him more willing to take risks, anger journalistic bigwigs, and search out new, more effective communications tactics. This trait drew a lot of early aid to Obama's side.

I long believed, in ways I couldn't articulate, that the old way of doing my job was an exercise in failure. Before Obama, it was hard to find a politician, especially one with a shot at the presidency, willing

---

22 His insistence on having a BlackBerry phone was seen as evidence of forward-looking digital prowess, something that, like the BlackBerry, has not aged very well.

to try something new.[23] The innovative efforts made under Obama often meant turning to more ideologically aligned media to communicate our message. Obama often gathered the progressive media for an off-the-record session to explain his strategy and policies. This was a privilege rarely bestowed on the White House Press Corps writ large. Whenever they saw Rachel Maddow, Eugene Robinson, and folks from the *Huffington Post* gathering to be escorted into the West Wing, the reporters from the more traditional outlets would make a beeline for my office. In 2015, Obama sat down for a series of interviews to amplify his recently delivered State of the Union address. There was nothing remarkable in and of itself about this. For years, White Houses put the president out to talk about the policies and ideas embedded in what is invariably the most important speech of the year. Sometimes those interviews are on the network morning shows. Sometimes they are with local television stations or key newspaper reporters. Obama did something very different. The president of the United States did interviews with a number of prominent YouTube influencers, including GloZell Green, a green-lipsticked comedian, and Bethany Mota, a nineteen-year-old fashion influencer. None of these folks would describe themselves as journalists. They were just online personalities with very large, highly engaged, mostly younger audiences. These are the exact people every politician desperately wants to reach but cannot do so through the usual media means.

I think the technical term for the White House Press Corps' reaction to the YouTuber interviews was "going batshit insane." My email in-box was on fire from reporters complaining about the sit-downs with the YouTubers. *Obama is seeking out softballs. He's*

---

23 I can also admit now that I liked sticking my thumb in the media's collective eye more than was constructive.

doing propaganda. He's scared of our tough questions. While I probably enjoyed their reaction a little too much, some of my White House
colleagues thought we went too far. We had needlessly poked the
media bear. Others were concerned we had demeaned the office of
the president. The mainstream media was petulant and wrote a series
of articles lambasting President Obama. The right-wing media used
the interviews to push the racist notion that the first Black president
of the *Harvard Law Review* wasn't smart enough to handle tough
questions.

Democrats are very sensitive to being accused of engaging in propaganda or snubbing the media. This was even truer after Trump.
Ironically, our response to the success of Trump's strategy is often to
do the exact opposite, out of spite. Too many Democrats are afraid
to embrace progressive media because Donald Trump successfully
embraces his media allies. But this is why we keep losing the messaging war.

The final ingredient for a successful progressive media is fun. Jon
Lovett tells a story about when he was writing a speech on climate change
for then senator Hillary Clinton. Very late the night before the speech,
he got a call from President Clinton's staff with edits on the speech. The
former president had crossed out a bunch of the language and offered
guidance the gist of which said, "This is going to be a great and fun
adventure. Defeating climate change and building this renewable-energy
world is going to be a blast. Politics doesn't have to be a slog."

I think about that story all the time. Our task is to make people
want to engage with politics. That is, of course, a tall order. Too
much of media makes politics seem scary, angry, and more than a
little corrupt. It's easy to get the impression that participating in politics requires sullying oneself. Too much progressive media focuses
on the bad parts of the process or the failures of Democrats. That's a

legitimate story. It's one that should be told. But it's not the only story. There is joy in people coming together to improve the community and better their country. It's fun and rewarding. How we talk about and cover politics should reflect that. Progressive media isn't just competing with CNN and MSNBC; we are competing with Netflix, TikTok, long walks, and everything else that people could be doing. If we want people to give us their attention, we should make it fun. There is a reason that *The Daily Show* might be the most influential piece of progressive media in the modern era. It was fun! Jon Stewart made you laugh. John Oliver succeeds for the same reason.

I would never want to go to a Trump rally.[24] It seems terrible to me. The rhetoric is offensive. The anger is palpable. The speeches are winding and bordering on incoherent. But the people in attendance are having a great time. They cheer. They laugh. The parking lot looks like a mix of the tailgate at a college football game and a Renaissance fair. It's fair to question their taste, but we shouldn't ignore what's happening. Obama rallies in 2008 had a similar feel. People waited in line for hours and clamored to get to the front. You didn't want to miss it. Progressive media needs to channel that spirit. Joyful, fun, and entertaining. Throughout the Trump years, I used to explain the jokes about serious things on *Pod Save America* by saying, "In times like these, you can laugh or you can cry. I choose laughter." I think the audience does, too.

If this sounds like one big pitch to get Joe Biden and Kamala Harris to appear weekly on *Pod Save America*, you are not totally wrong. But why wouldn't they want to be on a show that reaches millions of people every few weeks, an audience larger than every show on CNN and almost every show on MSNBC?[25] Democratic leaders must

---

24 If I went, I probably wouldn't make it out alive.
25 Hey White House, you know how to reach me.

embrace Democratic media just as they would embrace other allies, think tanks, grassroots organizations, and PACs. In the modern age, a progressive media is more important than the rest of our electoral coalition. If the last few elections have shown us anything, it's that winning the messaging war is a necessary ingredient for winning elections and saving democracy.

19

Starve the Trolls: How Liberals Can Stop Being Owned Online

In the days before Trump, it was a common assumption in American politics that Republicans were miserable at social media. They had fewer followers, made less of an impression, and always seemed be trying a little too hard.

During the 2012 campaign, the first campaign conducted largely on Twitter, Barack Obama set the standard for how a politician should behave on the internet. He spoke the lingo and possessed the effortless cool and self-confidence to poke fun at himself.

Obama's approach was perhaps embodied by an appearance on *The Tonight Show Starring Jimmy Fallon*[1] where Obama "slow-jammed the news" with the Roots, the *Tonight Show* house band and all-time great hip-hop group. The bit was a recurring segment in which guests read the news to the cadence of a 1990s R&B song. It's ridiculous, and no one looks good doing it...except Obama, who used the opportunity to hammer the Republicans for jacking up student loan costs. The clip went viral, the media went bananas, and Republicans folded within days. Using a short, humorous (bordering on absurd) video segment on a comedy show as opposed to an appearance on a

---

1 This was before Fallon affectionately mussed Trump's hair and angered the resistance and people generally opposed to the idea of treating racist authoritarian con men with kid gloves.

Sunday show or a *Washington Post* op-ed to drive a political message was the new politics. And Obama did it better than anyone else.[2]

And what was Mitt Romney's internet strategy? Awkward step-dad with a flip phone. If pleated khakis were a person,[3] they would be Romney. Whatever the internet and social media are, Romney didn't get it. The rest of the Republicans weren't any better. Social media was new(ish) and exciting(ish). And *new* and *exciting* aren't words often associated with Republicans. It's almost as if they resented having to communicate with people in any way other than being interviewed on Fox News. They were a party of old people who wanted to talk only to other old people, the old-fashioned way. In those days, even Facebook was too cool for them.

Flash-forward to the post-Obama era, and the Republicans are crushing the Democrats digitally. *We* are now Mitt Romney—not the Trump-impeaching, rare-voice-of-GOP-courage Mitt Romney, but the dorky, out-of-touch, can't-figure-out-which-way-to-aim-the-phone Mitt Romney of 2012. Right-wing figures now drive the conversation on the internet. Whether it's Facebook or Twitter, right-wing posts trend more often and get more engagement. Democrats are behind on a game we thought we'd mastered.

Did the Republicans gain an edge by mimicking Obama-era "internet cool?" Not even close. The right-wing yahoos who dominate the political internet, folks like Dan Bongino, Josh Hawley, Tucker Carlson, and Ben Shapiro, are the opposite of cool. They are people with the collective charisma of belly button lint.

It's our fault. Yep. You and me. This collection of fools is playing us for fools. Online liberals (myself very much included) have been unwitting soldiers in the GOP's online army.

---

2 Then or now.

3 Believe it or not, this book's fact checkers pointed out that Obama has worn pleated khakis.

Let me explain by using the example of the human internet punching bag and senator from Texas Ted Cruz.

Cruz Control

There is no person easier or more enjoyable to make fun of than Ted Cruz. He is deserving of all the online enmity directed at him and more. Cruz is cynical, shameless, and downright annoying. It's hard to know where to begin with him. He spent the last few years begging for acceptance from Donald Trump, even though Trump had called his wife ugly and accused his father of killing John F. Kennedy.[4] Maybe we begin when Cruz absconded to a luxury resort in Cancún while his constituents (who pay his salary) were stuck in a statewide blackout. If the two most annoying people in your high school class had a child, that child would be Ted Cruz.

Every time Cruz logs on to Twitter, he invites an avalanche of ridicule.[5] He leads with his very weak chin in every tweet. The counterpunch to his tweets is so obvious and impossible to resist. In recent years, he attacked Big Bird, accused Joe Biden of destroying America because of a shortage of Chick-fil-A sauces, and retweeted a Russian propaganda video in an ass-backward attack on "wokeness" in the US military. At one point, Cruz even expressed openness to the idea of Texas seceding from the union and suggested that podcast host Joe Rogan be president of "the Independent State of Texas." Every tweet elicited a response from thousands of online liberals, who dunked on Cruz or parried his tweet with a cutting comment.

Those responses are undoubtedly bright spots of enjoyment in

---

4 If democracy and the planet survive long enough, it's going to be super hard to explain this period in American history to people.
5 This is the one case where Twitter is real life.

what has been a pretty dark period in history. And who am I to deny people the pleasure of dunking on Cruz?

But ask yourself: Who gets more pleasure from your brilliant Twitter dunk than you?

Ted Cruz. You are feeding him.

Cruz (or someone on his staff) writes these tweets for the specific purpose of baiting liberals into Twitter fights. The angrier and more biting the replies, the better. It's not only Cruz who employs this strategy. "Owning the libs" by weaponizing liberal anger into online engagement is the primary Republican political strategy of the internet age. It's how we got Trump, and it's how we will get the next Trump if Democrats don't figure out how to properly respond to the antagonism.

To be fair to us, this is mostly Silicon Valley's fault. They built their platforms to reward the worst behaviors. They algorithmically perverted American politics. The algorithms that power Twitter and Facebook constitute an "attention economy." The type of attention is largely irrelevant to these rapacious profit engines. Hate and love are one and the same. All they care about is keeping you on the platform for as long as possible to collect as much data and show you as many ads as possible. If a post elicits a lot of engagement, the algorithm will show it to more people. Every time we comment in anger, dunk via a quote tweet (QT), or register our dislike or anger via an emoticon, we ensure that the offending post receives more engagement and is seen by more people. It feels good to you, but it feels great to Ted Cruz.

This isn't exclusive to Cruz. Trolling or "owning the libs" is the primary political strategy of the Republican Party in the Trump era.

Marjorie Taylor Greene, a junior member of Congress who has been kicked off her committee, grows in political power by fighting with liberals. Her Twitter feed was a nonstop stream of liberal rage bait. She stalks Rep. Alexandria Ocasio-Cortez on- and offline in the hope of picking a fight that will garner her attention. In one sense, Greene's strategy is working. She is a junior member of Congress who sits on no committees. She has barely the political power you do, but her star is rising in the Republican Party. No one should know her, or care about her, but according to a February 2021 Morning Consult poll, Greene's name ID was nearly as high as House Minority Leader Kevin McCarthy's. Even more disturbingly, after Greene became the focus of attention for her racist, anti-Semitic, unhinged views, her favorable rating among Republican voters increased by 11 points. She hijacked our attention and reaped the rewards. By constantly making fun of Greene for her batty conspiracy theories (Jewish Space Lasers), we are giving her the thing she desires most and deserves least: attention.[6]

In addition to spreading their message and building their brand, right-wing trolls want to use liberal outrage as proof of their conservative bona fides. We all laughed as Seth Rogen destroyed Cruz in a Twitter fight. But a Hollywood star telling the Texas senator to "fuck off" was a huge win for Cruz. For Republican politicians, the best way to be liked by the folks in their party is to be hated by the folks in the other party.

When we take the bait, we empower the trolls, enable their political strategy, and inadvertently spread disinformation and conspiracy theories. This is what the Right wants. And doing what your opponent wants you to do is always a bad strategy.

Later in this book, I will get into what can be done to change the incentives that make trolling an effective strategy. But between now and when the US Congress, federal regulators, and the captains of the tech industry adopt all my ideas, here are a few suggestions for how you can personally slow the spread of Republican propaganda:

---

6 If Trump was Kim Kardashian before Kim Kardashian, then Marjorie Taylor Greene is Scott Disick (IYKYK).

Allocate Your Attention Strategically

"Don't feed the trolls" is an easy thing to say and a hard thing to do. I say this from experience, because I fall for the trick more often than I would like to admit.[7] It's easy to get angry online and react without thinking. But always remember: Your attention is your greatest weapon. Think strategically about how you want to allocate it. Many of the worst people on the internet wake up every morning eager to hijack your attention. They want to use your outrage to build their brand and amass political power. Denying them the engagement they so desperately crave is how we fight back against the politics of "owning the libs."

In 2021, Anil Dash, an extremely thoughtful leader in the tech community, shared very good advice on how to think about online engagement in a Twitter thread:

> A reminder that may not be obvious: amplification on social networks has monetary value. Twitter's algorithm counts it as engagement[,] even if you shared a tweet to criticize it or mock it[,] and uses that signal to amplify the tweet further. Only RT what you would pay to promote...Do not reply to, retweet, or quote a tweet from a fascist unless you would give them your money. Apparently, some people would rather make that gift than change their behavior online, and I don't know what to do about that.

In other words, quote-tweeting or hate-sharing Cruz's content is the same as contributing to his campaign. If you wouldn't do the latter, don't do the former.

---

7 Thank you to the people on Twitter who ever so gently remind me when I violate my own rules.

Think about the causes, ideas, and politicians you want to contribute to and share their content. In the internet era, whom and what we give our attention to matters a lot. Do it wisely.

Share Screenshots, Not Posts

Whenever I talk, tweet, or write about ignoring the trolls, people respond with some version of the *Washington Post*'s pretentious marketing slogan "Democracy Dies in Darkness." The gist of this argument is that the only way to stem the rising Republican tide of racism, authoritarianism, and conspiracy is to shine a light on it. The point is not wrong—we cannot ignore these dangerous trends in Republican politics—but it's *how* we shine the light that matters.

One online engagement rule from Dash: If you need/want to push back on disinformation or highlight a dishonest or dangerous statement, take a screenshot of the statement and share that. This will allow you to make your point without giving the troll the engagement they crave.

Don't Spread Disinformation

Social media is awash in disinformation—conspiracy theories about the election, lies about Democrats, and mis- and disinformation about vaccines—and it's fair to say the internet is where reality and truth go to die. There is the natural and very well-meaning tendency to see bad info and correct the record. It seems like the right thing to do, and it is (has been) a cardinal rule of politics: Let no lie go unchallenged. And if we are honest with ourselves, the only thing more enjoyable than calling someone like Ted Cruz an "asshole" is calling them a "dumb asshole." Fact-checking falsehoods seems like the right thing to do. After all, that's what the media take real pride in. Folks like CNN's Daniel Dale became media stars for their valiant efforts to point out the bullshit. But fact-checking on a social media platform is a tricky business. How you do it matters. Commenting, liking, and quote-tweeting only feeds the engagement meter and therefore ensures that more people see the disinformation. Once again, the perverted incentives of the algorithms rear their ugly head. Doing the putatively right thing rewards the very people doing the wrong thing. This is not to say we should let the liars lie without a response. That would be bad, especially given that their platforms are too greedy, too afraid, and frankly too incompetent to stop the lies on their own. So, here's what you do:

- Use the screenshot trick to avoid triggering the engagement metric.
- Share the media fact-checked lies you stumble upon, understanding, of course, that the source matters to your audience. CNN and the *New York Times* will be immediately dismissed as fake news by your MAGA uncle. The Rupert Murdoch–owned *Wall Street Journal* less so. An influencer or TikTok star might be more influential to your young cousin than some over-the-hill former Obama hack who hosts a podcast.
- Flag the disinformation for the platform, and keep your expectations low about the outcome. No one likes a narc, but there's a chance it just might work and some content moderator will pull the offending post down or ensure it gets less promotion. It's worth a shot and takes about fifteen seconds.

If and when (most likely when) the platform fails to act to stem the disinformation, you can put pressure on its creators via their advertisers. Color of Change, Sleeping Giants, and others have spearheaded a successful advertising boycott of Facebook. At its peak, more than one thousand companies, including major brands like Coca-Cola and Procter and Gamble, either stopped advertising or significantly reduced their spending on the platform. This was a PR nightmare for Facebook, but it ultimately had little impact on its bottom line (which is a strong argument for antitrust action).

Laughs Travel as Fast as Lies

Abbie Richards is one of the most influential antidisinformation voices on the internet. In 2020, she created a chart that helped explain the spectrum of conspiracy theories—from "things that actually happened" (the JFK assassination) to "detached from reality" (QAnon). Richards isn't an academic, and she didn't publish her chart in a policy journal or unveil it at a conference.

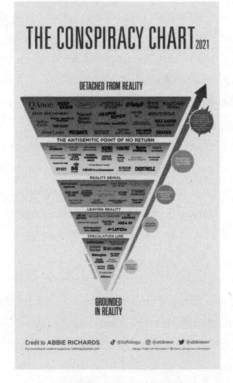

Courtesy of Abbie Richards.

The twentysomething former stand-up comic and environmental activist runs an antidisinformation TikTok account called "Tofology," which has more than 200,000 followers. Abbie's weapon against disinformation is not lectures. It's laughs. She makes viral videos that raise questions and poke fun. Her TikToks are some of the most effective content I have seen. What is notable about them—and is a lesson for all of us—is that she doesn't patronize or demean. The target of her humor is the conspiracy theories themselves, not the people who believe them. There are two types of viral content: anger and humor. Anger often powers the disinformation. Humor can be the antidote. But it must be empathetic, not elitist.

Serve Your Revenge Cold

Over the years, we have done dozens and dozens of *Pod Save America* shows. During every single one, we have received a request from a listener for advice about what to do when in the presence of their Trump-supporting, Fox-watching uncle/dad/dentist/coworker/yoga instructor.[8] What arguments and messages do we recommend for bringing their loved one back from the dark (red) side? This is a tough question, because it is usually asked in good faith and because the real answer is that there is almost certainly no hope. That person is gone and probably won't come back. The truth is depressing and demobilizing. And it's a real downer in front of a live audience.

At one point, Jon Lovett came up with an inspired answer. Stop trying to convert your MAGA uncle/dad/dentist/coworker/yoga instructor in the moment and, instead, go find two friends who aren't registered or even planning to vote and get them to vote. You'll cancel out the MAGA vote and spare yourself an infuriating and exhausting

---

8 I got this one once. For real.

conversation. It's a brilliant alternative to banging one's head against a wall.

A similar approach could be used with your online anger. Instead of responding to a troll, promote two progressive politicians or causes. Instead of dunking on some racist grifter, share information about how to register to vote, or volunteer for an organization working to defeat racist trolls. This may sound cheesy and less personally enjoyable, but I promise it is healthier for you and better for the cause.

Resisting the urge to express our outrage at outrageous conduct is hard. I fail to follow this rule at times. But we can and must do so. We liberals need to stop owning ourselves.

20

Build an Army of Keyboard Warriors

In May 2020, just as the campaign against Biden was ramping up, Donald Trump sent a cryptic tweet to his tens of millions of followers.

> Thank you to all of my great Keyboard Warriors. You are better, and far more brilliant, than anyone on Madison Avenue (Ad Agencies). There is nobody like you!

The response from Resistance Twitter was typical: derision and conspiracy mongering. We laughed at Trump's odd use of unnecessary parentheticals.[1] We wondered which nefarious groups Trump was communicating with. Was he speaking to the Proud Boys, the Russians, someone else? Was this a follow-up to the still-mysterious "covfefe" message of a few years before?[2]

Unlike other Trump social media musings, this tweet wasn't an oblique, deranged response to something random said on cable TV three days before.[3] Nor was it an attack on a B-list celebrity or junior member of congress. It also wasn't an attack on a reporter or a

---

1 Well, to be clear, as the author of a 2018 book titled *Yes We (Still) Can*, I most definitely did not laugh at the parentheses.
2 I am not the only one who remembers this, right?
3 We live in a golden age of entertainment, one where every movie and TV show ever made is at our fingertips, yet Trump DVRs cable news and watches it days later. This should have been included in the Articles of Impeachment.

complaint about a poll. Trump wasn't promoting Fox or denigrating CNN.

What made this Trump tweet unique was that it was smart. Really smart.

Now, to be clear, Donald Trump is not a smart man. Any person who believes that injecting bleach could be a wise medical course is in no danger of being admitted to Mensa. The former president often can't get out of his own way due to a twitchy Twitter finger and a level of insecurity that would make George Costanza look cocky. But Trump has an intuitive understanding of the modern media environment and how to communicate with his supporters.

His "Keyboard Warriors" are the army of online MAGA super-fans who flood social media with messaging, memes, and videos that deify Trump and demonize anyone and everyone in his way. Trump, whose life is defined by a desperate quest to be loved, understood the personal and political advantages of having millions of people expressing their approbation online.

Trump's army pumps out reams of low-quality content. Memes about "Crooked Hillary" or "Sleepy Joe," homemade videos of Trump body-slamming the media, and fan fiction about Trump as a conqueror and savior. There is even a guy who does oil paintings with Trump in famous historical settings—Trump crossing the Delaware, Trump at Gettysburg, etc. Some of it is dumb; a lot of it is schlocky; much of it is offensive, misogynistic, and racist.

But it works.

In the age of social media, when content is king and when quantity matters more than quality, Trump has millions of people pumping out content. They flood Facebook, Twitter, Instagram, and TikTok with content, making his message trend and ensuring that anyone and everyone sees positive stories about Trump and negative ones about his adversaries.[4] These folks see it as their job—nay, their calling—to ensure that Trump's message is spread far and wide.

Trump took time out of his not-so-busy day to thank the keyboard warriors because they helped him win in 2016 and would be critical to his reelection campaign. He understood their power.

Some look at Trump's army of racist rabble-rousers and despair. I see a model for exactly what Democrats need to do. The best way, the only way, to win the messaging wars is to build an army.

A Million Messengers

Like Trump, the Democrats have an army. Even in the middle of a pandemic, millions of Americans dedicated themselves to defeating Trump. People called and texted voters in their spare time. They donated what they could—often five or ten dollars at a time. There is no lack of enthusiasm on our side. The problem is that the Democratic Party treats its volunteers like telemarketers and an ATM.

Traditionally, we ask our volunteers to telephone strangers from a list, even though almost no one ever answers a call from an unknown number anymore. We have them walk for miles knocking on doors without knowing whether people are home. Sometimes, our volunteers and organizers are instructed to stand on street corners and parking lots, hoping to run into people who (a) are not yet registered to vote; (b) support our candidates; and (c) have the time and inclination to stop, talk to a stranger, and then fill out a piece of paper.

Plenty of research shows the value of a face-to-face conversation or a phone call. Yes, it's nearly impossible to register someone to vote

---

4 That is, everyone not named Donald Trump Sr. (He hates Don Jr. and could turn on him at any minute out of disappointment.)

over the phone, but there is value in every wrong number and incorrect address, because this information improves the voter file. But we must recognize the remarkable inefficiency of these activities. Anyone who has made phone calls for campaigns knows what I'm talking about. You carve out an hour of time you don't have, dial fifty numbers, and if you are incredibly lucky, you reach four people, of whom only two don't scream at you to stop calling them. Sure, you are able to leave messages with information about polling places, voter registration, and mail-in ballots, but is this really a good use of your time? Or, to put it a better way, is it the *best* use of your time?

It most certainly isn't.

In the age of the internet, nearly everyone is walking around with a supercomputer in their pocket. With Facebook, Twitter, Instagram, and their phone contacts, each of these people is connected to a couple hundred people on average. With the push of a button, they can send a message, a video, or an ad to that entire group. And people are much more likely to click on and trust information shared by someone they know.

Imagine a world where this army was empowered to persuade, shape the conversation online, and fight back against Trump's keyboard warriors; a world where the Democratic Party trusted them to carry out its message, combat conspiracy theories, and convince their friends and family to join the cause.

In the middle of the 2020 election, I decided to take matters into my own hands. For my entire career, I have been writing memos to candidates, senators, party leaders, and a president with strategic advice on what to say, how to say it, and to whom—insider information for insiders. I started writing *Message Box*, a newsletter I viewed as a strategy memo for the masses. I wanted to offer political messaging advice and polling analysis to the sorts of people who never get access to that sort of information—people running for school board, grassroots activists, and the folks trying to win the election one voter at a time on Facebook or via text.

This was admittedly a small-scale effort to turn volunteers into messengers, but it was proof of concept of the larger model I had been pushing for years. My readers began using the messaging I proffered in their campaigns and on their social media feeds. It wasn't everything; it was far from enough; but it was a start.

Adopting this approach at scale, however, will require a fundamental shift in how the Democrats do business.

The Best Way to Fight Disinformation

This grassroots-distributed messaging strategy is a key antidote to the right-wing disinformation plaguing our politics.

In the old days, before Mark Zuckerberg ruined everything, ignoring crazy conspiracy theories was an effective approach. If a politician or campaign acknowledged the absurd, the press covered it, and more people learned about it.

Ignoring the dumb stuff that emanates from the dark corners of the internet is no longer an option. The most common response from a political campaign to a false attack or conspiracy theory is to turn to the fact-checkers and the media and implore them to debunk it. But fighting back in the mainstream media is woefully insufficient. It's like appealing to the referees in a game when the other side doesn't recognize these officials' authority. Also, given how information bubbles work, the stories will mostly be seen by people who would never believe the attack to begin with. The mainstream media has neither the reach nor the credibility to play referee against disinformation and conspiracy theories. This assertion will annoy many reporters, but look at how woefully ineffective the media was at pushing back against the Big Lie about the 2020 election.

Getting the stories written is the first step. It is incumbent upon Democrats to get the stories, fact-checking, and other pushback in front of the public and in the hands of our supporters, and then to ask those supporters to spread the word to the people in their networks.

Yet, there is currently no concerted effort at the top levels of the Democratic Party to turn our army of volunteers into messengers. This lack has been driving me insane for years now. We are choosing to lose, and for the dumbest reasons possible.

The first impediment to adopting this newer, better approach to communications is structural inertia. Political communications and all public relations are currently centered on press management. Every decision is designed to answer the question: How do we work with the press to get our message out? The communications director develops the communications strategy and decides which interviews to do with which outlets and when to give speeches or make announcements to maximize press coverage. The press secretary is the spokesperson who responds to media inquiries, funnels their requests, and manages the relationship with the all-important constituency. For a long time, 90 percent of political communications was press management. This is no longer the case, but the basic staffing structure of the communications operations in campaigns, political organizations, Congress, and the White House is built on a long-outdated model. There have, of course, been changes and innovations over the years. The Obama White House had a large digital strategy office. We hired someone in the communications office whose primary job was to communicate with progressive publications and personalities. But in every case, these innovations were appended onto the old model. This marriage is always inefficient and a bit awkward.

We need to tear up the old staffing structure and rebuild it from the ground up. I fear that tinkering with the old communications director model is doomed to fail. Inertia and muscle memory will continue to push the campaign back into old habits.

A new model would focus on persuasion through content creation and distribution, not media coverage and press management. A content-first strategy requires thinking about a *New York Times* article, an interview on *Colbert*, and a campaign-created digital video in the same way. They are all a piece of content needing a separate distribution strategy. For a few years now, I have been pushing for campaigns to hire a chief content officer[5] to oversee persuasion writ large—whether in ads, social media, traditional press, or online organizing.

My appeals have fallen on deaf ears. I am sure I haven't yet made the best case for this new approach, but there is another problem. A new model is a threat to everyone thriving in the old one. I get that. I have no doubt that I would have been very resistant if some over-the-hill yahoo podcaster guy came around to suggest I get layered. Consider this: what's worse than getting layered or losing some stature? Losing another election to Donald Trump, that's what.

Another problem is that politics is filled with risk-averse control freaks.[6] Asking your supporters to make content or post things on the

---

5 Some will derisively call this a "minister of information," but there is a fundamental difference between a minister of information and a minister of *dis*information.
6 I say this as a risk-averse control freak. Just ask my former coworkers (or my wife).

internet is inherently risky. It means giving up control over the message. Political operatives of a certain generation have an incident from 2004 scarred into their psyche. MoveOn, an upstart political organization, had mobilized the opposition to the Iraq War using innovative digital techniques. MoveOn was a power player in a party largely uncomfortable with its proud liberalism and aggressive tactics. Like Trump, MoveOn's movement was powered by highly engaged, digitally savvy activists. It asked its supporters to make campaign ads as part of a contest. On paper, this was a very smart idea. It got people fired up and drew attention to the group. In reality, it was a political disaster. A couple of people made ads comparing President George W. Bush to Hitler,[7] and with the cynical help of the Bush campaign, the MoveOn contest became a raging political controversy that engulfed even John Kerry, Bush's Democratic opponent. The MoveOn ad contest was an abject lesson in relinquishing control of the message: when you did so, your opponent and the media could hold you accountable for things created by your supporters.

The technical term for the MoveOn contest's ads and the Trump memes is *user-generated content.* I am sympathetic to the risk. Over my many years in politics, I vetoed a lot of ideas encouraging user-generated content. This was a mistake, an archaic way of thinking about communications. It's penny-wise, pound foolish. There is no other option anymore. We need to loosen the reins, let go, and empower.

The necessity of closing the messaging gap with the Republicans outweighs the risk of some minor controversy. Hell, Trump never paid a real price for the crazy stuff his supporters made. Why should Democrats tie one hand behind their backs?

This is all scary and daunting—we are so much farther from

---

7 Comparing your political opponent to Nazis was long verboten, but things change, and you are now reading a book whose title contains a not-so-subtle allusion to Nazism.

success than we should be—but it's also empowering. Every person reading this book has the power to fight back against the disinformation, propaganda, and dangerous bullshit that powers Trumpism. We have access to the internet and a network of people who want to hear from us. It will be a while before the progressive echo chamber can compete with Fox and Facebook, but we must take control of our destiny.

The Republicans have Rupert Murdoch, Mark Zuckerberg, and Steve Bannon. The Democrats have you.[8]

That's good enough for me. If Democrats are willing to trust you, we will win.

---

8 No pressure.

21

Signs of Hope

I was in a political funk in 2021. The pandemic was dragging on. The early promises of the Biden presidency had turned into a frustrating lack of progress due to Republican obstruction and centrist Democratic obstinance. There was little effort to learn the lessons from the Big Lie.

The events of January 6, 2021, were a turning point. Trump is more firmly in control of his party today than when he was in the White House. Instead of being convicted or chastened, those who spread the Big Lie and incited the violence were only emboldened. "January sixth was practice" had become a rallying cry for the Right. And yet, too many Democrats seemed to be unaware of the danger and incapable of meeting the moment. It felt like everyone was watching the Republicans push America into authoritarianism, but no one was willing to do anything about it.

Whenever people asked me how I stayed hopeful amid the darkness of the Trump years, I would regale them with stories of the inspiring activists I met while traveling the country for *Pod Save America*. By the fall of 2021, it had been well over a year since I traveled for anything of consequence.[1] Sure, I did a bunch of virtual fund-raisers

---

1 I hadn't even been in the same room with my *Pod Save America* cohosts since the beginning of the pandemic.

and phone banks, but the rhythm of the events grew monotonous by the time the 2021 elections came around.

Log on.

Thank the volunteers/donors.

Talk about the importance of the election.

Take a few questions and log off.

Don't get me wrong, I was more than happy to help where I could, and grateful that I could do it without going farther than down the hall from my family. With an infant and a toddler at home during a pandemic, the convenience was a lifesaver. But being on Zoom is not the same as being in the room. The conversations I had on the road pre-pandemic happened on the margins—meet-and-greets backstage, while leaving the venue after a show, or while waiting in line to get my morning coffee. The Zoom experience was just different, less human.

But one night, I logged on for an event that gave me hope that we could beat the Big Liars.

DemCast is an organization started by Nick Knudsen and Lori Coleman. It grew out of the devastating defeat of November 2016. Nick and Lori, like so many others, were propelled into political activism out of a deep desire to do something to save their country from Donald Trump and all he stood for. So many important organizations like this came from Trump's election—SwingLeft, Run For Something, Indivisible, the Be a Hero Fund—and all of them played a huge role in taking back the House, Senate, and White House. But DemCast was unique. After some trial and error, Nick and Lori were building an army of online digital activists pushing messages on social media. Whether it was promoting Biden's accomplishments or informing the public of Republican obstruction, DemCast was recruiting volunteers, teaching them effective messaging, giving them tools and tips, and then setting them free to multiply the messengers.

I connected with Nick during the 2020 campaign and heard about what he was working on, but it wasn't until I joined a training session with hundreds of activists that I fully understood the power of what DemCast was building.

These folks understood the dangers of the right-wing media machine. They understood that they had the power to fight back. They weren't waiting for permission from the White House or from Democrats in Congress. They were the embodiment of Barack Obama's old adage "Change always comes from the bottom up." It wasn't everything, but it was a start. And it was inspiring. It shook me out of my funk and opened my eyes.

It wasn't just DemCast. The more I looked around, the more I found reasons for hope in the battle against the Big Lie.

Tara McGowan, a longtime Democratic digital operative, started Good Information, a public-benefit corporation that is fighting disinformation by investing in local news businesses. Good Information is the parent company of Courier Newsroom, a collection of progressive local news sites filling in the gap left by the decimation of local news and combating the disinformation merchants trying to exploit that gap. As Pat Rynard, the founder of Iowa Starting Line, a progressive digital outlet acquired by Courier in 2021, told the *Des Moines Register*, "Our new goal is going to be figuring out how to get good factual news in front of Iowans who get all their news in their social media feed, who don't subscribe to local newspapers, who don't watch the evening news."

Good Information and Courier are on the front lines in the battle against the right-wing billionaires funding right-wing local sites to push propaganda. I, for one, am very glad they're here.[2]

Also in 2021, Faiz Shakir, Bernie Sanders's campaign manager, launched More Perfect Union. This progressive digital media start-up

---

2 In 2021, because I believe so deeply in its mission, I joined Good Information's advisory board.

embodied the earlier admonition to tell the progressive story on its own terms. In clever and creative ways, it has created videos and other content that make the case for progressive policies. With an intense focus on workers' rights, union organizing, and the predatory behavior of large corporations, More Perfect Union tells the stories corporate media is unwilling to tell. Shakir told reporters that his outlet was, in part, a progressive response to right-wing video provocateurs like Ben Shapiro and PragerU. While a fraction of the scale of Shapiro and others, More Perfect Union is already making an impact. Its video about the horrendous working conditions at a Frito-Lay plant in Kansas garnered over a million views on YouTube—more than the number of viewers who tune into CNN most nights.

By focusing on criminal justice reform, Black history, and democracy, PushBlack, has quickly become "the nation's largest non-profit media organization for Black Americans. With more than 500,000 Instagram followers and nearly 10 million followers across all platforms, PushBlack has played a critical role in pushing back on Right Wing narratives about critical race theory and other racist messaging.

Others leapt into action, taking it upon themselves to create and promote content. MeidasTouch,[3] a group formed by Ben, Brett, and Jordan Meiselas, three brothers stuck at home and bored during the pandemic, has been flooding the internet with viral videos about Donald Trump and the Republicans. Don Winslow, a successful crime author, transitioned from an anti-Trump Twitter activist to a producer and funder of videos pushing progressive messaging. Not all the videos work; some miss; and few are designed to persuade undecided or swing voters, but quantity matters more than quality. And as mentioned previously, preaching to the choir is okay. Either we preach to our choir, or someone else does.

---

3 Get it? Because "truth is golden."

Some democrative operatives cringe at those efforts, but we should be encouraging risk taking. The more the merrier, in my view.

More and more reporters are willing to adjust their approach to fight disinformation. Several outlets now have reporters dedicated to covering right-wing disinformation.[4] CNN's Jake Tapper and Brian Stelter began aggressively pushing back against the Big Lie and those who promote it. Their refusal to normalize these right-wing lies and their willingness to explicitly call out Fox News is a model that others can and should follow.

Under public pressure from grassroots activists and frustrated subscribers, DirecTV stopped carrying OAN, crippling the pro-Trump conspiracy theory television network. DirecTV's decision proved that there is a price to pay for corporations profiting off right-wing disinformation—but if, and only if, a spotlight is shone. The Democratic National committee has invested time and money in an innovative and aggressive effort to fight disinformation.

And Crooked Media defied the doubters who believed the success of the company was dependent on Trump's presence in the White House. The company has expanded in multiple ways with a slate of new offerings, a beefed-up staff, and a new focus on video to fight back at what the Right is doing on YouTube. As an example, a new video series called *Tommy Gets Redpilled* has Tommy Vietor deep-diving into the conspiracy theories and disinformation making the rounds on the internet.

Don't get me wrong. There is so much more work to do. Too many are unwilling or unable to grasp the threat of the forces that brought us the Big Lie. Nor are they willing to contemplate the solutions necessary to win the war. But these efforts are a beginning, a reason for hope. And hope is a great place to start.

---

4 Talk about a soul-destroying beat. There should be a fund-raising drive every six months or so to send these folks on a nice vacation.

Epilogue

The Battle (against the Big Lie)
Goes On

I put the finishing touches on *Battling the Big Lie* right as the calendar turned to 2022.[1] The Democrats were staring down the barrel of a high-stakes midterm election in the most brutal of conditions. President Biden's approval ratings were as low as Donald Trump's at the same time in his presidency. Inflation was creeping up for the first time in forty years. And the public was in an objectively shitty mood—three quarters of Americans told pollsters that they were dissatisfied with the direction of the country.

You never want to lose an election, but this would have been a very bad election to lose. According to the *Washington Post*, "a majority of Republican nominees on the ballot this November for the House, Senate, and key statewide offices—291 in all—have denied or questioned the outcome of the last presidential election." And to make matters

---

1 "Wait, didn't your book come out in June of that year? Why so long?" Great questions. The publishing industry (filled with great people) moves with a speed that makes the United States Senate seem spry. At some point, someone will tell them about the invention of laser printers.

worse,[2] the biggest, proudest proponents of the Big Lie were running for governor, secretary of state, and attorney general in the battleground states that will decide the 2024 presidential election. The Right was sending an advance deployment of insurrectionists to seize the electoral apparatus and succeed where Donald Trump failed in 2020. When I say "insurrectionists," it's not liberal hyperbole. There were actual insurrectionists on the ballot. Pennsylvania Republicans nominated Doug Mastriano for governor. Mastriano was at the Capitol on January 6. In Arizona, the Republican nominee for secretary of state was a member of a Far-Right militia group. A candidate for Michigan governor had the FBI show up at his home to question him about his role in the assault on the Capitol.[3] Had these yahoos won, it would have posed an existential threat to the integrity of the 2024 election.

As the year went on, everyone began predicting a "Red Wave" that would wash Democrats out and Big Lie believers in. Democrats were despondent, and Republicans were downright cocky. As a natural-born pessimist, I mentally and professionally prepared for Democrats to lose. On Election Day, I flew down to Los Angeles to participate in Crooked Media's election night activities. On the short flight from Oakland to Burbank, I started sketching out my reaction to the ass kicking everyone expected. I had been writing the *Message Box* political newsletter for a couple years, and I knew I would need to have some thoughts for my subscribers after we knew the outcome. At the airport and on the plane, I wrote about seven hundred words with my reaction about what I thought was about to happen, what it all meant, and how Democrats should think about responding. As a big believer

---

2 Yes, worse is possible. Remember that when it comes to Republicans, worse is not only possible, it's probable.

3 This guy lost the primary to someone who believed the George Floyd protests were part of a Democratic plot to topple the US government as revenge for losing the Civil War. The Republicans are not sending their best (or perhaps this is their best).

in "preparing for the worst, and hoping for the best," this seemed like a good use of time as I was stuck on the runaway.

As it turns out, it was a terrible use of time. That newsletter never saw the light of day. Despite the relatively shitty fundamentals, it was a great night. Democrats didn't just hold the Senate majority; they picked up a critical seat for a 51-49 edge. This one seat meant that we didn't have to negotiate with Mitch McConnell about the rules of the Senate or committee makeups. The extra breathing room meant an easier path to confirming judges and other nominees. Although Republicans won control of the House of Representatives, they did so by a historically small margin—giving Democrats a real shot to take the House back in 2024. And perhaps most significantly, the Big Lie–believing candidates for governor, secretary of state, and attorney general in the battleground states lost.

In the days after the election, the pro-democracy coalition in American politics[4] crowed that the majority struck a decisive blow against the MAGA minority. Some even went so far as to say that Democracy had been saved—or at least preserved.

Were the 2022 elections a "battle against the Big Lie?" And if so, did the Big Lie really lose?

Yes . . . but also no. Per usual in Trump-era American politics—it's complicated.

Thanks to Democratic victories in places like Arizona, Nevada, Wisconsin, Pennsylvania, and Michigan, it is going to be much harder for MAGA extremists to steal the 2024 election. They tried to seize the levers of power and failed. So, in that sense, democracy is in a stronger position and the next election is more secure than before. If Republicans had done as well as people thought (and I feared), there was a

---

4 Democrats + nongrifting Never Trump Republicans.

very real chance Donald Trump or some other MAGA goon could've ascended to the White House without winning the election.

Adherence to the Big Lie (that the 2020 election was stolen) is the fundamental tenet of MAGA-ism. Repeating that lie was not enough. In order to win Donald Trump's support, Republican candidates needed to act on that lie. In doing so, they revealed that pushing the Big Lie came with a political cost. The closer a candidate was associated with MAGA extremism and relitigating the 2020 election, the more likely they were to lose. To put a finer point on it, in the purple states, Donald Trump—Mr. Big Lie, himself—was a giant bloated political albatross weighing down his candidates.

That's good news. In fact, I think you can safely call it great news, especially in the context of how a president's party normally does in the midterms. But,[5] winning the battle is not the same as winning the war.

Defeating candidates pushing the Big Lie is not the same as defeating the lie itself or the MAGA megaphone.

A January 2023. CBS News/YouGov poll found that 47 percent of Republicans considered what happened at the Capitol on January 6 to be "patriotism." Perhaps even more disturbing, 41 percent of Republicans said that the people who forced their way into the Capitol were mostly members of "Left-leaning groups." This belief persists despite a lack of supporting evidence and a series of high-profile hearings led by the daughter of the Republican vice president that proved beyond a shadow of a doubt what happened on January 6.

In the months after the election, conspiracy theories about vaccines and COVID continued to circulate. The right wing generated an absurd moral panic about Joe Biden taking away people's gas stoves.[6]

---

5 You knew there was going to be a "but."
6 He's not.

The failures of the conspiracy peddlers at the ballot box is not a sign that the Left has nullified the right wing's media advantage.

In fact, the problem could get worse before it gets better. After the hardcover edition of this book hit the shelves, Elon Musk bought Twitter. At one time, Musk was an Obama-supporting, quasi-progressive but had taken a hard Right turn in recent years and spent too much time online. In his own words, Musk had been "red-pilled" by Far-Right internet culture. One of Musk's first acts was to restore thousands of accounts that had been banned for violating Twitter's terms of service. Among those replatformed were Donald Trump, his fellow insurrection conspirators, white supremacists, holocaust deniers, and the biggest pushers of misinformation about COVID. Despite repeatedly claiming to be a free speech fundamentalist, Musk banned journalists from Twitter for various reasons that mostly amounted to personal pique. Musk's ownership of Twitter is a problem. He purchased the primary vehicle through which media and politicians communicate, and he is putting his thumb on the scale. Imagine if Rupert Murdoch didn't just own Fox, but instead owned all of Comcast and was making decisions about which channels and shows people could access.

Similarly, Mark Zuckerberg finally went full heel. Meta's stock went into the toilet. Facebook was becoming a wasteland. TikTok was eating his profits. To cut costs, Zuck stopped spending so much money to stop disinformation or protect users from harassment on Facebook. All the rhetoric about "meaningful interactions" and "connecting people" was gone. The mask was off, and Facebook was nothing more than a company making money from showing ads and monetizing invasions into people's privacy.

The news across the media landscape was not much better. The inexorable decline of the traditional media quickened. CNN and MSNBC were losing ratings and influence as more and more of the public cut the cord. Local newspapers continued to be gobbled up and treated as carrion by vulturous hedge funds. Even the *Washington Post*, which had returned to its prior glory during the Trump years, was losing subscribers and contemplating layoffs.

Put another way, the forces that allowed the right-wing propaganda and disinformation machine to prosper were weakening even as some of the candidates trying to benefit from that machine were being rejected by the electorate.

So, what the hell does that mean for the 2024 election and the future of American democracy?

This One's for All the Marbles

One general rule for politics: if anyone tells you that they know what is going to happen two months, let alone two years, from now, you should forever dismiss them. Mute them, block them, unfollow them, and never look back.[7]

In political terms, the 2024 presidential election is light years from when I am writing this (and perhaps when you are reading this).[8] To adhere to the deadlines of the publishing industry, I am writing this before we know who is running for president. Donald Trump announced his candidacy right after the midterms but has barely appeared in public since then. In fact, there is a chance that he will be sitting in prison when you are reading this. Joe Biden is expected to run for reelection but has not yet made a final decision. Florida governor Ron DeSantis, fresh off a big win in 2022, is leading the race to be the non–Donald Trump, but still very Trumpy, candidate.[9] Mike Pence is actively plotting a campaign despite the Republican Party's

---

7 This is why I am out of the prediction business.
8 Unless you are reading this in 2025. In that case, pretend I was correct.
9 In other words, all of the authoritarian assholery without the clumsy crimes and tacky tweets.

most committed voters recently endorsing his death by hanging. Other lesser lights (see: Cruz, Ted) and grifters (see: Pompeo, Mike) are also planning on running for president.

The candidates are not the only "known unknowns." What's happening in the economy? How high is inflation? What's the price of gas? Is Trump in jail? Is he running for president from his jail cell?

This is all a long way of saying I can't tell you what is going to happen in 2024.[10] But I think I can tell you what is at stake. In short, everything. The next presidential election will be for all the marbles—the rubber match to decide democracy. And despite everything we don't know, I sense an opportunity for Democrats to build on the success of 2022 and strike a fatal blow against the MAGA megaphone and the merchants of misinformation.

As outlined above, the world is in a moment of great disruption, transition, and uncertainty. I believe this a hinge point between two media eras. Cable television is fading fast. Talk radio is being replaced by podcasts. Newspapers are going the way of the dinosaur. Facebook is losing influence and users. Elon Musk is running Twitter into the ground. Even TikTok could get banned due to its ties to the Chinese government.

This uncertainty and change can be viewed two ways—with fear or with hope. I choose hope.

I wrote this book to help people understand the tremendous time, effort, and money that went into building the right wing's messaging apparatus. Telling that story can be defeating. Republicans have a forty-year head start and have already invested billions. That can make efforts to build progressive media seem hopeless. How could we

---

10 If I could see into the future, I would be doing something other than writing books. Something like high-stakes sports gambling and buying lots of lotto tickets.

ever catch up and compete? Are we destined to keep losing the information wars?

This period of rapid chaotic transition gives progressives the opportunity to make up lost time. The MAGA megaphone and the right-wing propaganda machine were built on cable television (Fox), radio (Rush Limbaugh et al.), and Facebook (Breitbart). All three are dying right before our eyes. We don't yet know what will replace them, but if Democrats can figure out what the future looks like and strategically invest our intellectual and financial capital, we could even the playing field long before anyone thought it possible. There is no better time than right now. This upcoming presidential campaign is the best chance we will have to battle the big liars.

The time is now. The opportunity is ours.

Acknowledgments

This book would not have been possible without Sean Desmond, a great publisher and friend. Sean pitched me on right-wing disinformation as the subject of a possible book long before the January 6 insurrection proved the power of the Big Lie. At every step of the process, Sean and the team at Twelve have shepherded this project, provided advice, and talked me off various ledges.

David Larabell and folks at CAA believed in me as an author long before I believed in myself. I am grateful for all the advice, support, and advocacy over the years.

Kristin Bartoloni and Alex Platkin of Silver Street Strategies are the best researchers in the business and provided immeasurable assistance in researching the topics covered in the book and fact-checking the final product. I am very appreciative of their efforts to keep me honest.

Melissa Sanders, who edits my *Message Box* newsletter, put in a herculean effort to edit the initial drafts of this book under a very tight timeline. She had tremendous patience with my multitude of typos and missing words as I wrote as fast as I could (and faster than I should) to meet various deadlines.

Many of the ideas and much of the information in this book was inspired by reading and speaking with a lot of very smart people over the years. In particular I want to thank Jon Favreau, Tara McGowan,

Jason Goldman, Clay Dumas, Anat Shenker Osorio, David Plouffe, Alyssa Mastromonaco, Cody Keenan, Ben Rhodes, Jen Psaki, Jennifer Palmieri, Tommy Vietor, Jon Lovett, and Tanya Somanader. There were several books that I turned to repeatedly during the research process: *Messengers of the Right: Conservative Media and the Transformation of American Politics* by Nicole Hemmer, *The Loudest Voice in the Room* by Gabriel Sherman, *An Ugly Truth: Inside Facebook's Battle for Domination* by Cecilia Kang and Sheera Frenkel, and *Twilight of Democracy: The Seductive Lure of Authoritarianism* by Anne Appelbaum, *After the Fall: Being American in the World We've Made*, *Ghosting the News* by Margaret Sullivan, and *Devil's Bargain: Steve Bannon, Donald Trump, and the Nationalist Uprising* by Joshua Green.

I am incredibly grateful to Jon Favreau, Jon Lovett, Tommy Vietor, and the entire Crooked Media team. Being part of *Pod Save America* and being able to help with Vote Save America has been so much fun and so rewarding. What you all have built is so impressive, impactful, and inspiring.

Kyla, the sweetest, smartest, funniest girl, sat next to me, using her toy laptop while I wrote. She brought some much-NEEDED joy to the process and made sure I took necessary breaks for science experiments, Sixers games, and going to see the garbage trucks on trash days.

A big part of my writing process was mentally composing paragraphs while holding a newborn Jack while he napped and I bounced him on a yoga ball. No matter how tired or stressed I was, Jack would crack me up with constant smiles and infectious giggles.

Finally, and most importantly, I want to thank Howli for all her support and inspiration. Writing this book in the middle of a pandemic in the year that our son was born was truly an insane decision. I would never have finished without your support and encouragement. You are the best mom, wife, and friend, and I am so lucky to have you, Kyla, and Jack in my life.